# A RHETORIC OF IRONY

# A RHETORIC OF IRONY
## Wayne C. Booth

THE UNIVERSITY OF CHICAGO PRESS

Chicago and London

THE UNIVERSITY OF CHICAGO PRESS, CHICAGO 60637
THE UNIVERSITY OF CHICAGO PRESS, LTD., LONDON
© *1974 by The University of Chicago*
*All rights reserved. Published 1974*
*Printed in the United States of America*
International Standard Book Number: 0–226–06552–9 (clothbound)
Library of Congress Catalog Card Number: 73–87298

For Lucille

# Contents

the impact of an unconscious (or, in the pathetic fallacy, malig-
nant) world on conscious man, or the result of more or less definable social and psychological forces. Tragedy's "this must be"
becomes irony's "this at least is," a concentration on foreground
facts and a rejection of mythical superstructures. Thus the ironic
drama is a vision of what in theology is called the fallen world.
[p. 285]

Well, yes, but how do you know all this? How did you decide? "Irony,
then, as it moves away from tragedy, begins to merge into comedy"
(p. 285). Perhaps, though I can think of other directions in which
many works everyone would call ironic have moved—as in fact Mr.
Frye at other points himself suggests.

How does he—how do we—know? Is there any way to get
hold of any corner of this large slippery subject with precision enough
to allow two readers to agree *and to know how they have agreed?* To
put the question in this form is to elect a rhetorical kind of inquiry,
and it is to make assumptions that should be stated openly from the
beginning.

I assume first that it is worthwhile to seek for as much clarity as a
murky subject in a murkier universe allows; if there is virtue in revealing ambiguities beneath what looked like simplicities, there is also
value in discovering clarities beneath what looked like confusions. I
assume secondly that some ironies are written to be understood, and
that most readers will regret their own failures to understand. One
hears it said these days that understanding is not really possible in any
normative sense: each man constructs his own meanings, and the more
variety we have the richer we are. But I never find anyone in fact tol-
erating all readings with equal cheer; critical practice assumes that
readers sometimes go astray. There is surely, then, some validity in the
notion of "going astray," and we can thus meaningfully pursue the
notion of finding one's way. Some readings are better than others, and
it is an impoverishment of the world to pretend otherwise.

But a third assumption is equally important: there are many
valid critical methods and there are thus many valid readings of any
literary work. I must stress this point from the beginning, because
when I come to particular readings I am often forced, seemingly by the
nature of the irony itself, to settle for a single reading. My air of certainty at such points—so-and-so cannot *not* have been ironic, whereas
so-and-so as clearly *must* be taken straight—should always be seen in
the light of the question I am trying to ask and the methods I am using.
When I ask "What does it mean—is it ironic?" and try to show "how
I know," my answers clearly do not rule out—in fact I hope they invite

—a wide variety of different comments derived from different critical interests. Thus I can be sure that almost every statement that I label non-ironic, Kenneth Burke could prove to be ironic in a dozen different senses; so could I, in another kind of inquiry, and without contradicting my original claim, since I would not be employing the same question about the same subject or pursuing that question with the same methods.

Finally I should make explicit what will be evident to every reader: the book is unabashedly in a tradition of evangelical attempts to save the world, or at least a piece of it, through critical attention to language. It is harder to believe in such salvation today than it was when I. A. Richards embarked on his rhetorical inquiries into practical criticism and the meaning of meaning; or when the American New Critics invited us to look closely at the individual literary work rather than only its background and sources; or when semanticists like Korzybski and popularizers like Stuart Chase and S. I. Hayakawa told us that if we would just look to our levels of abstraction we could escape the tyranny of words; or when philosophers like Wittgenstein and his progeny told us that if we looked closely at how we play our ordinary language games we could at last achieve salvation through intellectual clarity.

The list could be extended almost indefinitely. This has been a century of semantic and semiotic nostrums: the century of hermeneutical last-ditch stands. And here is another one, more modest than any I have named but still expressing the assumption that not just the practice of literary criticism but life itself can and should be enhanced by looking to our language. Unlike some of those earlier scourers of the language of the tribe, I cannot claim to have high general hopes. But then I do not, like some of them, think that if the *world* is not saved, all is lost. For me, one good reading of one good passage is worth as much as anything there is, because the person achieving it is living life fully in that time. The absurdity of this notion will be evident to everyone, but it seems only honest to get it out in the open from the beginning. Perhaps I should just add that I do not see how any such person can prove useless in the world.

Of all the authors who deserve more credit than I have been able to give in footnotes, I can mention here only a few. Kierkegaard's *The Concept of Irony* is to me one of the most interesting and profitable books ever written on an abstract idea—one of the very few books about Ideas which are not only delightful to read but from which one actually learns something. It is such a rich work that I cannot now state precisely where its influence leaves off and that of others begins. But I should make clear that I have in no way tried to do what Kierkegaard is doing. As his title says, he is struggling with a "concept"—that is, with an idea, which for anyone working in the Hegelian tradition means struggling with something that has a kind of autonomous reality, independently of its particular historical manifestations. The chapter headings of Part I show his driving interest clearly: The Conception Made Possible, The Conception Made Actual [in the life of Socrates], The Conception Made Necessary. It may be true that concepts have a life of their own of the kind Kierkegaard implies; I believe that they do and that his kind of inquiry thus not only is exciting but even has a kind of validity. But one cannot easily solve my kind of question while dwelling on his level: to deal with specific ironies in the "real world," to understand how they make themselves understood or fail to do so, is not done by looking at how abstract ideas interrelate conceptually in the "realer world." Nothing he says is of any use to me, directly, in Parts I and II, and even in Part III I generally draw back from his wonderfully wild line. But his is a splendid book, not likely to be improved on, a book which, like the similarly exhilarating conflations of irony in Kenneth Burke's monumental "rhetoric of everything," has in effect influenced every line.

D. C. Muecke, in his fine book *The Compass of Irony,* has done about all that we can expect to see done in ranging over the meanings of the word and sorting out differing and sometimes contradictory ironic worlds. I wish that I could have read Mr. Muecke's book before I wrote the first draft of mine; his help is evident everywhere in this final version, and I have again and again been tempted to say to my reader: go read Muecke and then we can carry on from there. My own classification of ironies, which comes only in Part III, was stimulated by his, though because of my exclusively rhetorical focus it finally bears little resemblance.

Readers of E. D. Hirsch's book, *Validity in Interpretation,* will see only part of my debt to him. Because of educational gaps nobody likes to confess to, his work first introduced me to Continental traditions in hermeneutics. Though he himself scarcely discusses what I call stable irony, it has not been surprising to me to discover, late in the game, that the tradition he works in has spawned a great number of studies, especially in German, only some of which I cite in the bibliography.

The recent death of Norman Knox must leave all students of irony saddened. His splendid tracing in *The Word "Irony" and Its Contexts: 1500–1755* is a permanent resource for scholars and critics.

I should finally make explicit an even larger debt that may be obscured by the widespread belief that "Chicago critics," of whom I am supposed to be one, are Aristotelians. I think of the book as in part an attempt to do with irony what Longinus did with another literary quality, the sublime. Irony, like the sublime, can be "used" or achieved in every conceivable kind of literature: tragedy, comedy, satire, epic, lyric poetry, allegory, congressional speeches—to say nothing of everyday speech. Like the sublime, it is a term that can stand for a quality or gift in the speaker or writer, for something in the work, and for something that happens to the reader or auditor. To study it rhetorically thus commits one to no general system or critical school: one need only assume—and I think it is an assumption that most of us should be able to share—that *one* important question about irony is how authors and readers achieve it together.

I am grateful to the Guggenheim Foundation for a grant that enabled me to write the first complete draft, and to the Rockefeller Foundation for a month of uninterrupted writing at the Villa Serbelloni.

I should like to thank Leigh and Patricia Gibby, D. C. Muecke, George P. Elliott, Sheldon Sacks, Nancy Rabinowitz, Robert Marsh, Ted Cohen, C. Douglas Barnes, and Kary Wolfe for detailed criticism. My wife has contributed most of all, not only by criticizing each draft but by enduring life with an addicted ironist. These eleven careful readers accumulated among them 748 suggestions, an average of 11.57 each. All of their points have of course been incorporated, even though some were flatly contradictory. Whatever faults remain can thus be traced, by any diligent reader, to the intervention or oversight of someone without whose.

The tacit conventions on which the understanding of everyday language depends are enormously complicated.

—Wittgenstein

The answers to those apparently simple questions: "What is a meaning?" "What are we doing when we endeavour to make it out?" "*What* is it we are making out?" are the master-keys to all the problems of criticism.

—I. A. Richards

I ask the reader to remember that what is most obvious may be most worthy of analysis.

—L. L. Whyte

Zu fragmentarisch ist Welt und Leben—
Ich will mich zum deutschen Professor begeben.
Der weiss das Leben zusammenzusetzen,
Und er macht ein verständlich System daraus;
Mit seinen Nachtmützen und Schlafrockfetzen
Stopft er die Lücken des Weltenbaus.

—Heine

We cannot use language maturely until we are spontaneously at home in irony.

—Kenneth Burke

# PART I STABLE IRONY

Since . . . Erich Heller, in his *Ironic German,* has already quite adequately not defined irony, there would be little point in not defining it all over again.

—D. C. Muecke

But irony was not for those people; their mental vision was not focussed for it. They read those playful trifles [of Pudd'nhead's] in the solidest earnest, and decided without hesitancy that if there had ever been any doubt that Dave Wilson was a pudd'nhead—which there hadn't—this revelation removed that doubt for good and all.

—Mark Twain, *Pudd'nhead Wilson*

Scaliger considers allegory as one part, or side, of a comparison. It differs from *irony,* in that *allegory* imports a similitude between the thing spoken and intended, *irony* a contrariety between them.

—Chambers' *Cyclopaedia*

We are all here on earth to help each other, but what the others are here for, God only knows.

—W. H. Auden

# ONE | The Ways of Stable Irony

E very good reader must be, among other things, sensitive in detecting and reconstructing ironic meanings. He may rejoice in this
requirement, as I do, and seek out occasions for ironic interpretation, or
he may try to avoid ironists and read only authors who speak "straight,"

> Not, ridle-like, obscuring their intent:
> But pack-staffe plaine uttring what thing they ment,

as Joseph Hall put it. But regardless of how broadly or narrowly he
defines irony—and the problem of definition is by no means a simple
one[1]—every reader learns that some statements cannot be understood
without rejecting what they seem to say.

There is reason to believe that most of us think we are less vulnerable to mistakes with irony than we are. If we have enjoyed many ironies and observed less experienced readers making fools of themselves,
we can hardly resist flattering ourselves for making our way pretty well.
But the truth is that even highly sophisticated readers often go astray.
The difficulty is that our errors are for the most part uncovered only by
accident. I once was discussing *Pride and Prejudice* with a very bright,
very sophisticated graduate student who was trying to convince me that
"the whole book is ironic"—whatever that might mean. Noticing something askew in one of his flights describing what Elizabeth and Mr.
Bennet "stand for," I asked him to say quite literally what kind of man
he took Mr. Bennet to be. "Well, for one thing, he's really quite stupid,
in spite of his claims to cleverness, because he says toward the end that
Wickham is his favorite son-in-law."

He retracted in embarrassment, of course, as soon as we had
looked at the passage together: " 'I admire all my three sons-in-law
highly,' said he. 'Wickham, perhaps, is my favourite; but I think I shall
like *your* husband [Darcy] quite as well as Jane's.' " How could he have
missed Mr. Bennet's ironic joke when he was in fact working hard to
find evidence that the author was *always* ironic?

1. The two best efforts at clarification are D. C. Muecke's *The Compass of
Irony* (London, 1969) and Norman Knox, *The Word "Irony" and Its Context:
1500 to 1755* (Durham, N.C., 1961). For accounts of how the word developed
historically, from ancient Greece to modern times, with special emphasis on the
astonishing flowering of new meanings in the eighteenth and early nineteenth centuries, see Knox, passim; Muecke, chaps. 6–7; G. G. Sedgwick, *Of Irony, Especially in the Drama* (Toronto, 1935); and J. A. K. Thomson, *Irony: An Historical Introduction* (London, 1926).

No matter how we might answer that question, the anecdote reveals a troublesome ambiguity about the word. For reasons that I cannot pretend fully to understand, irony has come to stand for so many things that we are in danger of losing it as a useful term altogether. Even if we rule out for now all non-verbal ironies, and all "cosmic ironies" and "ironies of fate" and "ironies of event,"[2] we are still faced with a very messy subject. But fortunately it is a subject which presents us with a real and concrete problem: we do in fact read and misread ironies. Often we accuse others of misreading, and sometimes we even confess to our own misreadings. I have here accused my student, who is unfortunately not present to give his own version of the incident, of *misreading*—not of having an interesting alternative hypothesis or of merely disagreeing with me or of discovering an eighth type of ambiguity; I have said that he made a flat mistake, and I feel a great deal of confidence that everyone who has read *Pride and Prejudice* attentively will agree with me. We feel as sure of ourselves as if we had the kind of statement from the author that Dickens once made in a footnote to a new edition of *Martin Chuzzlewit*: "The most credulous reader will scarcely believe that Mr. Pecksniff's [fallacious] reasoning was once set upon as the Author's! !"[3]

2. As I write this draft, "ironically" enough many years after the original date of promised completion and four years before publication (as it turned out, ironically), I read in the *Herald-Tribune* (International), "If there is a single irony in the miraculous flight of Apollo-13, it lies in the impact the near disastrous voyage will have on the space program. . . . One irony of the accident that aborted the flight is that the space agency now feels it must redouble its efforts to land an Apollo crew in the moon's Fra Mauro Hills. . . . The final irony of the flight . . . was that its brush with disaster caught everybody by surprise and yet caught nobody by surprise" (18–19 April 1970, pp. 1, 3). The irony is that such ironies, defined with such ironic indifference to precision, multiply on every hand, leaving the ironic critic caught in the ironic trap of defining a term that will not stay defined.

3. I borrow the citation from Simon Nowell-Smith: "In Chapter XX of *Martin Chuzzlewit,* Mr. Pecksniff congratulates himself at some length on the protection of his machinations by a special Providence. The passage ends:

" 'The precedents would seem to show that Mr. Pecksniff had good argument for what he said, and might be permitted to say it, and did not say it presumptuously, vainly, or arrogantly, but in a spirit of high faith and great wisdom meriting all praise.'

"Thus in 1843, and again in 1850. But a reader not attuned to irony took exception to the author's irreverence, and in 1858 Dickens altered the sentence to read, 'Mr. Pecksniff had (as things go) good argument. . . ,' and deleted 'meriting all praise.' Nine years later, working from his 1850 edition, he forgot that he had already conciliated his critic, and left the original sentence unaltered,"

Such flat assertions about error raise in themselves something of a problem, projected into a world in which many critics insist on the value of multiple readings, on the "open-endedness" of all ironic literature, and on the insecurity, or even relativity, of all critical views. If I am not being simply arrogant—if I can without blushing say "I *know* that Jane Austen intended Mr. Bennet's statement as meaning something radically different from what he *seems* to say"—then we have a real and specific problem, or set of problems: In what sense do I "know" Jane Austen's intentions? How is such a peculiar kind of knowledge possible, if it is? Here we seem to have a specific kind of literary fixity, a "stable irony" that does in fact present us with a limited set of reading tasks—regardless of the breadth or narrowness of our conception of irony in general.

## THE MARKS OF STABLE IRONY

To see clearly how readers perform such tasks, we must first be quite clear about how stable irony differs from all other kinds. If I am right, it is a kind that has never received adequate attention, being named fairly late by the Greek rhetoricians and then in effect quickly losing its name to less stable kin and to unintended "ironies of event" or "ironies of fate."[4]

What I am looking for is a way of making sense about a kind of interpretation that is demanded by most of the following quotations but not all. How do we talk about the precise and peculiar relationship between authors and readers of those passages which are unquestionably ironic?

1. "While everything around him bore a hostile aspect, he [Charles I] reposed himself [as his execution approached] with confi-

---

adding the footnote quoted above. "Editing Dickens: For Which Reader? From Which Text?" *TLS,* 4 June 1970, p. 615–16.

4. It is surprising that so little has been done with stable irony in detail, in a century when there has been so much detailed work on verbal interpretation. In I. A. Richards's three famous works *How to Read a Page; A Course in Effective Reading with an Introduction to a Hundred Great Words* (New York, 1942); *Practical Criticism: A Study of Literary Judgment* (London, 1929); and *Interpretation in Teaching* (London, 1938) there is almost nothing on irony— unless one chooses with Cleanth Brooks to define irony so generally that it becomes identical with Richards's "poetry of synthesis" and hence can be applied to all or almost all literature. Similarly, Ludwig Wittgenstein never discusses ironies in his pursuit of language games in *Philosophical Investigations* (London, 1953) and *Tractatus Logico-Philosophicus,* 1921, trans. D. F. Pears and B. F. McGuinness (London, 1961). Even E. D. Hirsch, Jr., whose *Validity in Interpretation* (New Haven, 1967) is the best on its subject in English, fails to make much use of stable ironies.

dence in the arms of that Being, who penetrates and sustains all nature, and whose severities, if received with piety and resignation, he regarded as the surest pledge of unexhausted favour."

2. "We Christians must recognize that neither the sciences, nor a great mind, nor the other gifts of nature are very considerable advantages, since God permits them to be completely possessed by devils, his chief enemies, and thereby renders them not merely unfortunate, but even worthy of infinite scorn; that in spite of all outstanding qualities, and miserable and impotent as we are, we are enviable to them, because our great God chooses to regard us with pity."

3. "The particular situation that confronts the religion of Western civilization is this. The concept of God has reached the limits of its usefulness: it cannot evolve further. Supernatural powers were created by man to carry the burden of religion. From diffuse magic *mana* to personal spirits; from spirits to gods; from gods to God—so, crudely speaking, the evolution has gone. The particular phase of that evolution which concerns us is that of gods. In one period of our Western civilization the gods were necessary fictions, useful hypotheses by which to live."

4. "The old, far-fetched notion of religion, which commended itself for so long to the rude intelligence of our ancestors, has fortunately given way, in our own time, to a more reasonable understanding of it. We find it difficult to think ourselves back into that complexion of mind, which conceived of religious truth as a body of philosophical statements and alleged historical facts; as, that grace was or was not indefectible; that it was Paul and not another who wrote to the Ephesians, and the like. Had such facts been demonstrable, is it not certain that in so many centuries of earnest controversy the common judgment of mankind must have resolved the question with 'aye' or 'no' long before this? And could it be credibly maintained that it might be a man's duty to resign his benefice, forgo the comradeship of his friends, and find himself a new way of living, merely because he had revised his notions about certain doctrinal points, without abating anything of his general zeal for righteousness? The wonder is, assuredly, not that we should have come to think otherwise, but that so defective an apprehension of religious truth should have so long dominated the superstitious fancy of human kind."

5. I approach the post office window and I hear the clerk and the customer just ahead of me in the three-man line quarreling:

CUSTOMER: All right, all right, let's pick it up. Get a bloody move on here. I can't wait all night.

4

CLERK: Now you look here. I'm sick and tired of you coming in here bitching all the time. You make my life miserable with your bitching.
CUSTOMER: If you'd spend less time talking and more time waiting on people, I wouldn't have to be here so long. Now I've got business that's important, and . . .
CLERK: Well, you can take your business and you know what you can do with it.

Since it is a London post office, I am a bit shocked but terribly fascinated. But as I lean forward to hear the continuation of the fight, they laugh, and the clerk says, "Well, how ya been, Sam?"

6. FIRST COLLEGE STUDENT: Boy, things are turning up good all over. I got my scholarship, I got a date with Jessie for tomorrow night, my dad just wrote and said I could have . . .
SECOND COLLEGE STUDENT: You know what, you lead a fine rich life.
FIRST COLLEGE STUDENT (showing pleasure): Oh well, things aren't *always* good for me . . .
He looks up and sees scorn in the other student's eyes. He blushes.
FIRST COLLEGE STUDENT (after a pause): You know what, you're a prince, a real prince.

Whatever differences of difficulty, subtlety, or skill in these examples, most of them present unequivocal and absolute ironic demands upon reader or auditor; two of them, in contrast, will be violated if read ironically. "Out of context," as we say, readers may find it difficult to recognize that number 2 (from Bossuet's *Sermons*) and number 3 (from Julian Huxley's "Religion as an Objective Problem") are almost unquestionably what we call straight, while others verbally so much like them, such as number 1 (from David Hume's *History of England*) and number 4 (from Father Ronald Knox's "The New Cure for Religion") are without question ironic. Numbers 5 and 6 reveal failures of speakers and interpreters to get together, but it is not easy to assign blame for the failure. What we can say is that regardless of theoretical definitions, the ironic examples share four marks that will give us a practical preliminary notion of the irony that for now concerns us:

1. They are all *intended,* deliberately created by human beings to be heard or read and understood with some precision by other human beings; they are not mere openings, provided unconsciously, or accidental statements allowing the confirmed pursuer of ironies to read them as reflections against the author. To me the sign on the pediment of the Royal Exchange, "The Earth is the Lord's and the

5

fullness thereof," is deliciously ironic, in one sense of the word. But I am reasonably sure that the architects did not intend my response. The story goes that the inscription "Arbeit macht frei" was carved over the entrance to German concentration camps. The irony that everyone sees in such a message is *not* the kind that will first concern us; if the same message were scrawled by an inmate in the dark of night, it would immediately enter our domain. Similarly I must put to one side ironies of event—the premature monsoon that undermines the invasion plans, the sudden stroke of lightning just as the orator raises his arm to make a dramatic point about God.

2. They are all *covert,* intended to be reconstructed with meanings different from those on the surface, not merely overt statements that "It is ironic that . . ." or direct assertions that "things" are or "the universe" is ironic.

3. They are all nevertheless *stable* or fixed, in the sense that once a reconstruction of meaning has been made, the reader is not then invited to undermine it with further demolitions and reconstructions. That he may choose to do so on his own, and thus can render any stable irony unstable, is irrelevant, so long as we take seriously the first mark and remain interested, for now, in intended ironies only.

4. They are all *finite* in application, in contrast with those infinite ironies (both stable and unstable) that we shall meet in Part III. The reconstructed meanings are in some sense local, limited. Though some of them are about very broad subjects like religion or the nature of God, the field of discourse even in these is narrowly circumscribed: Hume is not talking about the "nature of things in general" or the mysterious qualities of the universe but rather about certain specific religious doctrines attributable to particular men at a particular time. However complex his message may be, its interpretation is, like that of Father Knox, easily brought to term in a set of completed insights. This is not to say that one can catch all the meaning in a non-ironic paraphrase; as we shall soon see, most ironies, even stable ironies, are richer than any translation we might attempt into non-ironic language. But the stable irony with which we shall now wrestle does not mock our efforts by making general claims about the ironic universe, or the universe of human discourse. It does not say, "There is no truth," or "All human statements can be undermined by the true ironic vision," or (in the words of Edward Albee in *Tiny Alice*) "We do not know anything." On the contrary, it delimits a world of discourse in which we can say with great security certain things that are violated by the overt words of the discourse.

I realize that the mark of finitude and the mark of stability are not

6

clearly distinguished from each other in this account. I can do nothing about this without taking longer than would at this point be justified; in chapter 8 I return to the marks as I attempt a fuller classification of intended ironies.

I choose to begin, then, with the kind of irony rejected by Hans Castorp in Thomas Mann's *The Magic Mountain*. That aggressive and ridiculous moralist, Herr Settembrini, will have no irony *but* this kind: "Where irony is not a direct and classic device of oratory, not for a moment equivocal [sic] to a healthy mind, it makes for depravity, it becomes a drawback to civilization, an unclean traffic with the forces of reaction, vice, and materialism." To which Hans Castorp replies (speaking to himself): "But irony that is 'not for a moment equivocal' —what kind of irony would that be, I should like to ask. . . . It would be a piece of dried-up pedantry!"[5]

Irony as a direct and classic device—not only of oratory but of every kind of communication where it occurs—it is this irony, intended but covert, stable and localized, that we shall now pursue, without worrying about whether it is "dried-up pedantry."

The four marks of stable irony provide a subject that can be studied and not just speculated or preached about. But they do not yet distinguish irony clearly from other intended, non-literal (and hence more or less covert) invitations to read between the lines. There are many verbal devices that "say" one thing and "intend" another and thus invite the reader to reconstruct unspoken meanings. Metaphor and simile, allegory and apologue—to say nothing of metonymy, synecdoche, asteismus, micterismus, charientismus, preterition, or of banter, raillery, burlesque, and paronomasia—have all been discussed in terms similar to those employed for irony, and some of them have had an uneasy or confusing relationship with it.[6] What is more troublesome, some modern critics—for example, I. A. Richards, Cleanth Brooks, and Kenneth Burke—have suggested that every literary context is ironic because it provides a weighting or qualification on every word in it, thus requiring the reader to infer meanings which are in a sense not in the words themselves: all literary meanings in this view become a form of covert irony, whether intended or not. Since this entirely reasonable view can obscure the distinctions on which I shall depend, it

*[margin annotations in hand: "an elegance"; "an urbanity"; "summa"; "mention of a thing while seeming to pass it by"]*

5. *The Magic Mountain*, trans. H. T. Lowe-Porter (New York, 1939), pp. 281–82. I owe the citation, as I owe many, to Muecke. On Mann as ironist, see Eric Heller, *The Ironic German: A Study of Thomas Mann* (London, 1958).

6. See Knox, *The Word "Irony,"* chap. 2, "The Meaning of Irony: The Dictionary," esp. pp. 34–37.

will be necessary to look briefly at the way in which reconstructions of stable ironies differ from some other kinds of literary inference. In doing so, I shall not be trying to define a concept or fix a proper meaning for a word but rather to clarify one particular operation that is in fact performed together by authors and readers, regardless of their literary or critical presuppositions.

## STABLE IRONY COMPARED WITH "ALL LITERATURE"

If my friend comes into the room and says, "It's raining," my inferences about his intentions are ordinarily so quick and so automatic that they seem scarcely to be worthy of the name inference at all. But it is not hard to show that in fact my decision to accept his statement as a plain and simple effort to give information—if that is indeed what I decide— is highly complex, depending on an elaborate context of linguistic and social assumptions, as well as assumptions about his character and our relationship. We see this as soon as we note in any part of his statement or in its context any element that challenges the simplest literal interpretation. Suppose he comes in dripping wet, stands for a moment looking dejected, and then mourns, "It's raining." It is clear that he is no longer simply giving me information—I have the information already just from looking at him. But the precise content of his statement will not be clear to anyone reading my account here, because the three words "looking dejected" and "mourns" cannot tell enough about his character and our situation to show whether he is joking with a playful mournful tone or speaking from a mood of black despair. But as soon as we say this we see that the original statement depended just as fully on a complex set of assumptions about the context. My conclusion that "It's raining" meant literal information could have been reversed by knowledge about what kinds of statement he is accustomed to making, by knowledge of a quarrel we had just had or a bet we had made, by information about his rheumatism, by prediction of a hurricane on the radio that morning—in fact by any of innumerable contextual modifications which are brought to consciousness only when challenged.

If every human statement is thus surrounded with nuances that are assumed to be understood by speaker and listener (though often the assumption is unjustified), it is more obviously clear that elaborate inferences are always required when reading what we call literature. If, in a play, a character comes in dripping and says, "It's raining," the author may well want us to think about what it means to say something so obvious as all that. It may suggest literal-mindedness, or even stupidity. Or perhaps the character speaks it in an ironic tone, after the other character looks at him standing there, dripping, for about thirty seconds. In literature as in life, "It's raining" can mean an unlimited number of things, depending on the context.

One remembers what Hemingway does with simple, factual accounts of the rain at the end of *A Farewell to Arms*. Frederick Henry has walked through the rain up to the hospital: he has told us so, in just those undoctored, seemingly straightforward words. "I walked through the rain up to the hospital." At the hospital he learns that the woman he loves has died in childbirth. After forcing his way past the nurses into her room, he says, "But after I had got them out and shut the door and turned off the light it wasn't any good. It was like saying good-by to a statue. After a while I went out and left the hospital and walked back to the hotel in the rain." I've known students who accused Hemingway of writing a cold-blooded ending to the story. There's not a single emotive word in the passage; he's telling us, they say, that neither the author nor his hero can summon up any feeling. Everything is reported factually, unfeelingly. But to me it seems quite clear that the walk back to the hotel in the rain is intended to convey all the grief that a man could feel over a supreme loss. It may not entirely succeed, but it is evident that the words, though they are not ironic in the way of the misread ironies I reported earlier, cannot be taken in the simple literal sense that they might yield when read in another context. "After a while I went out and left the hospital and walked back to the hotel in the rain." A hospital inspector completing his rounds on a bad day? No, a hero expressing his grief, an author choosing a simple sign of that grief. Yet the same words could serve for both.

But if the reader is expected to use his powers of inference to make so much out of simple straightforward words like rain and hotel when there is real rain and a real hotel, are we not dealing with irony? The author in one sense says something less than he means, and it would be quite normal usage to call the passage ironic. The author has created ironies of event: "It is ironic that it should rain, on top of everything else; it is ironic that just when Henry has found true love, the woman should die." And some would say, "It is ironic that Hemingway should choose language that so markedly understates the emotion his character no doubt feels." There is no point in denying or trying to correct such usage; I have no quarrel with the many critics who choose to call such effects ironic and who therefore find all literature, or all good literature, ironic. Or rather, I have only a small quarrel, and it is one that we can bypass: such usage would leave us without a term for something quite important and quite precise, the special form of complex verbal reconstruction required by what I am calling stable irony.

9

*Stable Irony*

## The Four Steps of Reconstruction

In contrast to the general modifications of meaning that all words in any literary context give to all other words in that context, consider the transformations of meaning experienced in reading any passage of stable irony.

*Step one.* The reader is required to reject the literal meaning. It is not enough that he may reject that meaning because he disagrees, nor is it enough that he should add meanings. If he is reading properly, he is unable to escape recognizing either some incongruity among the words or between the words and something else that he knows. In every case, even the most seemingly simple, the route to new meanings passes through an unspoken conviction that cannot be reconciled with the literal meaning. Muecke cites a splendid bit from *Candide* that illustrates this requirement well: "When all was over and the rival kings were celebrating their victory with Te Deums in their respective camps . . ."

Even without any of the satiric context provided by *Candide* (chap. 3) or knowledge about Voltaire, the statement simply cannot be accepted at face value because it implies a proposition that nobody can accept: "Both sides can win a war," or perhaps "God can give victory to both sides in the same war."[7]

We should note two things for now about this first step, rejecting one proposition because we must reject an unspoken proposition on which it depends. It is not peculiar to irony, only essential to it. And the requirement may or may not be clearly "visible," as it seems to be here, in the form of some manifest inconsistency within what is said. Often an ironic statement is entirely consistent with itself, as in the passages from Hume and Knox above, but the reader is expected to catch what some would consider external clues. In fact the distinction between internal and external or extrinsic clues—relied on so heavily

---

7. I often generalize about "all readers" or "most readers," and I should say once and for all that if anyone can cite particular readers who do not fit, I shall not be the least bit shaken. Only if you can honestly say that *you* disagree will my own rhetorical purposes be undermined. Here, for example, if you can really argue in defense of the non-ironic acceptance of these implications about war, I have lost. But I hope no one will think he can escape the argument by imagining hypothetical readers, or by uttering general propositions about the relativity of all judgments. We are working rhetorically here, and that means that when we find ourselves in genuine agreement, we have found something real, regardless of what disagreements we can imagine "some readers" might concoct.

in much modern criticism—becomes strangely irrelevant when one is deciding whether a passage is ironic.

*Step two.* Alternative interpretations or explanations are tried out, —or rather, in the usual case of quick recognition, come flooding in. The alternatives will all in some degree be incongruous with what the literal statement seems to say—perhaps even contrary, as one traditional definition put it, but certainly in some sense a retraction, diminution, or undercutting: it is a slip, or he is crazy, or I missed something earlier, or that word must mean something I don't know about.

One possible alternative, usually unformulated except when controversy about a passage puts us in doubt about it, is thus that the author himself is foolish enough not to see that his statement cannot be accepted as it stands. "Voltaire *might* have been careless or stupid or crazy enough when he wrote the passage not to see what it means." We accept this alternative only when other more plausible ones fail to emerge and satisfy us.

*Step three.* A decision must therefore be made about the author's knowledge or beliefs—a decision like the one I made about my friend's character, situation, and likely intentions when he said "It's raining." My confidence that Voltaire was being ironic—and it is so great as to be virtual certainty—depends on my conviction that, like me, he sees and rejects what the statement implies: "Both sides can win a war." It is this decision about the author's own beliefs that entwines the interpretation of stable ironies so inescapably in intentions.

Note that the first two steps by themselves cannot tell us that a statement is ironic. No matter how firmly I am convinced that a statement is absurd or illogical or just plain false, I must somehow determine whether what I reject is also rejected by the author, and whether he has reason to expect my concurrence. It is true that the author I am interested in is only the creative person responsible for the choices that made the work—what I have elsewhere called the "implied author" who is found in the work itself. Talk about the "intentional fallacy" is sound insofar as it reminds us that we cannot finally settle our critical problems by calling Voltaire on the telephone and asking him what he intended with his sentence about rival kings. Our best evidence of the intentions behind any sentence in *Candide* will be the whole of *Candide,* and for some critical purposes it thus makes sense to talk only of the *work's* intentions, not the author's. But dealing with irony shows us the sense in which our court of final appeal is still a conception of the author: when we are pushed about any "obvious interpretation" we finally want to be able to say, "It is inconceivable that the author could have put these words together in this order without

11

having intended this precise ironic stroke." I return to this problem in Part II.

*Step four.* Having made a decision about the knowledge or beliefs of the speaker, we can finally choose a new meaning or cluster of meanings with which we can rest secure. Unlike the original proposition, the reconstructed meanings will necessarily be in harmony with the unspoken beliefs that the reader has decided to attribute to Voltaire. The act of reconstruction thus ends with a belief that can be made explicit: "In contrast with the statement Voltaire pretends to be making, which implies beliefs that he cannot have held, he is really saying such-and-such, which is in harmony with what I know or can infer about his beliefs and intentions."

The four steps can always be discovered in analysis, even in the simplest of cases. For example, my friend says, "Think it'll rain?"

1. Surface meaning is nonsense, since it *is* raining.
2. Alternatives: he hasn't noticed the rain—impossible—or he is cracking up and doesn't know rain from shine—unlikely—or he's kidding.
3. I decide that he cannot not know that it's raining.
4. I construct a meaning in harmony with that decision: his words mean "hello my good friend who understands me is it not a rainy day that we are enduring together by making something mildly humorous out of what might otherwise have been reason for grousing it is good to see you who thank God understand ironic joshing when you hear it and are not too critical even if it is rather stale and feeble."

Obviously these steps are often virtually simultaneous—or they may, for a given work, occupy a scholar's lifetime.[8] But the four can be isolated by anyone who challenges a reading at any point.

I suspect that many readers will feel that I am unduly complicating what is in fact a very simple, quick, and delightful leap of intuition. In reading a piece of irony I do not, they will rightly say, go

---

8. Controversy about them makes up a fair part of what critics write about these days. The bibliography of a single battle can be immense—e.g., whether or how Swift's portrait of the Houyhnhnms is ironic; or whether Billy Budd's "God bless Captain Vere" is Melville's praise or blame. One of the most astonishing developments in critical history is the outburst of articles and books about irony since the late 1940s. A simple tracing through any standard subject index will show it. In the International Index of Periodicals, for example, I find almost nothing from 1920 to 1949—an article by Hofmannsthal on "the irony of things," a dissertation on Menander. Suddenly, in the 1950s, the explosion occurs. I suspect that, by now, a bibliography of works with irony in the title would more than fill this volume.

step-by-step through any such laborious process as here described. "Sees by degrees a purer blush arise," Pope writes of Belinda in *The Rape of the Lock,* as rouge is applied to her cheeks by the sylphs. We catch the fun of "purer" in an intuitive flash, readers may say, without having to think about it. The pleasure depends on our *not* having to offer ourselves painstaking evidence for our conclusions.

Granted, the fun. Granted, the speed, when the process works as it should. Granted, even, the "intuitive," though the word really tells us nothing except that we may not make the steps consciously, and it may mislead us into forgetting how much intellectual activity is always involved. The fact that it is often more or less instantaneous should not trouble us in this age that has demonstrated just how rapid a complicated calculation can be—in "minds" much less highly elaborated than the human mind. It may well be that the steps are not sequential at all, and they might better be called something like elements, or even vectors. We often do take all of them "in a flash," and there may be in this some explanation of why irony is such a powerful weapon so much enjoyed by authors and readers alike. Perhaps no other form of human communication does so much with such speed and economy.

Once I begin to think about this four-step act of reconstruction, I see that it completes a more astonishing communal achievement than most accounts have recognized. Its complexities are, after all, shared: the whole thing cannot work at all unless both parties to the exchange have confidence that they are moving together in identical patterns. The wonder of it is not that it should go awry as often as it does, but that it should ever succeed. It is true that some stable ironies are in a sense obvious and not on the face of it wondrous at all. But looked at more closely, even the most simple-minded irony, when it succeeds, reveals in both participants a kind of meeting with other minds that contradicts a great deal that gets said about who we are and whether we can know each other. Talking of her growing friendship with Henry James, Edith Wharton wrote,

> Perhaps it was our common sense of fun that first brought about our understanding. The real marriage of true minds is for any two people to possess a sense of humour or irony pitched in exactly the same key, so that their joint glances at any subject cross like inter-arching search-lights. I have had good friends between whom and myself that bond was lacking, but they were never really intimate friends; and in that sense Henry James was perhaps the most intimate friend I ever had, though in many ways we were so different.[9]

9. *A Backward Glance,* 1934 (London, 1972), p. 173.

13

## Stable Irony

Irony as the key to the tightest bonds of friendship! Real intimacy impossible without it! This is scarcely the same creature that we saw Mr. Frye describing as what leads the writer to "turn his back on his audience."

### IRONIC READING AS KNOWLEDGE

To use words like "knowledge" and "knowing" for the ironic exchange may seem unduly ambitious to anyone who has taken part in controversy about how to read this or that ironic work. But I am not of course saying that we come to know other minds clearly in all our efforts at interpretation, only that we sometimes do so. All I would claim is that we have here discovered a form of interpretation that gives us knowledge of a firm (and neglected) kind, a kind quite unrelated both to ordinary empirical observation and to standard deductive or logical proofs.

It is no doubt true that according to some criteria of proof such knowledge is not knowledge at all, but rather only belief, or hunch, or intuition. But though the modes of proof are not quite those of the laboratory, this mutual knowledge of how other minds work does pass a very rigorous and simple test that should satisfy us, unless we are determined on a futile quest for absolute certainty. The test will be in our sense rhetorical, and it is circular; when we apply it, we imply a community of minds, and we depend, in the testing, on the validity of the process that is itself being proved to be valid. It takes at least two to play this game in which the rules are reflexively established.

The test can be stated in many ways, but we can take our beginning formulation from that famous skeptic, Bertrand Russell. In his middle years, trying to move out from the cold domains of mathematical and logical certainty into the dangerous quagmires of *"human knowledge,"* Russell found that absolute empiricism could not account for all of the beliefs that he "knew" were warranted, though he still felt somehow that empirical tests "ought" to prevail. ". . . In all empirical knowledge," he said, "liberation from sense [the senses] can be only partial. It can, however, be carried to the point where two men's [concurring] interpretations of a given sentence are nearly certain to be both true or both false. The securing of this result is one of the aims (more or less unconscious) governing the development of scientific concepts."[10]

10. *Human Knowledge: Its Scope and Limits* (New York, 1948), p. 93. The best-known extended discussion of a systematic "falsifiability" test is that of Karl Popper in *The Logic of Scientific Discovery* (*Logik der Forschung,* 1935; trans. Julius Freed and Lan Freed, London, 1959). See esp. chaps. 4, 6, and 10.

## The Ways of Stable Irony

The test as stated is surely cryptic, especially viewed thus out of its context, but I take it to mean that the goal of science is to construct statements about "the world" sufficiently unambiguous to allow any two investigators, using similar methods, to interpret them in identical ways. Since the interpretations would carry identical meanings, they would prove, on further investigation, either to be both false or both true. Who is to do this further judging is not specified. Russell characteristically reserves the highest marks on this test for logic and pure mathematics, where alone men can be sufficiently abstract to allow for identical views. If we ask how two pure mathematicians *know* that they place the same meaning on "371,294," as Russell claims they do, he would presumably be forced to rely on the experts themselves. One could not refer to further experts who would judge whether *these* saw

---

Current debates about what knowledge is and how we know are even more complicated than traditional discussions of epistemology. Fortunately they are not essential here, except for the point that ironic statements quite clearly complicate those debates further. Not only does irony threaten to undermine standard tests of knowledge like Karl Popper's. It seems to force us to straddle many standard distinctions. For example, almost everyone these days distinguishes between "knowing-*that*" something is the case and "knowing-*how*" to perform an act (e.g., Gilbert Ryle, *The Concept of Mind* [London, 1949], pp. 25–61); others are developing J. L. Austin's distinctions among kinds of speech acts, especially between descriptive statements and performatives. Stable ironic statements clearly give me "knowledge-*that*": I know that it is the case that X has said P and meant not-P. But they also both give and depend on "knowledge-*how*": I know how to do the dance they invite me to. They thus seem to me to be both descriptive and performative, in Austin's terms. I don't quite know what to do with this tidbit, except to hope that some professional philosopher will digest it, and then do something with my further observation that "ironic performatives" can apparently be employed in each of J. L. Austin's speech acts: locutionary, illocutionary, and perlocutionary (*How to Do Things with Words* [Oxford, 1962], esp. chap. 8). A good brief introduction to both the standard issues and the bibliography of the relation of literature and knowledge is Martin Steinmann's "Literature, Knowledge, and the Language of Literature," *College English* 34 (April 1973): 899–911. (Ted Cohen, whom I trust on Austin more than I trust myself, tells me—too late for me to do anything about it—that I have a couple of things wrong here: "As I read Austin, the distinction between descriptive statements [constatives] and performatives—which Austin abandons because, as I read him, it cannot be drawn—is a distinction between kinds of utterances or sentences, not between kinds of speech acts. The 'theory of speech acts' is formulated in response to the performative/constative breakdown." I am sure that—as Kenneth Burke has his "God" say again and again at the end of *The Rhetoric of Religion*—it's even more complicated than *that*. Mr. Cohen has made a beginning on the project of talking philosophically about irony in his "Illocutions and Perlocutions," *Foundations of Language* 9 [March 1973]): 492–503.

the number in the same way, not without falling into an infinite regress: who is to judge what the new experts really see?

So far as I know, Russell never pushed his little test into the domains of literary interpretation. If we do so we find that for a vast number of our readings of literature the test simply will not work. Many of the literary works we value cannot be interpreted unambiguously by any two readers, no matter how skilled they are. We read their interpretations and we cannot say "both are true or both are false." Rather we say something like "both are interesting," or "both are illuminating," interesting or illuminating in different directions. It is thus clear that much of our talk about literature could never count as knowledge for Russell, or indeed for any of the modern theorists who have made the so-called criterion of falsifiability crucial to knowledge. For most of us this would not mean that it had no cognitive value whatever, by other standards, but that is another matter.

Now the interesting thing is that stable irony clearly passes the test—as indeed would any figurative language that achieves "stability." "Wickham, perhaps, is my favourite; but I think I shall like *your* husband quite as well as Jane's." Either Mr. Bennet and Jane Austen are playing with irony or they are not; there are no two ways about it, and if you and I elect an ironic reading, we shall prove either both right or both wrong. In Russell's terms, we have here a form of literary interpretation sufficiently freed of the distractions of "sensation" to be firmly known. What is more remarkable, the known object can be described either as a literary work or as an intention of a human being: our hard knowledge is of a stuff that in some views is totally inaccessible.

The question of who is to decide about our rightness or wrongness is of course begged in this formulation, but no more so than it is begged in Russell's. Scientific experts judge the falsity of scientific propositions; experts in irony judge the falsity of propositions about irony. And though it may be more difficult to recognize who the latter experts are, that they exist is undeniable to anyone who has ever been a party to successful ironic communication: he has known the condition of expertise in himself (see chapter 7).

In this view knowledge of some subjective responses is thus not "merely subjective." I do not claim to know something that is implacably and totally private or idiosyncratic; I know only those convictions that I think are at least potentially shareable because they can be soundly argued for. If it is objected that I will call "knowledge" many convictions which will finally turn out to be mistaken, that is no real objection, since it applies to every definition of knowledge. No definition can prevent error; the virtue of this one is that it does draw

16

a practical, operational line between those personal feelings and convictions which, because based on some kind of *"common* sense," are inherently shareable and those which are inescapably private.

The point is not to pretend here to having constructed a new and tricky epistemology but rather simply to underline the intellectual peculiarity of this kind of knowledge: though much discourse about many kinds of literature cannot pass any such test as we are describing here (but can still be good discourse for all that) some discourse about some stable irony can do so with a rigor that might equal that of laboratory scientists. It would be disastrous, I think, if all discourse aspired to the condition of such clarity, in the name of scientific rigor, but it is important to recognize the precision sometimes achieved in this one kind.

The test helps us to distinguish this kind from some other "ironic interpretations" that generally get more attention. I have already put to one side all those readings that depend on seeing all literature, or all good literature, as ironic; such readings are self-evidently valid to anyone who accepts the broadened definition, self-evidently false to anyone who does not, but the test is found not in the passage read but in the critic's definition. When Cleanth Brooks decided that even "Tears, idle tears, I know not what they mean" was ironic, nothing in Tennyson's poem required him to reject or seriously modify any meaning seen on the surface, as we say, by every reader: only his definition of irony as the effect whenever one part of a literary work modifies or qualifies the meaning of another part led him to his decision.[11]

11. *The Well Wrought Urn: Studies in the Structure of Poetry* (New York, 1947), pp. 153–62. By the same criterion Mr. Brooks is of course able to show that Keats's "Ode on a Grecian Urn" and Wordsworth's "Intimations" ode are ironic: like all good poetry, they subject every assertion, every word, to qualifications imposed by other parts, other words. ". . . irony is the most general term that we have for the kind of qualification which the various elements in a context receive from the context. This kind of qualification . . . is of tremendous importance in any poem. Moreover, irony is our most general term for indicating that recognition of incongruities—which, again, pervades all poetry to a degree far beyond what our conventional criticism has been heretofore willing to allow" (pp. 191–92). Mr. Brooks seems to waver between calling all poetry ironic and calling all *good* poetry ironic. In either case the term is so general that it would cover every part of every organic whole, every detail in any well-planned building, every note in every melody. Even if I am wrong in that extension, it is clear that his broadened definition would make the term useless for the kinds of discrimination I am attempting here. See also his "Irony as a Principle of Structure," in *Literary Opinion in America,* ed. Morton Dauwen Zabel, rev. ed. (New York, 1951), pp. 729–41. A rereading of these works confirms Mr. Brooks's hope expressed in the preface to the first: "If the worst came to the

If two readers agree on such a decision, we could not argue that their claim was either true or false, except in the sense that it follows from the definition. But when you and I encounter in Samuel Johnson's dictionary a definition of irony illustrated with the sentence "Bolingbroke was a holy man," we know together that Johnson's satiric intentions determined his choice of *holy,* and thus our ironic reconstruction of its meaning. Whether we are right or wrong in our decision about Johnson's intentions is a question of fact. Regardless of our general theories about literature or irony, our "interpretations of the given sentence are nearly certain to be both true or both false." What is more, we both have a pretty good idea about the kinds of evidence that would be required to prove us wrong. And in this case—though not by any means in all cases of intended stable irony—we know that we have no such evidence, and we are therefore justifiably confident about our knowledge.

A second kind of ironic reading is equally unable to pass our present test. Private interests or associations can lead to "ironic" reversals of any passage. Especially in a time when critical reputations can be gained by discovering clever new readings that no one else would ever have thought of, temptations to reversals are for some critics hard to resist. Any statement can easily be turned into its opposite and made more "interesting." Any work can be revised, turning the three little pigs into villains, the wolf into a tragic hero.[12]

Once you get the hang of it, you can go on indefinitely improvising reversals that will seem clever to some people but that are worthless to all. They are in one sense permitted—nobody will ever pass any laws against improvisation. But what we are dealing with is by comparison rigorously controlled; it is a process we are required to undertake by incongruities that no mind can live with comfortably. Asked why I do not remain satisfied with Johnson's literal meaning about Bolingbroke, I would be able to say, "Because something which my mind found intolerable pushed me to examine the statement's foundations; I found them unsound and was forced to conclude that Johnson would agree with me—it was not just something I didn't like but some-

---

worst and the account of poetic structure itself had to be rejected, some of the examples might survive the rejection as independent readings."

12. I relish such transformations when, as in *Rosenkranz and Guildenstern are Dead,* by Tom Stoppard (New York, 1968), they make something new out of the original without claiming that "that was what Shakespeare really meant all the while." But see my "The First Full Professor of Ironology in the World" in *Now Don't Try to Reason with Me* (Chicago, 1971) for an enthusiastic spreading of other kinds of relish.

thing that I could not believe this author could seriously intend in this context." But when I am told by G. Wilson Knight that Claudius is the moral center of *Hamlet*,[13] or when Wayne Burns asks me to see Sancho Panza as *the* moral center of *Don Quixote*,[14] for a variety of personal reasons I may agree or disagree, but I know that nothing in the work itself requires me to agree.

## MEANING AND SIGNIFICANCE

But the phrase "in the work" is not, as we shall see again and again, unambiguous. Discovering an ironic intention in a work depends on that third step in the ironic reconstruction: the decision that the author cannot have intended such and such a meaning. Whether we see this step as taking us outside the work itself, it certainly opens us to debates about whose picture of the author, and of other relevant features of the context, is correct. Saving the problem of delimiting contexts for later, one can use here a distinction from the hermeneutic tradition, between "meaning" and "significance."[15] For the time being, we are seeking a kind of hard knowledge about "meanings," and we are relegating to "significance" all of the indefinitely extendable interpretations that any work might be given by individuals or societies pursuing their own interests unchecked by intentions.

Consider for a moment a fresh example, the statement by the narrator of Samuel Butler's *Erewhon:*

> . . . my swag was so heavy that I was very nearly drowned. I had indeed a hairbreadth escape; but, as luck would have it, Providence was on my side.

The interpretation of the meaning of this sentence is a highly complex matter; it cannot be purely intrinsic to the sentence, not only because the sentence comes from a large and intricate satirical work but because the reader must infer the author's intended meanings of all the words, and particularly of luck and Providence, before his reconstruction of the ironic joke is completed. But though the process is complex, the results are nearly certain. Any reader who fails to see some sort of joke about how belief in luck and belief in Providence both relate and clash has missed the ironic point. If someone tells me

---

13. *The Wheel of Fire,* rev. ed. (London, 1949), pp. 32–38.

14. *The Panzaic Principle* (Vancouver, B.C.: Privately printed, 1965), 32 pp.; reprinted in *Paunch* 22: 1–31. See also, for a variety of extensions of "the Panzaic principle," *Recovering Literature: A Journal of Contextualist Criticism,* ed. W. K. Buckley, Jr., et al. (La Jolla, Calif.), vol. 1 (Spring, 1972).

15. See Hirsch, *Validity in Interpretation,* esp. pp. 8 ff., 38, 39, 140 ff.

that for him luck and Providence "mean the same thing in the sentence, sort of like Fate, and there is no special conflict between the speaker's surface meaning and the author's intended meaning," I can say that I know he is wrong; every fellow "investigator" I have tried the passage on has confirmed my view that there is an ironic meaning.

Nothing like the same clarity obtains when we move to the sentence's "significance"—the whole range of social and historical association and of approval and disapproval that a given sentence or a given work takes on as it moves out into space and time from its intending author. The significance of Samuel Butler's sentence will be different, for example, for a confident believer in divine Providence and for Samuel Butler, even if both would agree about its meaning. A true believer might want to say that the sentence "is just one of many examples to be found throughout *Erewhon* of Butler's determination to attack the church and its beliefs; in this respect it is representative not only of Butler's apostasy but of a whole tragic historical movement in the later nineteenth century: a generation of gifted men in effect crippled their spiritual lives by conducting petty quarrels with superficial errors, or seeming errors, of the church. Butler's joke about Providence and luck, clever enough in itself, is finally a sad manifestation of those many adult little boys who, in the Victorian period, thought that to thumb their noses at authority or tradition was the same as to think profoundly about human life and its spiritual problems. That's what the sentence means *to me.*"

Such a statement, like the contradictory one that could easily be made in Butler's behalf, need not be ruled out of the realms of honest inquiry. Though it cannot be verified as a statement about meaning in our sense, it still offers itself as a kind of knowledge about the work: a general truth about it, a truth that other men ought to accept whether they do or not, and a truth that can be supported with good reasons. Two readers who were honestly committed to pursuing the question of Butler's significance could presumably discuss long and profitably, learning from each other the significance that *Erewhon* had to Butler's world and to later times. What is more, with a little care they could presumably reach a kind of agreement that could be called knowledge, according to criteria never admitted by Russell. The believer might come to agree, for example, that "for unbelievers in 1872, the book should have had such and such significance." The unbeliever might come to agree that "for believers in 1974 the book *has* such and such significance." It is possible that if they talked long enough and pursued their differences with sufficient open-mindedness, one or the other might go a step further and say, "I was wrong in accepting the picture I at first offered of the book's significance." But in doing so he would not be repudiating all of his previous knowledge about the book's significance; he would be in fact changing his whole world view, and in his new world view, knowledge about the book's significance to the two conflicting groups would still constitute a genuine and largely unchanged —though steadily expanding—element.

Running constant throughout any such debate would be agreement about meaning. No party to the various discussions will take any originator seriously who suggests that Butler was really defending the church or was really a Satanist alluding to Beelzebub with his reference to Providence; or that for Butler Providence suggests Fate and Fate suggests Karma, and that there is thus a strong likelihood that he was satirizing those in his time who toyed with Eastern philosophy. Yet I suspect that if I worked up an article defending any one of these absurd readings, I could get it published, as things stand, so confused have we become about what makes a contribution to meaning.

In short, some debates about ironic readings could be more often brought to profitable term if critics made clear which kind of contribution they are attempting: an expansion or redefinition of *terms*; an explication or illumination of *meanings*; an exploration of *significance* the work has or had for a given body of readers; or an exhibition of the *critic's private sensibility*. Even this last, which I cannot resist putting pejoratively, need not be useless: the final significance of any work might be thought of as the accumulation of what all "private sensibilities" could make of it. It might even be that in a time of heavy conventionality among critics, when received opinions carried undue weight, a romantic pursuit of private readings could in fact free readers from radically deficient readings. But we do not live in such a time—or if we do, our received opinions are those that exalt the private and idiosyncratic and novel. If we are to get our bearings, we can afford for a while to probe again for what oft was thought, instead of seeking what ne'er was thought, regardless of how badly expressed.

## STABLE IRONY AND OTHER FIGURES OF SPEECH

Though what I have said should serve to dramatize how strikingly stable irony differs from what is often called irony, I must now say something more about how the four steps in its reconstruction differ from those we take with some other literary devices that "say one thing and mean another." (I must ignore all acts of deliberate deception, even though in some definitions they would be considered ironic: e.g., flattery and other hyperbole not designed to be seen through—"Darling! How absolutely devastating!"; advertising euphemisms; plain lies.)

## Metaphor

In reading any metaphor or simile, as in reading irony, the reader must reconstruct unspoken meanings through inferences about surface statements that for some reason cannot be accepted at face value; in the terminology made fashionable by I. A. Richards, there is a *tenor* (a principal subject) conveyed by a *vehicle* (the secondary subject). It is not surprising, then, that many casual definitions of irony would fit metaphor just as well, and that the two have sometimes been lumped together in criticism.[16]

All the world's a stage . . .

1. As in reading irony, here one is first required to go beyond the surface meaning, but what is rejected is primarily the grammatical

---

16. An uncommonly serious effort to distinguish them was made by Reuben Brower in *The Fields of Light: An Experiment in Critical Reading* (New York, 1962), chap. 3, "Saying One Thing and Meaning Another." His discussion of irony, though brief, is far more perceptive than most.

I cannot pretend to explain why, with all the casual reliance on undifferentiated "irony" as a pseudo-explanation of literary effects, there is so much less serious discussion of how it works than there is of metaphor. Except for the work of Grice (see chap. 9, n. 1 below) and Cohen (n. 10 above) I know of very little by professional philosophers on irony, and there are scores of articles and books on metaphor. Though they tend to ignore rhetorical questions in favor of topics like "the truth value of metaphor," there is a good deal of interesting work on "how metaphors can be understood, identified and assessed" (Ina Loewenberg, "Truth and Consequences of Metaphors," *Philosophy and Rhetoric* 6 [Winter 1973]: 30–46; the footnotes to this article provide a good starting bibliography of current issues about metaphor—most of them not directly rhetorical in my sense).

Perhaps the most extensive effort in English to place irony in a general aesthetic theory is Monroe Beardsley's *Aesthetics: Problems in the Philosophy of Criticism* (New York, 1958). Beardsley defines a literary work as "discourse in which an important part of the meaning is implicit." Such a "semantic definition" of literature as "meaning" of course leads him to classify kinds of literature according to their degrees of "secondary" or implicit meanings; metaphor and irony tend in this view to become treated in similar terms, since both are ways in which discourse becomes "self-controverting." A metaphor is "a significant attribution that is either indirectly self-contradictory or obviously false in its context" (pp. 138, 142), and the irony I call stable is for him simply the clearest instance of what is the essential ingredient of all literature. I can fortunately dodge a quarrel with this view, because I am not attempting a general theory of aesthetics; in practice, there is a radical difference between what the two figures require us to do: though both may be said to be in one sense "self-controverting," the powerful shock of negative recognition essential to irony is secondary or muted or perhaps sometimes even non-existent in metaphor.

22

form of the claim. There is nothing secret or covert about it now; even when the clues given in similes (like, as) are missing, we know at once that the author means a comparison: the world is like a stage. (There may be metaphors which are not condensed similes, metaphors in which something more like true identity is intended—"Our birth is but a sleep and a forgetting:/The Soul that rises with us, our life's Star . . ." —and these are clearly even less like irony.) The process is therefore not usually one of repudiation or reversal but of exploration or extension. There is no moment of shock when incompatibles are forced upon our attention, with the demand for active negative judgment; or if there is, the shock is relatively muted, and it is caused only by the misleading form of the statement (identity claimed where similarity is meant), not by any absurdity or impossibility in what is said. The essential process, as most writers on metaphor have stressed, is addition or multiplicaton, not subtraction.

2. As the open invitation to add unspoken meanings is accepted, with or without further words from the author, we face a need for choice only if and when we come to meanings that *are* incongruous, and these will ordinarily not be the first we think of; in fact, if they come to mind too early, we conclude that the metaphor is clumsy or inapt. Usually they arrive late and without much strength: we have no difficulty ruling from our attention, in the life-stage metaphor, the selling of tickets, fire insurance laws, the necessity for floodlights, and so on. And even these might be incorporated meaningfully into the metaphor's range by an aggressively metaphoric mind.

3. Thus no moment of conscious decision about the author's beliefs is thrust upon us. Except for the unspoken "metaphorically speaking," everything implied by the statement is in harmony with it from the beginning: as the author says and as he clearly believes, the world is like a stage in this way, and in this way, and in this way, and . . .

That we do not find ourselves forced to a decision does not, of course, mean that no decision is made. I suspect that even the simplest communication of the most literal meanings would prove on close analysis to depend on steps and judgments as complicated as any we find in irony or metaphor. The point is, however, that irony dramatizes each moment by heightening the consequences of going astray.

4. Though there may be a point of decision, then—this far I will go with the stage metaphor and no farther—it is not a decision like the one between two Voltaires, one a fool and one an ironist. Shakespeare (or Jaques) offered us a metaphor and we accepted it (and him) without question. It may not be disastrous if no decision is made at all. Some modern critics have even argued, quite wrongly I think, that a

decision to stop adding should *not* be made, since the more metaphoric associations one can find in a passage the better.

Obviously metaphors can themselves be used ironically; when they are, the fourfold process of interpreting irony sets in. "Policemen are pigs" or "Marilyn is a gazelle" may be straightforward metaphors or ironic ones;[17] to decide that they are ironic we must take the same steps as we would with a non-metaphorical irony: "For such and such reasons I am forced to reject the possibility that the metaphor is straightforward; it does not fit its context read in that way. The author *may* be simply careless or mad, but because I can think of an unspoken assumption or set of assumptions that he probably accepts and that harmonize with a reconstructed message that makes sense of the passage, I decide that he means the metaphor to be read ironically." If someone suggests, for example, that Shakespeare's metaphor is really ironic—used to characterize Jaques negatively, not as a poetically respectable metaphor connecting the world and stages—I can ask for evidence that each of the four steps is required.

We see then that although the reader of metaphor usually comes to a point at which he must say, "No—this far and no farther," in irony the negatives press in on him from the beginning. Some critics have even said that irony is finally negative,[18] so evident is it that the first step in reading it is a resounding "no" and a pulling back to discover some possible way of making sense that can replace the rejected nonsense.

### Allegory and Fable

Prolonged doublings of meaning, as in allegory and fable, work much like metaphor. Though there may be a moment of shock when the requirement to see more than is said is recognized, it will be a requirement to add meanings, not to see incompatibles and then choose among them.

All readers of Bunyan's *Pilgrim's Progress*, for example, soon recognize, even if they overlook the author's "Apology" and its announcement that the author "Fell suddenly into an Allegory," that they must reconstruct everything that is said. Reading about "a Man

17. You have trouble imagining a context where this would happen? It's easy. A writer wants to satirize the New Left, and he writes, "There was once a member of the New Left who desperately needed a policeman to save her from a maniacal intruder in her Greenwich Village apartment. 'Police, police!' she shouted, hoping that someone would hear her through the open window. Her boy friend, lounging beneath the window, knew that she just had to be kidding, and mumbled, 'Policemen are pigs.'"
18. See Muecke for examples, esp. chaps. 7 and 8.

cloathed with Raggs, standing in a certain place" they move easily to a
second order of meanings about Christians and their pilgrimage
through the world. But there is no repudiation of the literal pilgrimage,
merely an addition to it. Within a page "the man" meets Evangelist,
and we experience no shock, because everything about the style has
prepared us for a kind of biblical experience. When we then read the
following passage, no shift of direction is required to accommodate the
personifications of abstract qualities:

> The Neighbours also came out to see him run, and as he ran,
> some mocked, others threatned; and some cried after him to re-
> turn: Now among those that did so, there were two that were
> resolved to fetch him back by force. The name of the one was *Ob-
> stinate,* and the name of the other *Pliable.*

Though there is a good deal of dramatic irony (see below, pp. 63–67)
in the counsel that Obstinate then gives Christian, because we see how
mistaken he is, the allegorical transformations are not in themselves
ironical in our present sense: the reconstructed meanings are added to,
not subtracted from, what a strictly literal reading would yield.

This distinction is not merely of theoretical importance. For the
reader there could not be a greater difference between the traps laid by
stable irony and the invitations offered by allegory. A naive reader
who overlooks irony will totally misunderstand what is going on. A
naive reader who reads an allegory without taking conscious thought,
refusing all invitations to reconstruct general meanings out of the literal
surface, will in effect obtain an experience something like what the
allegory intends: the emotional and intellectual pattern will be in the
direction of what it would be for the most sophisticated reader. One can
see this clearly in talking with children who have read C. S. Lewis's
Narnia books without being aware of the Christian allegory. To talk
explicitly of the death and rebirth of the lion as "like the story of
Christ" neither surprises the child nor offends him; a mild additional
pleasure is added, but the essential experience remains the same. But
when someone is corrected about misreading an irony, he is shocked;
he is being asked to repudiate all of his original response and move in
an entirely new direction.

There is such a thing as ironic allegory, of course, and its effects
are often the effects of stable irony. The explicit attack on communist
(and other) totalitarianisms that we reconstruct in reading Orwell's
*Animal Farm* is re-created against the grain of the literal evaluations
offered on the surface of the tale.

Sometimes, as in Swift's *A Tale of a Tub,* an allegory is partly ironic and partly straightforward. The Grub Street hack who narrates the satiric allegory of Peter, Martin, and Jack can blame their achievements through pretended praise ("It will be no difficult Part to persuade the reader, that so many *worthy* Discoveries met with great Success in the World," section IV) and then, two sentences later, he will attack them directly ("In short, what with Pride, Projects, and *Knavery,* poor Peter was grown distracted . . ."). "He [Jack] was besides, a Person of *great Design and Improvement in Affairs of Devotion,"* we read in one paragraph in section XI, and in the next, "When he had some *Roguish Trick* to play . . ." (my italics).[19] The point is that these required shifts, which provide an intense kind of challenge in some ironical allegory, are neither different from the shifting tone one meets in many non-allegorical ironic works nor essential to allegory.

## Puns

Like every other figure except irony itself, puns can be used either ironically or straight. Puns of all kinds are close to stable irony in intending a reconstruction; they are all more or less covert and most of them yield rigorously limited or local interpretations. But many of them are more like metaphor than irony, lacking the step of negation. "When we were at the circus, the heat was in-tents." This folk pun requires a leap of reconstruction, but it does not require us to repudiate the surface meaning, which makes perfectly good sense in itself (when the pun is spoken, not written); when we do recognize the pun we must still keep the original meaning unmodified as part of the reconstruction.

Puns which are both aural and visual, like those in Joyce's *Finnegans Wake,* come closer to our account of irony. When Joyce refers to "muddlecrass" students or offers "end of muddy crushmess" as a yuletide greeting, the invitation to reconstruct the meanings is clearly intended and inescapable; the translation is (unlike many required by Joyce) relatively stable and finite; at least part of the reconstructed message can be called covert; and the primary, non-pejorative meanings of "middleclass" and "Merry Christmas" are undermined in the

19. Herbert J. Davis has described this "inconsistency" well: "What I would contend is that here, just as all his other later disguises, Swift simply makes use of a mask as it suits him; it is never permanently moulded over his face, and it always allows him to use his own voice. It is a mask which he holds in his hand, like a comedian, which may be withdrawn at any moment to show a sardonic grin or a humorous smile" ("Swift's Use of Irony," *The Uses of Irony: Papers on Defoe and Swift,* by Maximillian E. Novak and Herbert J. Davis [Los Angeles, 1966], p. 44).

process of reconstruction. It would not trouble me too much if we therefore called such passages stable irony, except when we are in fact adding rather than subtracting. It is often hard to sày what is the overt and what the covert meaning in Joyce's puns, and we often do not know whether the several readings of a portmanteau word are equally repudiated or equally embraced. They can thus seldom be called stable irony, even when we must consider them ironic in some other sense.

The effect is different when puns are used in full stable irony. When Vindici, disguised as Piato in Tourneur's *The Revenger's Tragedy,* tries to convince his mother that she should in effect sell his sister, her daughter, she replies, "Oh fie, fie! the riches of the world cannot hire a mother to such a most unnaturall taske." Vindici answers:

> No, but a thousand Angells can[.]
> Men haue no power, Angells must worke you to't.
> The world descends into such base-borne euills
> That forty Angells can make fourscore deuills. [II.i][20]

Vindici intends irony, and even those of us who have no knowledge of Elizabethan coinage are driven to see that the surface meaning of "Angel" cannot account for such a speech. Those Angells are not both angels and coins, they are devilish coins, and yet they pretend to be angels.

For reasons that are perhaps by now obvious, Joyce's puns, like yours and mine, are most effective when they go all the way and become ironic in this respect: not "I yam as I yam," in which the yam contributes nothing that I can see, but rather "Do you hold yourself then for some God in the manger, Shehohem, that you will neither serve nor let serve, pray nor let pray?"

### STABLE IRONY AND SATIRE

A great deal has been made of the inevitable presence of victims, real or imagined, in all stable irony. But for several reasons this is slightly misleading. It is true that irony often presents overt victims: Johnson's "Bolingbroke was a holy man"; Kierkegaard's "the audacious pen-strokes of recent philosophic investigators." It is also true that even in the most amiable irony one can always imagine a victim by conjuring up a reader or listener so naive as not to catch the joke; no doubt in some

20. The example is used by Peter Liska to make a different point in *"The Revenger's Tragedy:* A Study in Irony," *Philological Quarterly* 38 (1959): 242–51.

uses of irony the fun of feeling superior to such imagined victims is highly important. But we need no very extensive survey of ironic examples to discover—unless we are choosing the examples to dramatize the use of victims—that the building of amiable communities is often far more important than the exclusion of naive victims. Often the predominant emotion when reading stable ironies is that of joining, of finding and communing with kindred spirits. The author I infer behind the false words is my kind of man, because he enjoys playing with irony, because he assumes *my* capacity for dealing with it, and—most important—because he grants me a kind of wisdom; he assumes that he does not have to spell out the shared and secret truths on which my reconstruction is to be built.

Even irony that does imply victims, as in all ironic satire, is often much more clearly directed to more affirmative matters. And every irony inevitably builds a community of believers even as it excludes. The cry "Hail, King of the Jews," an example cited by Thomas Hobbes, was intended initially to satirize Christ's followers who had claimed him as king; presumably the chief pleasure for the shouting mob was the thought of the victims, including Christ himself. But what of Mark as he overtly reports the irony ironically in his account of the crucifixion?[21]

It is true that Mark may in part intend an irony against the original ironists, but surely his chief point is to build, through ironic pathos, a sense of brotherly cohesion among those who see the essential truth in his account of the man-God who, though *really* King of the Jews, was

21. Curiously enough, John changes the whole point: Pilate writes the inscription, "Jesus of Nazareth the King of the Jews," and the Jews then protest: "Write not, The King of the Jews; but that he said, I am King of the Jews." But Pilate, more favorable to Jesus than in the other accounts, says, "What I have written I have written"—a new and weaker irony substituted for the strong one in Mark.

Further elaboration can weaken further:

FIRST SOLDIER:    Hail! comely King, who no kingdom
                     hast known.
                     Hail! undoughty duke . . .
FOURTH SOLDIER:  Hail! strong one, who may scarcely
                     stand up to fight.
                     Whee! rascal, heave up thine hand
                     And thank us all who are worshipping thee . . .

(York Tilemakers' Play, from *York Plays,* ed. Lucy Smith, no. 33, lines 409–20, as quoted by Earle Birney, "English Irony before Chaucer," *University of Toronto Quarterly* 6 [1936–37]: 542.)

reduced to this miserable mockery. The wicked and foolish insolence of those who mocked the Lord with the original "Hail" is no doubt part of Mark's picture, but it is surely all in the service of the communion of Saints.[22]

And there is a curious further point about this community of those who grasp any irony: it is often a larger community, with fewer outsiders, than would have been built by non-ironic statement. Ironists have often been accused of elitism. For Kierkegaard, irony "looks down, as it were, on plain and ordinary discourse immediately understood by everyone; it travels in an exclusive incognito. . . . [It] occurs chiefly in the higher circles as a prerogative belonging to the same category as that *bon ton* requiring one to smile at innocence and regard virtue as a kind of prudishness."[23] But it seems clear that Mark's irony builds a larger community of readers than any possible literal statement of his beliefs could have done. If he had said simply, "Those who gathered to mock Jesus did not know that he was in fact King, king not only of the Jews but of all mankind, quite literally the Son of God," a host of unbelievers would draw back, at least slightly. But the ironic form can be shared by everyone who has any sympathy for Jesus at all, man or God; even the reader who sees him as a self-deluded fanatic is likely to join Mark in his reading of the irony, and thus to have his sympathy for the crucified man somewhat increased.

Similarly, when Johnson calls Bolingbroke a "holy man," he catches more of us in his net than he would have with "Bolingbroke is an unholy man." *Unholy* is relatively narrow and at the far end of the scale of blame that Bolingbroke's critics might be willing to apply. But *holy* as irony can be accepted and enjoyed by everyone who is in any degree suspicious or critical of Bolingbroke; it is a kind of contradiction, but by no means strictly an opposite, of a wide range of views, all the way from "not always quite as virtuous as he ought to be" to "vile." All readers will be required to reconstruct the message in a form that goes *against* Bolingbroke, but each will reconstruct it according to his own estimate of the man. And each will be likely to assume that Johnson sees it the same way, thus adding to his negative judgment of Bolingbroke, however mild, the strength of his pleasure in joining the shrewd ironist. Though victimization of bad readers is present in

22. The dialectical relation of affirmative and negative in such ironies is illuminated by Kenneth Burke's repeated jest, "Yes, I know you are Christian, but who are you Christian *against*?"

23. *The Concept of Irony, with Constant Reference to Socrates,* trans. Lee M. Capel (London, 1966), p. 265.

much stable irony, it is thus far from essential, unless one wants to say that the reader is victimized by being caught in a net of collusion cast by the skillful author.

In short, irony is used in some satire, not in all; some irony is satiric, much is not.[24] And the same distinctions hold for sarcasm.

It is scarcely surprising that such a powerful and potentially deceptive tool as stable irony should have been deplored by moralists. But it would be a serious mistake to see it as only in the service of the spirit of eternal denial. Though the devil is a great ironist, so is the Lord; the great prophets have used irony as freely as the great sinners. It can be found on almost every page of many great writers, but you will also find it sprinkling the conversation of the railroad workers in Utah and—I am told—the street sweepers in Bombay. As my family recently walked toward the cathedral, highly visible before us, in Angers, a cement worker looked at us and said, at first without a smile, "The Cathedral is that way"—pointing to it—"and the Palace of Justice is there"—pointing to the sign on the building right before our eyes: "Palais de Justice."

I knew that he intended an ironic stroke, though I could not at first be sure whether we were to be excluded as mere victims—stupid American tourists who would not recognize the deliberate absurdity of

24. There is one kind of ironic attack which takes the form of pretended satire and often expresses genuine distance or hostility, but which social custom requires to be taken without deep offense. What in some English dialects is known as flyting, what some anthropologists have named "joking relationships," takes place in many cultures. As A. R. Radcliffe-Brown describes the practice in some African tribes, this form of teasing depends on "a relation between two persons [or even two tribes] in which one is by custom permitted, and in some instances required, to tease or make fun of the other, who in turn is required to take no offence. It is important to distinguish two main varieties. In one the relation is symmetrical; each of the two persons teases or makes fun of the other. In the other variety the relation is asymmetrical. . . . The joking relationship is a peculiar combination of friendliness and antagonism. The behaviour is such that in any other social context it would express and arouse hostility; but it is not meant seriously and must not be taken seriously. There is a pretence of hostility and a real friendliness." Reporting on an extensive literature about this relationship, Radcliffe-Brown theorizes that it is a mode of "organising a definite and stable system of social behaviour in which conjunctive and disjunctive components . . . are maintained and combined ("On Joking Relationships," *Structure and Function in Primitive Society* [New York, 1952; Free Press Paperback, 1965], pp. 90–91, 95). It seems likely that an anthropologist who went into a society looking not only for teasing patterns—pretended satire—but for other patterns of ironic usage would find a much more complicated world than this one in which nephews can insult their uncles with impunity.

such obvious and uncalled-for directions. But we were clearly welcomed within the circle of ironists as soon as I said, "Oh, yes, and the workers are *here* (pointing at them) and the Americans are *here* (pointing at us)." His laughter told me that he now knew that I knew that he knew that I . . . The circle of inferences was closed, and we knew each other in ways that only extended conversation could otherwise have revealed. Total strangers, we had just performed an intricate intellectual dance together, and we knew that we were somehow akin.

But there is as little social unity in a coterie of ironists as there is truly honesty among a band of thieves.

—Kierkegaard

If a person, against whom *irony* is level'd, is so arrogant and self-sufficient as to be persuaded that he is possessed of all the virtues and great good qualities to which he is entirely a stranger, he will be, like the man in the almanack, insensible of a smart, though all his beholders see him stuck full of darts.

—*The Craftsman,* 1731

But if what I have written be the strongest Irony, and consequently the greatest push that I could make . . .

—Defoe

# TWO | Reconstructions and Judgments

## RIVAL METAPHORS

I t is in a way surprising that we do not have a distinctive verb for the unique and complex process of reading stable irony. One would think that, like those primitive tribes who develop a variety of distinct terms for different ways of cutting with an axe, we would have developed something more precise, for understanding stable irony, than "interpret" or "decipher" or "translate" or "understand" or "dig" or any of the many other expressions for taking another person's meaning. Discussions of irony, especially since the term began its imperialistic wanderings through the whole of man's discourse, have been marked by an effort to find either a literal term or the proper metaphor to name the marvelous art of reading it. Recently the most popular metaphor has been that of seeing behind a mask or a "persona." In this view the reader is thought of as unmasking an *eiron,* or detecting behind a "mask-character" or persona the lineaments of the true speaker. This metaphor has at least the great advantage, over terms like "decipher" or "decode" or "translate," of suggesting the complexity and uniqueness of persons, not the substitution of one simple message for another simple message. The meaning of an irony in this view inescapably includes the dramatic engagement of person with person— in the form of peering and unmasking. And the metaphor has the final advantage of entailing "personal feelings" and suggesting the presence of drama.

Since no metaphor can capture the thing itself, we need not repudiate any of these. Reading irony *is* in some ways like translating, like decoding, like deciphering, and like peering behind a mask. But these all, in my view, underplay the complexity of what the reader is required to do. Conscious of a loss in grace and warmth, then, I turn to the building trades, to "reconstruction," implying the tearing down of one habitation and the building of another one on a different spot. In playing with the notion of reconstructed buildings and relocated inhabitants, we can see more clearly the almost incredible intricacy of the *pas de deux* that I reduced to "marks" and "steps" above.

We have already seen that ironic reconstructions depend on an appeal to assumptions, often unstated, that ironists and readers share. In this they resemble—and can help to illuminate—all other forms of verbal communication; we never make all of our shared assumptions explicit, and if we encounter readers or auditors who are determined to deny all "unproved" assumptions we are always in trouble. As the

classical rhetoricians taught, conviction about any belief that is not
thought to be self-evident is produced by a speaker's finding beliefs
that the listener will accept and that are thought to imply the desired
conclusion. I do not convince you that our king is a menace by saying
so (though saying so may in itself plant suspicion if you have an assumption that I am worth attending to); I must convince you that I
know of qualities and actions of his that you will think *imply* a threat
to your welfare or a violation of your values. If I cannot find some
point of contact with your notions of what implies threat, some point
on which we can stand in agreement as we explore our disagreements,
I can never hope to change your mind. The process is not of course
confined to what is conventionally thought of as rhetoric; all communication, including education and inquiry, can only move from the
known to the unknown.

From Aristotle until the nineteenth century, treatises on rhetoric
as the art of persuasion always included an account of the intellectual
"locations" that could provide such points of agreement. Once found,
these locations—what the Greeks called *topoi,* the Latins *loci,* and the
English *places*—were used almost literally as platforms on which
speaker and listener could securely stand while conducting an argument; there were, of course, *"common* places," yielding points useful in
arguments on any and every subject, and "special places" useful only
for certain subjects or kinds of argument. Sometimes rhetors constructed for themselves mental blueprints of entire edifices containing
many places. Such buildings were recommended most often as aids to
memory—an orator could move through his building and find not only
his places but recall his chosen sequence with what seems to us almost
incredibly detailed memory. But they were also aids to successful
communication and were useful pedagogical devices. Though study of
the "topics" may seem to modern readers uninvitingly routine and
repetitive, they often served to liberate from needless confusion and
endless quibbles about what we call semantics.[1]

This notion of a complex dwelling place can be useful, stretched
far beyond its original application, in clarifying what we do as we read
irony. The reconstruction implied by conventional formulas about
irony would be a very simple one. Irony, the dictionaries tell us, is
saying one thing and meaning the opposite. If we apply the metaphor
of locations to such a definition, there would seem to be no great act
of reconstruction required; the reader is asked simply to move from

1. The original source is Aristotle (esp. the *Rhetoric* and *Topics*), but the
topics really came into their own, as it were, with Cicero's elaborate developments, especially in his *Topica.*

one platform, on which the speaker pretends to stand, to another one, on which he really stands—one that is somehow "opposite," across the street, as it were. But perhaps the implied intellectual motion is really "downward," "going beneath the surface" to something solider or more profound; we rip up a rotten platform and probe to a solid one.

"Ignore the hungry and they'll go away"

(Relief Fund appeal, London, 1970)

"Give to our fund or the hungry will die"

Fig. 1

There's nothing especially wrong with this view, except that it still radically obscures the complexity of what we do, and how we manage to do it. How did we know that the first platform was shaky?

Obviously each statement stands for much more than itself, implying a whole world—or "building"—of related beliefs. The first suggests inhabitants who could accept such implications as "It doesn't matter if people die from hunger," "The way to deal with problems is to ignore them," "Out of sight, out of mind," and "Let them eat cake." The second statement could be embraced only by someone who believed that "It is bad for anyone to die of hunger," "When there is a social ill, one should do what he can to cure it," "Some organizers can be trusted to take upon themselves the charitable duties of their fellows," and so on. Thus I do not reject the printed statement because of any literal untruth. I reject it because I refuse to dwell with anyone who holds this whole *set* of beliefs. And then, because I cannot believe that the author of the statement can be that kind of person, I am forced (through psychological and intellectual pressures which I will not even pretend to understand or explain) to make sense out of the statement by concluding that it is ironic.[2]

2. I suspect that many different current theories of how the mind makes sense out of conflict might fit the facts of what we do. Theories of "cognitive dissonance" are especially tempting: the mind leaps to an ironic interpretation whenever the dissonance produced by a straight reading becomes too great to bear. Some of the most interesting questions about 'how we interpret' are being raised by "structuralists," though they tend, like many other close readers, to give us their elaborate results rather than telling us how they achieved them. See, for example, "Charles Baudelaire's 'Les chats'" by Roman Jakobson and Claude Lévi-Strauss (*L'Homme* 2 [1962]; widely reprinted, as in *Structuralism: A Reader,* ed. Michael Lane [London, 1970]), in translation by Katie Furness-Lane. "Structuralism" has of course become a catch-all term, and those who call

35

Note once again that it does me little good to say that *I* reject the structure of beliefs implied, unless I have good reason to believe that the author intends my rejection. The process of reading the irony is thus better represented by the metaphor of reconstructing a whole building, any final statable message being only a kind of roof, or perhaps capstone, for a whole collection of propositions that make up a solider structure than the one implied by the original overt statement. (In each structure there will be some kind of coherence between the grounds, as reasons, and the conclusions, but of course the connections need not be strictly logical.)

What is more, the process is in some respects more like a leap or climb to a higher level than like scratching a surface or plunging deeper. The movement is always toward an obscured point that is intended as wiser, wittier, more compassionate, subtler, truer, more moral, or at least less obviously vulnerable to further irony. Since there is always a sense in which part of the new view is a look back upon the old inferior dwelling, the moving van is perhaps better described as traveling upward to a nicer part of town. In place of the simple two-platform plunge, implied by all definitions of irony as "saying the opposite of what you mean," we now are yielded the elaborateness illustrated by figure 2.

Thus in every successful interpretation of stable irony we find not only that the four steps described in chapter 1 have been taken, with the resulting clarity about the invitation to come live at the higher and firmer location, but also that there is a strong sense of rejecting a whole structure of meanings, a kind of world that the author himself obviously rejects. There is also usually—some have said always—a possibility that some readers may choose to dwell in happy ignorance in the shaky edifice, thus adding to its absurdity.

Successful reconstruction obviously does not require that the reader finally accept without question the superior edifice. He may conclude that the choices should be drawn differently, with perhaps a

---

themselves structuralists are often not concerned to distinguish whether they are dealing with poetic structures, structures of intention in poets, structures of interpretation in readers or between readers and poets, or mythic or linguistic structures in the societies from which literary works spring. For good current efforts to come to terms with structuralism, see recent issues of *New Literary History* (e.g., "French Structuralism and Literary History: Some Critiques and Reconsiderations," by Robert Weimann, in vol. 3 [Spring 1973]) and *Novel* (e.g., "The Contributions of Formalism and Structuralism to the Theory of Fiction," by Robert Scholes in vol. 6 [Winter 1973]).

Because of the vogue, I want to insist that according to at least three separate definitions of the term this book is a work of structuralism.

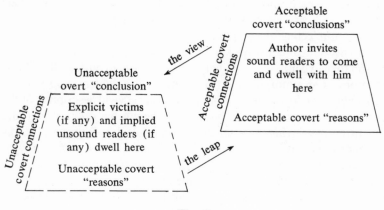

Fig. 2

third edifice, even higher, for whose inhabitants the author of the original irony is himself an ironic victim. "Ignore the hungry and they'll go away" may be vulnerable to this kind of further undermining. Some readers of the slogan have called it "sick humor." "Somehow the hungry are the victims of that humor," my friend in London said. Stable irony is always in this sense potentially unstable, but there is no doubt that stability was intended. No critic of the irony chooses to accept the original statement at face value, or fails to understand precisely what its invitation is. The act of reconstructing *meaning* is itself thus clear and accurate and stable enough: the two dwellings are seen for what they are and the invitation to leave one and choose the other is accepted. That such a choice can be then undermined with further ironies, intended by the reader who now becomes an intending ironist in his own right, is part of the significance the text may acquire.

## ADVANTAGES OF "RECONSTRUCTION"

In sum, the metaphor of buildings and reconstructions, clumsy as it may seem, has several advantages:

1. It reminds us of inescapable complexities: in addition to whatever one takes as a final message, there are always other unspoken beliefs that may or may not serve as firm foundations; there are always inferential processes between these foundations and the conclusions that rest on them; there are always both an incongruity of content and an intended difference in "elevation" between the two "conclusions," one of them not stated; and there is always thus an implied claim to superiority of total vision in the final view of those who see the irony and thus a potential look downward on those who dwell in error. The

metaphor suggests thus a choice between two large structures of beliefs each so tightly associated that to reject or accept any one of them may well entail rejecting or accepting a whole way of life.

This is no doubt why explaining an irony is usually even less successful than explaining an ordinary joke, and why to mistake literal talk for irony is an unforgiveable sin. I once had a student who wrote a paper about the joys of deer hunting, including a vivid description of the thrill that "coursed through" his veins as he cut the deer's throat and watched the life dying in those "large, beautiful, child-like eyes." It was evident to me that he was satirizing blood sport. But I found, in what seems now to have been one of the most ineffectual conferences I have ever had with a student, that my ironic reading was to him plain crazy. I made the mistake of lingering over his bloodthirsty phrases, trying to explain to him why I had thought them ironic. But he was simply baffled, as well he might be; to read irony in any one of his statements was to misunderstand his entire perception of what his life and the deer's were all about. Wrestling with irony, he and I were not talking only about "verbal" matters; we were driven into debate about how a man should live.

2. The metaphor also dramatizes the possibility of an unlimited variety of "distances" between the dwelling places. The differences can be of any size and in any direction on any axis of belief, knowledge, or value—any direction, that is, except "downward." What is up for some ironists will of course be down for others; when ironists pretend, as they sometimes do, to invite us downward, it is downward only on their victim's scale but still upward on the ironist's own. An atheist satirizing the naive piety of a believer—"It almost broke my heart to have to undeceive him, dragging him down from the heights to grovel with me in the facts of life as it is lived"—is inviting us to look down on the rejected position just as much as God is when he says to Job:

> Where were you when I laid the earth's foundations?
> Tell me, if you know and understand.
> Who settled its dimensions? Surely you should know.
>                        [38:4–5, NEB translation]

When Hume makes wry fun of the beliefs underlying the admirable resignation of Charles I when facing death (p. 3 above), he can do so only by assuming that his view of things is superior to that of Charles, and this is of course to invite the reader to join him in his higher position, even though for a believer it is to assume a more worldly and therefore a lower position. When ironists write the devil's dictionary, they have no doubt who is the supreme lexicographer.

38

3. The metaphor clarifies what many commentators have noticed, namely, that there are often many rejected propositions and many victims, not just one. "When all was over and the rival kings were celebrating their victory with Te Deums in their respective camps . . ." —in the "dwelling" rejected here by Voltaire we see not only a whole crew of ridiculous kings and priests but also a host of naive believers and poor readers, some of them not even obliquely mentioned in the presented words.[3]

4. The metaphor helps to explain what is meant by saying that the "words" *require* reconstruction. In many ironies, perhaps in most, the words themselves do not require retranslation. They are in fact words which in other contexts would be accepted in precisely this form without demur. It is always something in their surroundings, and it is usually something merely implicit in their "place," that gives them away.

5. Perhaps most important, to talk in these terms about what we do makes it impossible to think of irony as something that can be fully paraphrased in non-ironic statement. The act of reconstruction and all that it entails about the author and his picture of the reader become an inseparable part of what is said, and thus that act cannot really be *said,* it must be *performed.* All figurative speech can be seen as a mutual performance in this sense, beyond paraphrase. Any terminology that, like I. A. Richards's *tenor* and *vehicle,* suggests otherwise is misleading.

## REQUIRED JUDGMENTS

In reading stable irony we are always required to make a series of precise judgments. Not only must we take the four steps described in chapter 1, which include (1) a judgment against the overt proposition and (2) a decision about where the author stands; we now see that it is almost impossible to escape two additional judgments, about (3) whether the reconstructed building is indeed a good place to dwell in,

---

3. Muecke uses the word *innocent* to describe the victim, and particularly the reader who may be victimized. The word may be misleading because we must keep in mind how often in irony the "innocent" is in fact the ironist with whom we choose to dwell, as his innocence undermines the falsely sophisticated (e.g., *The Good Soldier Schweik.*) See also Blake's couplets:

> Thank God, I never was sent to school . . .
> To be Flog'd into following the Style of a Fool.
> The Errors of a Wise Man make your Rule
> Rather than the Perfections of a Fool.

(*Blake: Complete Writings,* ed. Geoffrey Keynes [Oxford, 1966], p. 550.)

and (4) whether the ironist was justified in forcing us to go to all of this trouble—is he, finally, writing or speaking well? The last three of these are shared with the reader of non-metaphorical passages, but irony transforms even these. The first is shared in some degree with readers of other figurative writing, but again irony dramatizes and heightens the choices until they are scarcely recognizable. In looking more closely at how the ironist's way of making these four invitations to judge can increase—or diminish—rhetorical force, we can begin to learn why stable irony has proved so durable and widespread, even as critical theory has neglected it, or even denigrated it, in favor of instabilities and ambiguities.[4]

1. As we have seen (pp. 21–27), all non-literal language, every "abnormal" way of saying anything, invites us to reject a lower literal interpretation and climb to a better one. "He looks at life through rose-colored glasses"—we are faced here with a demand for a metaphorical reconstruction that is superior, in truth, in perceptiveness, in imaginative skill, to the literal reading which is trivial or even nonsensical. But note again that the rejected meaning is, in all metaphor and simile, so uninviting or irrelevant that there is really no contest. "Business is a rat-race." "She is an elephant." "My love is like a red, red rose." The strictly literal meanings are so obviously unlikely that only the metaphoric meaning has sufficient appeal to be considered seriously. Though a literal image of rat-races, elephants, or roses may remain part of our final reconstruction, insofar as they do they in no sense cancel or subtract from the non-literal views that the reader has come to. But in stable irony (whether employing metaphor or not) the superiority of the new meaning is an aggressive or competitive superiority—the rejected meaning is in some real sense a rival or threat. Someone *could* say it and mean it literally, yet it must be totally rejected—though of course it is still somehow kept in mind, as part of our awareness of the irony. "A Daniel come to judgment." The satiric force when Shylock's

4. Stable irony seems to be used, at least in oral form, in all cultures. I have been unable to find anyone from any land—in a rather casual sampling over the years—who could not think of examples from his own people. Sometimes it is built firmly into the usual terms for things—in western America tall men nicknamed Shorty; in one part of India a blind man called, in everyday speech, "man with a thousand eyes." For a first-rate anthropological discussion of a culture that lives with and by stable ironies (and unstable as well) see *Wax and Gold: Tradition and Innovation in Ethiopian Culture,* by Donald N. Levine (Chicago, 1965). The metaphor of wax and gold is used by Ethiopians to describe what happens in their ironies: the wax mold melts away, under interpretation, leaving the gold of true meaning—a striking parallel to my account of irony as essentially requiring a negative or "subtractive" step.

enemies in *The Merchant of Venice* turn his statement into irony comes precisely because he has earlier applied the same metaphor to Portia *without* irony. When irony succeeds, somehow the energy our minds put into recognizing this type of conflict and making our choices is transferred to one element or another in the ironic scene: either negatively against the victim, as in the standard (but often challenged) reading of Shylock, or affirmatively on behalf of the final reconstruction: having decided for myself that the ostensible judgment must be somehow combatted, I make the new position mine with all the force that is conferred by my sense of having judged independently. After all, I built this superior dwelling place "for myself."

2. The initial act of judgment, uniquely forceful in irony, will thus work strongly to support or weaken the second judgment, one which the reader of ironies shares with all other readers: where, really, does this author stand? Put in this form, the judgment may not seem necessarily to include an act of evaluation. But, clearly, in the very act of building a position that is coherent, plausible, humanly tenable, we are inescapably steeped in value choices.

All authors, to repeat, invite us to construct some sort of picture of their views and to judge them as in some sense coherent or plausible or challenging. But ironic authors obviously offer that invitation more aggressively, and we must answer it more actively: since the reader has in a sense put the final position together for himself, he can scarcely resist moving immediately to the third judgment: "Not only do I see it for what it is, but it must be sound since it is my own." Even short of that agreement, he has inevitably judged it to be in some sense better, since more plausible, than the position implied by the overt statement.

3. All readers are invited to agree with whatever message they cringe at the very suggestion of a message, even the purest poets, ask us to join them in whatever opinions, views, attitudes, or emotions they present or imply, and we have difficulty resisting a decision for or have discerned. Even the least didactic authors, even those who would against them. Even if an author presents no argument or position, claiming strict objectivity, indifference to the reader, or aesthetic impassivity, the reader will find himself choosing, perhaps unconsciously, to accept or reject the pose, or stand, or tone, or claim to poetic craft. But irony dramatizes this choice, forces us into hierarchical participation, and hence makes the results more actively our own.

4. The final judgment is also shared by all readers, but it is usually muted in all the arts that, unlike irony, work to conceal their art. Irony obtrudes itself and thus obtrudes its author's claim to skill. It risks disaster more aggressively than any other device. But if it

succeeds, it will succeed more strongly than any literal statement can do.

We can distinguish the workings of the last two kinds of judgment in the famous scene in *Julius Caesar* when Mark Antony reverses the crowd's mood by hammering relentlessly on the ironic "And Brutus is an honorable man." For the populace, when Mark Antony says for the first time that "Brutus is an honorable man," the invitation is simply to agree or disagree. If any of them takes the further step of judging that Mark Antony does not believe what he says, they will probably decide that he is a liar, not an ironist. But to us in the theater audience, knowing from the first word of praise that Mark Antony is contradicting his own views and working for a hidden purpose, there is a further invitation, this one from Shakespeare: in his invitation to ascend to *his* platform and watch the victims take Mark Antony's bait, he invites us to judge whether he, Shakespeare, is clever or wise or perceptive or subtle. After all, he is claiming to be clever in a way that he would not be if his presentation were direct. If we make this judgment favorably, our alignment with him is peculiarly heightened beyond what would be produced by any literal statement, even the most passionate: he and we are now engaged together in silent collusion as we watch the speaker play with his victims.

It is only as the scene proceeds that Mark Antony begins to produce this second effect between himself and *his* audience. As they begin to perceive that he is ironic—since it is impossible on any other hypothesis to reconcile his praise for Brutus with the rest of what he says—they do not just translate into the opposite conclusion: "Brutus is really *dis*honorable." They are forced to make the ironic leap in order to stand with Mark Antony on his platform (a good deal higher, one might say, than the literal one on which he stands) and they must feel themselves drawn to his conclusions by the acrobatic skill which they themselves have shown. And all of this energy now works against Brutus, who has been so stupid—or so it seems—as to lie to them again and again about being an honorable man. Meanwhile, needless to say, with each further step in the dramatic portrayal of these ironies *we* are more tightly caught in Shakespeare's own rhetorical net: the more intended ironies we discover in the scene, the cleverer we think him— and the cleverer we consider ourselves for joining him on his vantage point at least one degree higher even than Antony's.[5]

The full force of this ironic invitation to join the wise and the just

5. For a brilliant discussion of the rhetoric of this scene, including its ironies, see Kenneth Burke's "Antony in Behalf of the Play," *The Philosophy of Literary Form* (Baton Rouge, 1941), sec. 3.

in looking down on repudiated worlds can be seen in a further example. In the *Institutio oratoria* Quintilian tells of a speech by Cicero: "Believe me," Cicero said of Clodius, "your well known integrity has cleared you of all blame, your modesty has saved you, your past life has been your salvation."[6] Presumably every listener at the time recognized the irony, though the words taken out of context are not clearly ironic. But no listener could simply translate the statement into literal terms—something like, "Believe me, your well-known dishonesty has led everyone to blame you, your boastfulness has damned you, your past deeds have been your damnation." The literal statement, if spoken directly by Cicero, would indeed invite the listener to judge whether Cicero is right in his condemnation. But the ironic statement does so much more forcefully, because it contains the invitation to a further judgment about both his cleverness in the use of irony and the fairness of employing such a weapon of contempt. Partisans of Clodius, we can be sure, would feel considerably more affronted by the ironic version, because the assumption that Clodius is so bad that ironies about him will be self-evidently clear is in itself "obviously unfair." They may even have seen the irony as a sign of desperation or dull-wittedness—one usually does not think ironic attacks are clever if they are made against objects that do not deserve attack. On the other hand, those who were already moving toward Cicero's extreme position would be given a strong additional boost toward it by their admiration for his cleverness, such as it is, and by their pride in joining him; if he is "right" in his wit he is probably "right" in his judgment. And of course their pleasure in their own shrewdness and vitality is all transferred to the judgment against Clodius.

It is hard to think of any stable irony that does not, for the proper reader, add this kind of complex intellectual force to whatever other effects are at work. An ironic statement of friendship or love, however feeble the irony, will be stronger than a simple "I love you"— unless it is reversed because the irony has been missed, or weakened because it is seen as a hint of *blame disguised as disguised blame*. "You don't thrill me when you hold me, no, not much"—even this drab stroke, from a recent popular song, implies an intellectual sharing: we not only love each other, we understand each other. It thus runs the risks, and may reap the rewards, implicit in all stable ironies.

## SOME PLEASURES AND PITFALLS OF IRONY

The conclusion seems inescapable: reconstructions of irony are seldom if ever reducible either to grammar or semantics or linguistics. In read-

6. Loeb Classical Library, trans. H. E. Butler, 8. 6. 56.

ing any irony worth bothering about, we read life itself, and we work on our relations to others as they deal with it. We read character and value, we refer to our deepest convictions. For this reason, irony is an extraordinarily good road into the whole art of interpretation. Though ironic statements are only a small part of all that men say to each other—even in this highly ironic age—they bring to light the hidden complexities that are mastered whenever men succeed in understanding each other in any mode, even the most flat and literal.

But it is also clear by now why irony causes so much trouble. An aggressively intellectual exercise that fuses fact and value, requiring us to construct alternative hierarchies and choose among them; demands that we look down on other men's follies or sins; floods us with emotion-charged value judgments which claim to be backed by the mind; accuses other men not only of wrong beliefs but of being wrong at their very foundations and blind to what these foundations imply—all of this coupled with a kind of subtlety that cannot be deciphered or "proved" simply by looking closely at the words: no wonder that "failure to communicate" and resulting quarrels are often found where irony dwells.

Successful reading of irony depends on reserves of tact and experience and even wisdom that are likely at any moment to prove lacking in any of us, and yet irony offers special temptations to our weaknesses, especially our pride. Those who under-read and those who over-read will usually think of themselves as good readers. The critic who asks us to ironize our straight readings may seem to be corrupting a beloved object and repudiating our very souls. When Marvin Mudrick sees more ironies in *Emma* than I think the book invites, he attacks *my* book, in a sense, and I cannot help feeling that he is attacking me.[7] All of us who love irony are likely to destroy other men's sacred objects with the same error, as I labored to destroy the pleasures of deer-hunting for my student.

For reasons that are now obvious, most readers have a deeply moral feeling about right interpretation. "If other readers don't see things my way, they *ought* to." Our pride is more engaged in being right about irony than about many matters that might seem more important—being logical or consistent, for example. If I am wrong about irony, I am wrong at deeper levels than I like to have exposed. When I am "taken in," my profoundest beliefs and my most deeply rooted intellectual habits are under judgment. But is it not also true that I am equally under judgment, if not by my fellow men then by the mocking spirit of irony, when I see ironies that are not there?

7. *Jane Austen: Irony as Defense and Discovery* (Princeton, N.J., 1952), esp. pp. 91, 165, 206.

My wit is short, ye may wel understonde.
—Chaucer

But those who aim at Ridicule
Shou'd fix upon some certain Rule,
Which fairly hints they are in jest,
Else he must enter his Protest:
For, let a Man be ne'er so wise,
He may be caught with sober Lies.
—Swift, "Cadenus and Vanessa"

The only shield against irony, therefore, is absolute circumspection, a shield no man can lift.
—D. C. Muecke

Isn't it wonderful, Hedda, how everything has worked out?
—George Tesman, in Ibsen's *Hedda Gabler*

Well, if the FBI said [Ronald] Kaufman did it, then he did. That's for sure.
—Jerry Rubin

# THREE | Is It Ironic?

Irony that gives trouble can range from the simplest everyday kidding to the most complex literary and philosophical disguises. Scholars have difficulty, for example, deciding which parts of Kierkegaard's book *The Concept of Irony* are themselves ironic.[1] Some sections are "unquestionably" so, as stable as the most direct thrust of a Swift or Pope: ". . . whether we dare abandon ourselves with a clear conscience to rejoicing over the audacious pen strokes of recent philosophic investigators" (p. 194). Others that do not in themselves look clearly ironic become so when one understands the general run of Kierkegaard's arguments against Hegel's reading of Socrates: "One statement of Hegel expresses quite simply but with much pregnancy of thought how the daimonic is to be understood" (p. 189). But there are vast numbers of passages in this as in other books by Kierkegaard about which even experts are in disagreement, though they are never in disagreement about whether Kierkegaard intended vast numbers of stable (and unstable) ironies.

Similarly, there are many lively controversies about whether this or that modern novel is ironic. William Empson at one point bursts out against all the critics who do not read *Ulysses* as he does: "By the way, I have no patience with critics who say it is impossible to tell whether Joyce means a literary effect to be ironical or not; if they don't know this part [the union of the Blooms and Stephen at the end] isn't funny, they ought to."[2]

No doubt there are many controversies that can never be resolved; we must be willing to live with whatever confusion cannot be avoided. But a too ready tolerance of confusion can deprive us of a great deal of fun in literature, and it can of course be disastrous in daily life. Readers of *Mein Kampf* who thought that Hitler must have meant something different from what he said were making a risky mistake. The fable of "the boy who cried 'Wolf!' " is generally taken—quite properly—as speaking against the boy with his pseudo-ironic alarms; he is no ironist in our special sense, because he provides no proper clues and in fact does not intend stable irony but a sadistic practical joke.

1. See Lee M. Capel's "Historical Introduction" to his translation (London, 1966), pp. 7–41.
2. "The Theme of *Ulysses*," *Kenyon Review* 18 (Winter 1956): 36. See my *The Rhetoric of Fiction*, pp. 325–26, and passim, for examples of controversy about such matters.

But surely the fable also says something about those who cannot tell the difference in tone between one cry of "Wolf!"—the cry of the "put-on" artist—and the desperate cry of "Wolf!" by one prospective victim to other prospective victims.[3]

It is sometimes assumed that the effort to clarify or to rule out false interpretations is somehow anti-literary because it is against the spirit of irony. I shall work on the contrary assumption unproved: that with certain kinds of irony the mind's irrepressible desire to be clear is the very source of whatever pleasure or profit is to be found. A thoroughly muddled world is a world that cannot really enjoy *Gulliver's Travels* or *Animal Farm*; it is a world that will fall blithely into the traps set by Defoe's *Shortest Way with the Dissenters,* Samuel Butler's *The Fair Haven,* and Leonard C. Lewin's *Report from Iron Mountain,* all of which were taken in great straight doses by some readers.

How do we avoid such mistakes? More affirmatively, how is it that authors ever manage to succeed in enforcing their complex and unspoken demands upon us? For various reasons, modern critics have tended to stress the value of diversity in interpretation, and they have had no difficulty finding innumerable examples of conflicting interpretation by responsible and sensitive readers, and of conflicts between such readers and the stated intentions of authors. "Both irony and ambiguity are 'pluralistic' ways of speaking, evasions of committed speech"[4]—this is a commonplace about irony, and like most commonplaces it is true enough when confined to its proper domain. But the irony that disorients by resisting univocal interpretation, the irony that evades committed speech, is only a branch of a great and ancient art; even those modern works which are rightly celebrated for their rich ambiguity reveal, on close inspection, large tracts of stable irony— what Muecke calls "rhetorical irony"—about which no careful reader experiences any ambiguity whatever.

---

3. For an interesting and useful distinction between stable irony and the "put-on"—an "ironic" statement that the ironist does not expect to be reconstructed (and may not himself even understand)—see Jacob A. Brackman's account in *The New Yorker,* 24 June 1967, pp. 34–73. See also D. C. Muecke's distinction between overt and covert irony, on the one hand, and "private irony" on the other (*The Compass of Irony,* esp. pp. 59–60).

4. See Barbara Herrnstein Smith, *Poetic Closure: A Study of How Poems End* (Chicago, 1968), p. 254, and Claudette Kemper, "Irony Anew, with Occasional Reference to Byron and Browning," *Studies in English Literature* 7 (1967): 705–19, esp. pp. 708–11.

## Is It Ironic?

### CLUES TO IRONY

Considering how much has been written about irony, one finds surprisingly little about how we manage to understand it. The first problem is how we recognize that we should even begin reconstruction.

Quintilian went about as far as anybody until recently, when he said that irony "is made evident to the understanding either by the delivery [assuming a speaker, not a writer], the character of the speaker or the nature of the subject. For if any of these three is out of keeping with the words, it at once becomes clear that the intention of the speaker is other than what he actually says."[5]

The triad of delivery, speaker, and subject was repeated through the centuries in innumerable treatises on rhetoric; whenever irony came up, Quintilian was either quoted or echoed. But, even putting aside the fact that Quintilian was interested only in the relatively simple and brief ironies used in orations, his account is clearly oversimplified. Muecke rightly comments that merely to have one of the three "out of keeping with the words" is not enough to reveal irony, "for an apparently ironic 'delivery' [could] . . . be the result of mere ineptitude or inadvertence; to be sure it is not we need to know more of the speaker or his views."[6]

How, then, do you and I recognize—often with great sureness—an ironic invitation when we see one? It is not hard to explain why we often do not—why, for example, when we make our way through Swift's *A Tale of a Tub* with its manifold reversals from irony to straight invective through many shades in between, we disagree at many points about where Swift would have us stand. What is puzzling, once we think about it, is that we have no difficulty whatever when we encounter a passage like this:

Last Week I saw a Woman *flay'd,* and you will hardly believe, how much it altered her Person for the worse.[7]

To explain how we know that "you will hardly believe" is ironic, we must be able to answer such questions as, What is the equivalent of

5. *Institutio oratoria* 8. 6. 54.

Of contemporaries, Muecke has done most with this problem. See especially, in addition to *The Compass of Irony,* "The Communication of Verbal Irony," (unpublished paper read to the Twelfth International Congress of the Fédération Internationale des Langues et Littératures Modernes, Cambridge, 1972).

6. *The Compass of Irony,* pp. 57–58. See also Norman Knox, *The Word "Irony" and Its Context,* pp. 141–61.

7. Section IX, "A Digression concerning . . . Madness . . ."

"delivery" when there is no actual delivery? What is in fact "out of keeping" with what? Is it "the words" only? How do we know what "the subject" is if the words belie it? And how do we recognize "the true speaker" if we are given nothing but the words of a false representative?

Before attempting to construct an adequate description of the clues which we in fact use in making our reconstructions (regardless of our critical theories), I should like to dramatize once again the curiosity of what we do. I shall now quote from two works which I assume that the reader is not likely to know, and I ask him to note at what point he becomes "certain" that he is or is not dealing with irony:

[1]   The first large iron foundries like the Carron Works or Coalbrookdale date from round about 1780: Howard's book on penal reform was published in 1777 and Clarkson's essay on slavery in 1785. This may have been no more than a coincidence, because at that time most people thought of the application of mechanical power to industry as something to be proud of. The early pictures of heavy industry are optimistic. Even the workers didn't object to it because it was hellish but because they were afraid that machinery would put them out of work. The only people who saw through industrialism in those early days were the poets. . . .

Meanwhile the spirit of benevolence was growing. Prisons were reformed, Sir Frederick Eden published the first sociological survey called the *State of the Poor,* and overshadowing everything else was the movement to abolish the slave trade. . . . The trade was prohibited in 1807, and as Wilberforce lay dying in 1835, slavery itself was abolished.

One must regard this as a step forward for the human race, and be proud, I think, that it happened in England. But not too proud. The Victorians were very smug about it, and chose to avert their eyes from something almost equally horrible that was happening to their own countrymen. England had entered the war with France in the first triumphant consciousness of her new industrial powers. After twenty years England was victorious, but by failing to control her industrial development she had suffered a defeat, in terms of human life, far more costly than any military disaster.

[2]   While the Victorian architects were busy erecting tasteful reproductions of Chartres Cathedral and the belfry of Bruges (so useful for factory chimneys) and covering the rather inefficiently drained marshes on the outskirts of Westminster with the stucco palaces of the nobility and gentry, it must not be imagined that the needs of the humbler classes of the community were in any way overlooked. In all the great new towns of the Midlands and the Industrial North large

housing estates sprang up on which, by the exercise of remarkable fore-
thought and ingenuity, so great was the anxiety lest the worker should
be too far removed from the sights and sounds of the factory or mine
which was the scene of his cheerful labour, a quite fantastic number of
working families were accommodated. In order that the inhabitants
might have the privilege of contemplating, almost ceaselessly, the visible tokens of nineteenth-century man's final triumph over nature, many
of these estates were carefully built alongside the permanent way, or
even, if there was a viaduct handy, actually underneath it . . . .

If there is any reader who is not sure that the first passage, from
Sir Kenneth Clark's *Civilisation* is not ironic, while the second passage,
from Osbert Lancaster's *Here of All Places,*[8] is ironic in almost every
word, I shall be much surprised. "Certainty"—a word we are often
urged to avoid, since no one, it is said, can be certain of anything—
is the only possible term for my own conviction about the Lancaster—
yet I have never met the man, have never read anything else by him
that I can remember, and have read only part of the book from which
the excerpt comes!

It is important not to cheat at this point by bringing into the discussion either general principles about the uncertainty of everything or
imaginary readers who might see things another way. Everyone "here"
sees it the same way—as the skeptical reader can confirm by asking
himself how much he would be willing to wager against me if I argued
that Lancaster was *not* ironic. About the non-ironic quality of Clark's
passage one is, curiously enough, considerably less certain; it might
easily be turned into irony by what happens in the next sentence, or
the next after that. But this possibility does not occur in considering
the Lancaster; no succeeding sentence could possibly "straighten" the
whole thing again. Irony thus often produces a much higher degree of
confidence than literal statement.

One widespread dogma of this century is that there are at most
three kinds of statements, experiential (testable by reference to "hard"
data or "the facts"), analytical (derived through logical or mathematical "deduction" from self-evident or axiomatic principles), and what
is left over—moral and aesthetic and political and metaphysical statements that have no cognitive value whatever and are therefore sum-
marizable under some such term as emotion or faith or mere opinion.
On the one hand we have the rigorous "scientific" search for certainty;
on the other hand the *doubtful*. The distinction lies back of much
twentieth-century philosophy (e.g., Bertrand Russell's early effort to

8. *Civilisation: A Personal View* (London, 1969), pp. 321–24. *Here of All
Places* (New York, 1958), p. 88.

turn all philosophical questions into scientific or logical questions, or A. J. Ayer's claim, in *Language, Truth, and Logic* (1936) that "emotive statements" convey no knowledge. In literary criticism the notion has been stated and resisted again and again.[9] But belief in the distinction underlies many efforts to make the humanities and social studies quantitative and hence, presumably, scientific.

There may be a way in which our certainty about Lancaster's ironic intent could be rendered into strictly experimental or analytical language, but I doubt it—too many of the inferences on which it is based are qualitative, emotive, and moral. What is more, since the statement is in one sense internally consistent, there is nothing "out of keeping" between the words and the character of the speaker, or the "delivery." When we come to "subject," the third in Quintilian's triad, we discover that most of our clues in this case indeed come from clashes between what is said and what we think we know about the subject, but we find that what we know consists mainly of value judgments (the reproductions were *not* tasteful; the labor was *not* cheerful; the estates were *not* carefully built; etc.). None of these could be easily proved by established methods; most are at least questionable. Yet from them we build a conclusion that is unshakable.

The processes by which I come to my convictions about the intentions of the authors implied by such passages are, then, sufficiently remarkable to justify tracing in detail. I have already followed the path of my inferences through four steps and four judgments, and I have developed a metaphor which does some justice, I think, to the complexities of the process. But it is now time to explain further how the steps are possible, by charting the kinds of evidence one uses. I am aware that much of what I shall say on this score may seem obvious to some readers. But this does not trouble me: in a sense the greater the obviousness the stronger the demonstration that we have overstressed "failures of communication" and disagreements and undervalued our agreements.

Any one of the clues I turn to now can be stated in the form of an inference about an implied author's intentions: "If the author did not

9. See, for example, I. A. Richards's distinction between cognitive statements and emotive, or "pseudo"-statements (like poetry), in *Science and Poetry* (London, 1935). For an extended discussion of the destructiveness of this dichotomy, when used uncritically, see my forthcoming *Modern Dogma and the Rhetoric of Assent* (Notre Dame and Chicago, 1974). One of the great mysteries of modern intellectual life is the survival of this distinction even though it has been "decisively" refuted by professionals in field after field. I cite only one brilliant attack, now almost a quarter of a century old: W. V. Quine, "Two Dogmas of Empiricism," *Philosophical Review* 60 (January 1951).

intend irony, it would be odd, or outlandish, or inept, or stupid of him to do things in this way." Every clue thus depends for its validity on norms (generally unspoken) which the reader embraces and which he infers, rightly or wrongly, that his author intends. Rhetorically speaking, it makes no difference whether we think of these norms as being intrinsic or extrinsic. In short, the debate between the objective critics who want the work of art to be autonomous and other kinds of critics who want to relate it to values in life outside the work is irrelevant here —at least for a time. The only relevant distinction between what is inside and what is outside will be technical: Can I, as with the Lancaster passage, make all necessary inferences about the implied author's norms on the basis of the text itself (though in fact I rely on knowledge about industrialism and what has been said about it) or must I—as in much satire and a great deal of twentieth-century poetry, drama, and fiction—search for 'external' clues about the author's probable intentions?

### 1. Straightforward warnings in the author's own voice

In spoken ironies, especially in conversation, we are accustomed to catching a variety of clues that are not in themselves ironic—direct nudges of the elbow and winks of the eye. In written irony the same kind of nudge is sometimes given—often to the distress of readers who prefer to work things out on their own.

*a) In titles.* Occasionally an author will use a direct epithet in his title to describe one of the qualities of his speaker. Thomas Mann's *Felix Krull, Confidence Man,* Ring Lardner's "Gullible's Travels," Bruce Bliven's "Diary of a Worrier," T. S. Eliot's "The Hollow Men" —these all give us quite directly information that we can immediately use in suspecting "secret" intentions behind the narrator's words. "My narrator-hero is a con-man, and I invite you to stand up here with me (somewhere, somewhere up here, a new place that you'll have to work out with me as we go along) and observe him behaving and speaking like a con-man." "My narrator is gullible; stand with me up here to observe him." "Mine is a worrier." "My spokesmen are hollow, and they dwell in a location made of the beliefs and sufferings of such men." *Praise of Folly—The Dunciad*—"Memoirs of Martinus Scriblerus"—And so on.

Such direct, unmistakable invitations are in fact quite rare, possibly because they reduce the reader's fun in figuring things out. There is nothing of the kind, for example, in the passage by Lancaster. But only the most careless of readers will fail to make use of such aids when they are offered; for one thing, they can make a great difference in what happens in the first moments of reading: the reconstruction of details of meaning can begin at once, with little time spent on deciding whether to reconstruct at all.

But even at best, direct clues cannot solve very many problems for us. They leave us with the task of deciding to what degree Felix Krull cannot be trusted, precisely what it means to be "hollow," whether being gullible is finally a vice or virtue in this context, and so on. But at least we have been alerted not to identify the "I" with the implied author—and this already means that every statement must be scrutinized with more than ordinary skepticism.

Often the warning of titles is less specific and more subtle: "The Love Song of J. Alfred Prufrock" tells us that we are not about to read "the love song of T. S. Eliot." The explicit disavowal in itself would not take us very far: many a poet has adopted a pseudonym without intending stable ironies. But the choice of name is our first hint that the speaker will prove to be another hollow man: "The Love Song of J. Alfred Prufrock" promises a very different poem from, say, "The Love Song of Danny Deaver," but the promises are so delicately made that it is difficult, after reading the poem, to separate what the title then means from what it conveyed at the moment when the poem was begun. Similarly, *Joseph Vance: An Ill-Written Autobiography,* by William de Morgan—well, this will obviously not be simply de Morgan's autobiography, and it will be written in some way characteristic of "Joseph Vance." But *how* different Vance will be from de Morgan, just how much distance there will be between the dwelling place of *eiron* and of author and reader, we can only discover as we read the work. "Caliban upon Setebos"—thus Browning identifies his speaker in advance, for those who know Shakespeare's *The Tempest.* We have been warned not to assume that the opinions expressed are simply Browning's. But the complex task of determining the poem's placement of Caliban remains.

*b) In epigraphs.* Nineteenth-century ironic essays frequently began with quotations from famous ironists as clues to ironic intentions. The author assumed that to quote from Rabelais or Erasmus or Butler or Swift would announce to the reader that effects like theirs might be expected. In our time such epigraphs have gone out of style in essays, but they are still used in novels and poems, where they can often be the clearest clue we have that the author does not identify with one or more of the speakers of a work, and thus that ironic undercutting *may* follow. Hemingway began *The Sun Also Rises* with two epigraphs, one quoting Gertrude Stein, "You are all a lost generation," and the other quoting Ecclesiastes to explain the title of the novel. The author never appeared again directly; having warned the reader that he *perhaps* saw these characters as in some sense lost he then left them to speak entirely for themselves. Or rather one should say that he˙pretended to. Every word chosen spoke for him, but not directly.[10]

    *c) Other direct clues.* The most obvious warning of all is a direct statement by the author that, as William Gerhardi prefaces *Futility*: "The 'I' of this book is not me." Lawrence Durrell spends a full page at the beginning of *Balthazar* trying to warn the reader that the "I" of the novel becomes an object, that is, a "character," to be viewed ironically, as "entirely imaginary." Vladimir Nabokov uses a postscript to *Lolita* for the same purpose: "My creature Humbert is a foreigner and an anarchist, and there are many things, besides nymphets, in which I disagree with him."

    There are two important points to remember about such direct warnings—whether in titles, epigraphs, or supplementary statements: it is foolish to ignore them when they are offered, but it is dangerous to take them at face value. They may or may not be reliable clues as to what the work achieves. The author, for all we can know in advance, may turn things upside down once more.

    Why not, then, give real help? In 1899 one Alcanter de Brahm published a work, *L'Ostensoir des Ironies,* in which he suggested that ironists use a special punctuation mark (¿), "le petit signe flagellateur." Such a blatant clue, as Muecke says, would almost always reduce the value of the irony. And it would, in any case, simply postpone the decision a reader must make, because there would always be the possibility that the *mark* was being used ironically, and that the *words* should be taken straight![11]

    Just how confusing a warning network can become, in the conscious thought of the author himself, is shown in the two prefaces Kenneth Burke wrote for his novel *Towards a Better Life*.[12] In the first preface, written when the book was published in 1931, Burke wrote:

> I must impress it upon the reader that many of the statements made in my story with an air of great finality should, as Sir Thomas Browne said even of his pious writings, be taken somewhat "tropically." They are a kind of fictive moralizing wherein, even though the dogmas are prior to the events, these dogmas are

10. See *The Rhetoric of Fiction,* chaps. 1 and 10.
11. I learned of Alcanter de Brahm from Muecke's book (p. 56), and of the author's real name, Marcel Bernhardt, in a letter from Muecke. He suggests that Bernhardt "should have called himself 'Alcanter de Brahm¿'"
12. Berkeley, 1966. Quotation from first preface, pp. xv–xvii; from second preface, pp. vi–vii.

not always to be read as absolutely as they are stated. What is right for a day is wrong for an hour, what is wrong for an hour is right for a moment—so not knowing how *often* or how *long* one should believe in the dubious aphorisms of my hero, I should say that there is more sincerity in their manner than in their content. *Facit indignatio versus,* which I should at some risk translate: "An author may devote his entire energies to rage purely through a preference for long sentences." . . . I had . . . to select . . . a hero so unpleasant that the reader could not possibly have anything in common with him. He laments, rejoices, beseeches, admonishes, aphorizes, and inveighs, to be sure, but always in a repellent manner—. . . he lacks that saving touch of humour which the reader wisely and deftly summons to sweeten his own personal dilemmas. He is a very frank, a very earnest, a very conscientious man, in whom one should place slight confidence. . . . I can say nothing in his favour except that he is busy. . . .

If you can reconstruct that passage into explicit guidance about how much acceptance or rejection to grant Burke's hero, you are a very subtle reader indeed, perhaps the very reader that the young Burke was hoping for. If you are, like me, thoroughly discombobulated, you will not be much helped by reading the second preface, written thirty-four years later:

I have found that the title of this work can be misleading, if the words are read without ironic discount. . . . [The progression in the plot from worse to worse, instead of "towards a better life"] was a necessary part of the development.

On the other hand, there is also a sense in which an ironic discounting of the title must in turn be discounted. My later study of various literary texts, viewed as modes of "symbolic action," has convinced me that this book is to be classed among the many rituals of rebirth which mark our fiction. And though I did not think of this possibility at the time, I noticed later how the theme of resurgence is explicitly proclaimed. . . .

Faced with such complex disclaimers from the confirmed ironist, we might well be tempted to retreat into the cowardly doctrine that the author's intentions (and of course his warnings about them) do not interest us; if we trust the teller and not the tale, we commit the intentional fallacy. Or we might put it that all ironies are essentially unstable after all.

We may all find this kind of strategic withdrawal sometimes necessary, but it is not available to us here: we are interested precisely in deliberate intentions, and it will be more important to us that Burke is finally "convinced" than that it took him thirty-four years to become so. And for now we can continue with less complex examples, warned by Burke that explicit warnings can be undermined.

What do we do when Erasmus, for satirical purposes, uses almost exactly the same kind of untrustworthy demurrer as Burke's? "If anything I have said seems sharp or gossipy," Erasmus has "Folly" say at the conclusion of *Praise of Folly,* "remember that it is Folly and a woman who has spoken." His title has in itself warned us from the beginning that irony will be at play: nobody, we infer, can *really* build his castle on the belief that foolishness is praiseworthy. But when such warnings as this quotation occur, condemning folly as in fact foolish, how do we decide whether to discount *them* too? Every reader of the book discovers early that many of Folly's opinions are Erasmus's and many are not. But the reader could never be sure of this by relying only on direct warnings at the beginning.

In short, if we look at the first kind of clue, the author's direct statement in title, epigraph, postscript, or whatever, and ask how we *know* that the author speaks to us in a more direct tone in them than in his other words, we discover that the direct statement is always at best only a hint; our confidence begins to rise only when we come to other clues. Unless what the voice says or does conflicts in some clear way with what we can be sure the author would say, we will not *know* that the passage is ironic.

## 2. Known Error Proclaimed

If a speaker betrays ignorance or foolishness that is "simply incredible," the odds are comparatively high that the author, in contrast, knows what he is doing. Many comic writers rely on an initial absurdity to set the tone for an entire tale, as Mark Twain does at the beginning of "Baker's Bluejay Yarn": "Animals talk to each other, of course. There can be no question about that; but I suppose there are very few people who can understand them. I never knew but one man who could. I knew he could, however, because he told me so himself." Mark Twain knew that *you* would know that *he* knew that his speaker is talking nonsense here.

There is no limit, except for the conventions of agreement, to the kinds of knowledge that a speaker can violate:

*a) Popular expressions.* "You could a heard a bomb drop," says the narrator of James Thurber's "You Could Look It Up" concerning a moment of complete silence. "Well, I'll own up that I enjoyed wearin' the soup and fish and minglin' amongst the high polloi and pretendin' we really was somebody," the narrator of Ring Lardner's, "Gullible's Travels" says, early in the story. Taken by themselves the confusion of pins with bombs and the double error about *hoi polloi* might conceivably mean that Thurber and Lardner are themselves ignorant of the standard expressions: not ironic, just ignorant. But in a context of other "incredible" errors, probabilities become certainties: Thurber and Lardner are communicating with us from behind their narrators' backs.

*b) Historical fact.* Nabokov begins *Ada* (1969) with the following reversal of the first sentence in *Anna Karenina*: " 'All happy families are more or less dissimilar; all unhappy ones are more or less alike,' says a great Russian writer in the beginning of a famous novel (*Anna Arkadievitch Karenina,* transfigured into English by R. G. Stonelower, Mount Tabor Ltd., 1880)." The reconstruction will begin only if we know Tolstoy's opening, or if we see that he has the wrong translator, the wrong publishing location (two more jokes), and the wrong date—to say nothing of a masculine patronymic with a feminine name. The inference that Nabokov could not have stumbled into this comedy of errors is unshakable, begun in our notions of general human probability and clinched by bits of "historical" information: Nabokov is also Russian, he has written about Tolstoy, he is fond of this kind of joke, and so on.

David Riesman reports that when his ironic essay "The Nylon War" was printed in 1951, "[I] began to get letters and calls asking me if the 'war' whose fictitious date had by then been passed) had actually gotten under way! It was like a page out of *The Invasion from Mars* that people could feel so remote from the current of probabilities as to take my tale for literal fact. . . . The disorientation from reality that this misreading indicates is frightening."[13]

"Today—August 1, 1951—the Nylon War enters upon the third month since the United States began all-out bombing of the Soviet Union with consumer's goods . . ." No reader is helpless with a printed text when he has this kind of fact that can be checked—if checking is necessary. Even if a reader felt that he had not been keeping up on events closely enough and had missed the "war," he has only to go to the library to see what did, in fact, happen in August 1951. But he will do so only if he has developed the habit of thinking critically about historical fact.

*c) Conventional judgment.* To talk of historical "fact" is misleading. Any piece of knowledge is useful to the stable ironist (and to

13. *Individualism Reconsidered* (Glencoe, Ill., 1954), p. 412.

his reader) only insofar as it can be presumed to be held by someone else. Except for unstable or private ironies or "put-ons," not now our concern, general fashions of belief (or even conventionally held errors) are more useful in reading irony than esoteric but solidly grounded knowledge. When Fielding wrote of Mrs. Partridge, in *Tom Jones,* that she was "a professed follower of that noble sect founded by Xantippe of old," it was of no importance to him or his readers to ask whether Socrates' wife was in fact a "Xantippe," a virago; what was important was whether readers in general could be assumed to believe so. The point of "noble" depends on the reader's knowledge not so much of historical fact but of conventional notions of valid judgment. If he can assume that *Fielding* would assume that *he* would assume *Fielding*'s assumption of such knowledge in all readers—our old circularity—then the ironic interpretation is certain. It may be objected that this absurd building up of assumptions could go on indefinitely. Surely we have reached a point beyond which we could easily move toward infinity ("but *Fielding*'s assumption is based on the probability of the *reader*'s inference, but the *reader* must assume . . ."). But no interpreter of stable irony ever needs to go that far, even though some ironies, as we see in Part III, do lead to the infinite.[14]

To sustain the objection about this passage, the objector will have to provide *his* grounds for stopping along the path at some earlier point. And I think that he will always find that his stopping point is in some sense conventional—rhetorical in the sense that it is based on the kind of inferential relationship between readers and intending authors I have described; hard facts are only as hard, in reading irony, as is allowed by authors' and readers' assumptions about what is hard and what soft.

14. In this way we rediscover, in our practical task of reading ironies, why Kierkegaard, in his theoretical task of understanding the concept of irony, should have defined it finally as "absolute infinite negativity." Irony in itself opens up doubts as soon as its possibility enters our heads, and there is no inherent reason for discontinuing the process of doubt at any point short of infinity. "How do you know that Fielding was not being ironic in his ostensibly ironic attack on Mrs. Partridge?" If I am answered with a citation of other "hard" data in the work, I can of course claim that Fielding was ironic in his use of *them*. But how do I know that he was not really pretending to be ironic in *their* use, not in fact ironically attacking those who take such data without irony? And so on. The spirit of irony, if there is such a thing, cannot in itself answer such questions: pursued to the end, an ironic temper can dissolve everything, in an infinite chain of solvents. It is not irony but the desire to understand irony that brings such a chain to a stop. And that is why a rhetoric of irony is required if we are not to be caught, as many men of our time have claimed to be caught, in an infinite regress of negations. And it is why I devote the following chapters to "learning where to stop."

The conventional knowledge in Fielding's time about the "historical" Xantippe is not now nearly so widely shared by readers who find themselves engaged with Fielding. As any college teacher knows, *English* English literature, as distinct from *American* English literature, gets more remote from even his very bright students in each generation, because the community of knowers sharing any one such "fact" shrinks from generation to generation. It is true that an intelligent reader ignorant of the Xantippe convention can reconstruct from the passage itself (using other steps that I shall describe) the essential inference that Mrs. Partridge is not noble and that she is "in fact" a virago. But this will still not give the precise ironic shade to the sentence that is given if the historical convention about Xantippe is already known.

Most irony depending on commonly held historical judgments is much more transitory than "the noble sect of Xantippe," which is after all still clear to perhaps a majority of the readers of *Tom Jones*. When the 1964 Republican Convention was being held in San Francisco, Art Buchwald wrote a column from convention headquarters which began like this: "So far this has probably been one of the most exciting conventions in the history of American politics." Practically every reader must have known immediately that Buchwald was being ironic, though one can assume a small handful of the irony-blind who would write in to inquire how he could say such a stupid thing, when everyone knew that it had been one of the dullest conventions in history.[15] But by now, nine years later, I assume that there are many who will have to stop and think for a moment if they come to the statement cold (now just which convention *was* the one in 1964? Oh, that Goldwater one!) and many others who will have no usable memory at all. An ironist would be foolish to let very much hang on the assumption that his reader would know such a reference, and a decade or so from now the knowledge will be useless: no reader will be able to say, as he must: "The author simply could not be that badly informed. *Everyone knows* . . . Ergo . . ."

We can see from this again that even flat contradictions of fact—and in great number—cannot always by themselves prove to a reader

15. Mr. Buchwald tells me that almost every ironic column produces a collection of angry letters from the irony-blind. When he wrote a defense of a British social worker's plan to provide assistance to unwed fathers, the indignation ran high indeed: "What is the world coming to, where such things are even ALLOWED to be published. . . . If this new idea of yours is going to come under United Fund, we're quitting. [signed] Indignant mother of 1 daughter and 2 lovely granddaughters."

that irony is present. His estimate of what kinds of ignorance or error or misjudgment are humanly probable is always called into play, a very different thing from judging what is true. It is clear that in the passage by Lancaster with which we began this chapter, we do not depend very much on plain, "demonstrable" historical inaccuracy—whatever that might be—in deciding that the "great towns of the Midlands" with their "large housing estates" and "cheerful" inhabitants are to him miserable, inhuman, and unnatural blights. Rather we depend on judgments about what a man, even a man defending this historical development, might reasonably *say* about it—on the words "cheerful" and "privilege" and "quite fantastic." Whatever factual discord the passage contained would be insufficient to justify our certainty.

But there are deliberate factual discords so obvious that no reader could require more. On the occasion of his seventieth birthday dinner, Mark Twain began his speech, "I have had a great many birthdays in my time." So far, if this were spoken by a stranger, we would not know for sure whether it was deliberate ironic understatement or simply bumbling obviousness. "I remember the first one very well . . ."—and even if we had never heard of Twain, we would know where we stand.

## 3. Conflicts of Facts within the Work

All the examples in the previous section led us to rely on knowledge or conventional judgments brought to the work, knowledge on which we base our guesses about whether the author shares his speaker's ignorance. But many works of stable irony provide within themselves the knowledge necessary for establishing that a speaker's ignorance is not shared by the author. Whenever a story, play, poem, or essay reveals what we accept as a fact and then contradicts it, we have only two possibilities. Either the author has been careless or he has presented us with an inescapable ironic invitation.

> Now lap-dogs give themselves the rousing shake,
> And sleepless lovers, just at twelve, awake.[16]

Here the "fact" that the lovers are sleepless becomes a satirized poetic cliché as soon as the real facts are revealed. When there are two contradictory statements like this, there is no way of knowing in advance whether the first or second voice will be repudiated; but usually one or the other must be, and the probability is that the final voice will triumph, as it does here, unless we are given explicit evidence against it.

The process of decision may be easy, as in most of Pope's underminings, or hard, but it will always be complex when viewed closely, as

16. Alexander Pope, *The Rape of the Lock,* lines 15–16.

we see if we try to *prove* that in the poet's view the lovers *in fact* slept very well.

It is clear that if the final voice triumphs, then we have here simply the reverse of "advance warning" (clue no. 1 above). A very great proportion of ironic essays could be said to have this essential structure: (*a*) a plausible but false voice is presented; (*b*) contradictions of this voice are introduced; (*c*) a correct voice is finally heard, repudiating all or most or some of what the ostensible speaker has said.

Logically there is one further possibility in any conflict of facts or claims to fact: both voices may be false. It is comforting to find that the realms of irony are sometimes actually inhabited by the creatures that logic would predict. Muecke cites some splendid examples of what he calls "Double Irony," a form "in which two equally invalid points of view cancel each other out":

> The penguins had the most powerful army in the world. So had the porpoises.[17]

Reading the first sentence, we might think for a moment that we were hearing the author's voice conveying a plain fact. But reading the second sentence does not simply substitute it for the first. The author suddenly transcends what might be called the local scene, in which one judgment or another could be accepted without irony, and invites us to a higher view, unstated, from which both implied jingoists below can be observed with equal amusement and scorn.

It is when such internal cancellations are multiplied that we finally lose all sense of stability and sink into the bogs of unstable irony. The successive annihilation of seemingly stable locations has been widespread in modern literature,[18] and critics have often claimed that the effects of such instability are somehow superior to the illusions on which stable irony are based. Regardless of whether such judgments about the superiority of non-judgment are valid, the important point is that each local cancellation on which total cancellations are based depends for its immediate effect on shared "knowledge." Anatole France's "factual" conflict holds only for those of us who will not—at

17. Anatole France, *Penguin Island* (1908), Book 4, chap. 4. "Les Pingouins avaient la première armée du monde. Les Marsouins aussi."

18. In Jean Cayrol's *Les corps étrangers* (Paris, 1959), for example, the narrator tells one contradictory story after another about his life; there is simply no way that I can discover to accept anything he says as valid. The final paragraph starts again, with one more unreliable version of a life that perpetually recedes from us: "Je vais tout te dire. Je te jure que je ne vais pas arranger ma petite vie. Tout. Je suis né dans un petit village de Seine-et-Marne, un soir d'hiver, dans une famille d'une grande noblesse. Mon père qui avait servi . . ." (p. 189).

least for the moment—allow violations of an unstated logical law: if A is greater than B, in a given dimension, B cannot be greater than A in that same dimension, provided we keep our definitions univocal. We in the ironic community here are thus a crowd of arrant dogmatists, even as we savor France's underminings of other dogmatists.

*Dramatic irony.* Drama has always been especially given to effects depending on the author's providing, early in the play, information that will point to an ironic effect later on. Soliloquies, for example, are used in some plays to prepare us, with what we take as hard fact, for the ironic reconstruction of what characters later say and do. Speaking only to himself—and thus, by convention, conveying to us spectators some thoroughly reliable data about motives—Iago says, "I hate the Moor," and "Nothing can or shall content my soul / Till I am even'd with him, wife for wife"; he then tells us in detail his plan for revenge. Forewarned in this way, not even the dullest spectator can fail to see that everything he says to Othello later is false: everyone is prepared to savor the complex (but not difficult) reconstructions required, from this point on, of almost everything that Iago and Othello say. Only the subtlest of literary critics have been able to resist the ironic thrills that result from sympathizing with Othello as he is victimized by Iago.

Dramatic irony, as this kind of effect has been called since about the beginning of the nineteenth century,[19] is of course by no means confined to plays, and it does not depend on the convention of soliloquies. It occurs whenever an author deliberately asks us to compare what two or more characters say of each other, or what a character says now with what he says or does later. Any plain discrepancy will do, though it is true that conventions like the soliloquy or the epistolary technique in novels are especially useful because especially sure.

Since they *are* sure and hence relatively easy to interpret, I shall not dwell on them at length here.[20] But we should look for a moment

19. Muecke, p. 50. The bibliography of dramatic irony is enormous, ranging from Connop Thirlwall, *On the Irony of Sophocles,* The Philological Museum, vol. 2 (Cambridge, 1833); through J. A. K. Thomson, *Irony: An Historical Introduction* (London, 1926), esp. chaps. 3 and 4; to Bertrand Evans, *Shakespeare's Comedies* (Oxford, 1960).

20. The effects are easy of course only when the information can be treated by the reader or spectator as hard knowledge. To the degree that it becomes questionable, the effects of dramatic irony are weakened, and other effects like curiosity, mystery, and metaphysical wonder begin to take over. In reading *Faust* for example, one could take Mephistopheles as the real devil and his operations as unequivocally evil; the sealing of the pact would then produce a "straight" frisson of anxiety for Faust's future. But Goethe has other goals in view; for most readers Mephisto is laden with ambivalence—a figure of both threat and promise—and the result is a pattern of ironies very different from

at two examples, the first to illustrate that even though in one sense not difficult, such effects do not allow for passive reading, the second to show that in calling them "easy" I am not judging literary quality.

The first example is from the opening of Jane Austen's epistolary novelette, *Lady Susan.*

LETTER 1.

*Lady Susan Vernon to Mr Vernon.*

MY DEAR BROTHER

I can no longer refuse myself the pleasure of profitting by your kind invitation when we last parted, of spending some weeks with you at Churchill, & therefore if quite convenient to you & Mrs Vernon to receive me at present, I shall hope within a few days to be introduced to a Sister whom I have so long desired to be acquainted with. My kind friends here are most affectionately urgent with me to prolong my stay, but their hospitable & chearful dispositions lead them too much into society for my present situation & state of mind; & I impatiently look forward to the hour when I shall be admitted into your delightful retirement. I long to be made known to your dear little Children, in whose hearts I shall be very eager to secure an interest. I shall soon have occasion for all my fortitude, as I am on the point of separation from my own daughter. The long illness of her dear Father prevented my paying her that attention which Duty & affection equally dictated, & I have but too much reason to fear that the Governess to whose care I consigned her, was unequal to the charge. I have therefore resolved on placing her at one of the best Private Schools in Town, where I shall have an opportunity of leaving her myself, in my way to you. I am determined you see, not to be denied admittance at Churchill. It would indeed give me most painful sensations to know that it were not in your power to receive me.

Yr most obliged & affec: Sister

S. VERNON.

Here we have a perfectly straightforward presentation of a loving sister and concerned mother, beloved by all who know her and certain to be warmly received by her brother and his wife. Or do we? If we

---

what we are at this point trying to understand. See Hans-Egon Hass, "Über die Ironie bei Goethe," *Ironie und Dichtung,* ed. Albert Schaefer (Munich, 1970), pp. 59–84: "Goethes eigene Position entspricht weder der Fausts noch der Mephistos, sie wäre auch nicht durch einfache Summierung dieser beiden Gestalten zu bezeichnen. Sie liegt vielmehr in dem polaren Kraftfeld, das durch die Wechselbeziehung der beiden hier vereinseitigten Positionen geschaffen ist" (p. 79). I think it could be shown, however, that this is a point more heavily leaned on by late modern critics than by anyone in Goethe's time; even for liberated romantics, the devil still had more of the devil in him then.

read the lettter closely, doubts begin to arise. If she is as loving as she implies, why has she not been to visit them and the children before? Are not things a bit too "dear" and "kind" and "most affectionate"? What does the letter suggest about her own care for her daughter? And why the sudden change of tone in the last two sentences? Are we seeing something peremptory or even threatening, in that final flat statement?

Though he thus may doubt, no reader can be sure from these words alone that Lady Susan is writing hypocritically, and in many literary forms it might be difficult to lead quickly to a self-betrayal. But when everything is told in letters the author can quickly provide the equivalent of a soul-baring soliloquy by having Lady Susan write letter 2 to a confidante:

*Lady Susan to Mrs Johnson.*
You were mistaken my dear Alicia, in supposing me fixed at this place for the rest of the winter. It greives me to say how greatly you were mistaken, for I have seldom spent three months more agreably than those which have just flown away. At present nothing goes smoothly. The Females of the Family are united against me [now all doubts are confirmed, in a flood, because we have caught her plainly in her first outright lie]. You foretold how it would be, when I first came to Langford; and Manwaring is so uncommonly pleasing that I was not without apprehensions myself. I remember saying to myself as I drove to the House, "I like this Man; pray Heaven no harm come of it" But I was determined to be discreet, to bear in mind my being only four months a widow, & to be as quiet as possible,—& I have been so; My dear Creature, I have admitted no one's attentions but Manwaring's, I have avoided all general flirtation whatever . . . except [with] Sir James Martin, on whom I bestowed a little notice in order to detach him from Miss Manwaring.

And so the self-betrayals flood on, one damning detail after another. We are not the least surprised when she concludes by describing her true feelings about "that insupportable spot," her brother-in-law's home: "Were there another place in England open to me, I would prefer it. Charles Vernon is my aversion, & I am afraid of his wife."

It would be hard for any reader to miss the basic irony here; the self-portrait in letter 1 simply cannot be harmonized with the self-portrait in letter 2, and even the most inexperienced reader will recognize that Jane Austen is calling Lady Susan a hypocrite behind her back. It is true that to savor every stroke of the contrast requires us to be constantly alert. (What does it mean, for example, for her to pursue Manwaring while saying "pray Heaven no harm come of it"?) But the basic dramatic irony that builds throughout the work toward Lady Susan's final unmasking needs no interpreter: the reader with his eyes open cannot lose his way.

But it is equally obvious that the mind must be on the alert, to catch every invitation to inference that is offered here. Only the reader who has read the first letter with attention to every word—no speedy readers permitted!—will catch in retrospect every damning trait. There is another form of active engagement called for as well: our human sympathies and antipathies are worked upon with each detail. Lady Susan is a liar and hypocrite who has neglected her child shamelessly. She can also be described as a clever woman trying as best she can to live by her wits. There can be no doubt that Jane Austen expected and desired our condemnation of the first qualities to outweigh our admiration for the second. It is also clear that for some reason many modern readers feel much less aversion to such characters than the author intended (the most famous example is that of the Crawfords in *Mansfield Park* who—being much less obviously vicious than Lady Susan—have won the sympathy of many modern critics). Regardless of where one stands in this moral debate, it is clear that a kind of morally active engagement is invited by the irony in a form that few readers can resist. And the full reconstruction is by no means an easy one, though the recognition that ironies are present, our first step, is simple.

The same "easy" clarity yielding an intensely active response can be found in many plays, at moments of greatest dramatic irony. The moment when Orgon, hiding under the table, watches Tartuffe, the religious hypocrite, trying to seduce Orgon's wife, Elmire, is one of the greatest in all comic literature, but the irony on which it depends must be evident to even the densest spectator. Elmire has planted Orgon under the table, in full view of the audience, in order to trap Tartuffe. Tartuffe has obliged with a chain of more and more damning, cynical propositions, finally insulting the hidden Orgon:

> Why worry about the man? Each day he grows
> More gullible; one can lead him by the nose.
> To find us here would fill him with delight,
> And if he saw the worst, he'd doubt his sight.[21]

Elmire, desperate because the watching Orgon does not come out of his shelter, even though Tartuffe has by now provided more than enough evidence of what he is, finally sends Tartuffe offstage to check carefully whether Orgon is spying. Orgon crawls out from under the

21. Richard Wilbur translation, IV.v.

table—as every spectator has been expecting him to do for some time. Elmire turns on him with an irony which no spectator has ever misunderstood but which is no less delicious for that:

> What, coming out so soon? How premature!
> Get back in hiding, and wait until you're sure.
> Stay till the end, and be convinced completely;
> We musn't stop till things are proved concretely. . . .
> Wait, and be certain that there's no mistake.
> No jumping to conclusions, for Heaven's sake! [IV, vi]

As Tartuffe returns, Orgon hides briefly behind Elmire and then finally leaps out at the hypocrite. The leap has by now been expected for a long time, as stage time goes; Molière has worked with great skill to play upon the expectations of the spectators as they watch Tartuffe slip his neck into the noose and then wait, and wait, and wait, for Orgon to hang him. The subtlety, if that is the word, is all in the dramatist's formal skill in building toward the greatest possible delight in the unmasking. The audience need not be subtle; they need only be awake and morally engaged and every ironic touch will be evident.

### 4. Clashes of Style

If a speaker's style departs notably from whatever the reader considers the normal way of saying a thing, or the way normal for this speaker, the reader may suspect irony. The effect is easy when there is a quick temporary clash of meanings—what in fact amounts to a direct conflict of information conveyed: "The Marchese del Dongo was given a high position, and as he combined the most sordid avarice with a host of other fine qualities . . ."[22] But such clashes are not really stylistic at all:

22. Stendhal, *The Charterhouse of Parma,* trans. M. R. B. Shaw, chap. 1.
Since many critics have seen the question of irony as entirely a question of style, some of the fullest discussions of stable irony have scarcely mentioned irony, substituting terms like "decorum" or more recently simply "tone." The two chief sources for classical and Renaissance discussions of decorum were Cicero (e.g., *Orator,* ed. and trans. G. L. Hendrickson and H. M. Hubbell [Cambridge, 1939], pars. 70–74, 101, 123; and *De officiis,* trans. W. Miller [Cambridge, 1947], I. 93–146); and Quintilian (*Institutio oratoria,* e.g., 9.3.102; 11.1. 1–93). The former says that "no single kind of oratory suits every cause or audience or speaker or occasion," and he of course adds to these four—or rather holds them constantly under the control of—the notion of purpose. For a characteristic modern discussion of tone, characteristic especially in how much it drops from earlier discussions, see Cleanth Brooks and Robert Penn Warren, *Modern Rhetoric* (New York, 1958), pp. 350–82. Unfortunately this snide comment can almost as well be applied to my own discussion, as anyone will recognize who is familiar with Renaissance treatments of decorum and the various

Quintilian is wrong, I think, in distinguishing such an effect as a *trope* —a mere verbal matter—from the true *"figure* of irony."[23] The clash we experience is a clash between the blame of "sordid avarice" and the praise granted by "fine."

In contrast, a true stylistic clash must be based on recognizing different ways of saying what, in substance, would seem to amount to identical messages. Whenever, in the normal course of perusing a piece of precisely executed writing, whether discursive or imaginative, whether prose or verse, one encounters any radical tergiversation from those perhaps ineluctable norms of expression with which one is accustomed, one should promptly recognize that there is a strong likelihood that irony is being adumbrated.

You noticed, of course, what happened to my style in that sentence, and I hope you deplored it. The sudden departure from my usual way of writing into a kind of useless extravagance of vocabulary should have alerted every reader to an ironic shift, even though there was no point to the irony except teasing illustration. The same general message about irony could have been conveyed in styles of many different kinds: "When you're reading anything that seems to have been written carefully, and you run into something odd in the style, watch out: it may be ironic." "Some writers ya gotta watch out for; they'll sneak in a sudden hunk of . . ." Etc. Modern humorists have specialized in such stylistic shifts, as in *The New Yorker* cartoon of the criminal testifying before the judge: "So den I got piqued and bashed him one." When Mark Twain describes the Greek chapel, in *Innocents Abroad,* as "the most roomy, the richest and the showiest chapel in the Church of the Holy Sepulchre"; when Jane Austen has her narrator of "The History of

---

figures that either achieve it, inadvertently violate it, or—in irony—deliberately violate it. Something of the complexity of the subject, even in modern hands, is illustrated in the controversy between T. McAlindon and Mark Sacharoff in *PMLA* 87 (January 1972): 90–99, concerning whether Shakespeare deliberately ironizes the style of most of the characters in *Troilus and Cressida.* Although I do not agree with quite all of Mr. McAlindon's decisions about irony in the play, I think he has the theoretical argument all his own way, because unlike Mr. Sacharoff, he does justice to the way in which almost every figure can be either decorous or ironic, depending on the five variables mentioned by Cicero (see McAlindon's original article, *PMLA* 84 [January 1969]: 29–43). Both authors recognize the extent to which Shakespeare's skill is under judgment in such debates, though Mr. Sacharoff is much more inclined to see the breaches of decorum as "daring innovations" than as either irony or the extravagance that Dryden deplored (p. 93).

23. Quintilian tries to maintain a distinction between verbal tropes and figures of thought, but he admits that rhetoricians in his own time obscure the distinction (see 6.3. 68; 8.6. 54; and 9. 1. 3 and 7).

England" say, "It was in this reign that Joan of Arc lived and made such a *row* among the English"—it is conflict in stylistic levels, not any incompatibility of bits of knowledge or belief, that gives the show away.

Note how E. B. White adds to his indictment of James Agee in the following piece with a strong shift "downward" toward the colloquial and "upward" toward the pretentious.

### Critical Dilemma

Some time ago, Mr. James Agee wrote a piece for the *Partisan Review* deflating a number of plays, among them "Oklahoma!," which he said were so bad he had not bothered to see them. We commented briefly at the time on Mr. Agee's critical method, which would seem to spare the critic the irksome experience of becoming acquainted with the material he is criticizing. We thought the matter would end there, but the *Partisan Review* apparently broods a good deal about these questions. . . .

Actually, we think we understand why a critic shuns "Oklahoma!" if he learns from sources he considers reliable that it is a debasement of art. Having placed it in the category of pseudo-folk art, he stays away because of a deep dread that if he were to attend a performance, at some point in the show he might find himself having fun. No conscientious critic wants to risk the debilitating experience of enjoying something which is clearly on an inferior artistic level. It upsets everything. When the intelligence says "Nuts" and the blood says "Goody," a critic would rather be home writing his review sight unseen, from information supplied by friends.[24]

The contrast between the third-to-the-last and the next-to-the-last sentence is especially skillful; the word "upsets" does indeed upset everything, or at least nails down the inverted meanings that the earlier sentence has established.

As in our discussion of conflicts of knowledge, we can see here why it is often assumed that reliance on conflicts that seem inescapably contained within a given piece, as in the last passage, is fairer or more artistic than reliance on unspoken conflicts with standards that the reader must bring to his reading. Yet there is obviously a great deal of splendid stylistic irony, some of it easy and some of it hard, that provides no visible norm. What is more, even the visible violation of the standard of consistency depends on standards that are by no means independent of what the reader brings to the passage: how does the author know that the reader will recognize a sudden shift in stylistic level when he sees one?

24. From *The Second Tree from the Corner* (New York, 1962), p. 154.

Some violations are indeed so obvious that they might seem not to rely on the complicated processes of recognition and testing that I have described:

### Why the Little Frenchman Wears His Hand
### in a Sling

It's on my visiting cards sure enough (and it's them that's all o' pink satin paper) that inny gintleman that plases may behould the intheristhin' words, "Sir Pathrick O'Grandison, Barronitt, 39 Southampton Row, Russell Square, Parish o' Bloomsbury." And shud ye be wantin' to diskiver who is the pink of purliteness quite, and the laider of the hot tun in the houl city o' Lonon— why it's jist mesilf. And fait that same is no wonder at all at all (so be plased to stop curlin' your nose), for every inch o' the six wakes that I've been a gintleman, and left aff wid the bog-throthing to take up wid the Barronissy, it's Pathrick that's been living like a houly imperor, and gitting the iddication and the graces. Och! and wouldn't it be a blessed thing for your spirrits if ye cud lay your two peepers jist, upon Sir Pathrick O'Grandison, Barronitt, when hé is all riddy drissed for the hopperer, or stipping into the Brisky for the drive into the Hyde Park. But it's the illegant big figgur that I 'ave, for the rason o' which all the ladies fall in love wid me.

Here Poe's use of the dialect of the stage Irishman alerts us to the possibility that the narrator is a fool. But it is not yet proof of anything other than itself: his talk is "sub-standard." An author could very well portray a wise or good man speaking in an illiterate dialect, as Mark Twain shows the goodness of "nigger Jim" through Huck's and Jim's illiterate speech. But the dialect alerts us, without our even having to think about it, to the fact that Poe is not speaking in his own voice, and it thus prepares us for the many ways in which this foolish man gives himself away by violating our other standards of behavior and speech. Even in the first sentence, his ridiculous pride in his garish visiting cards and his choice of the word "interesting" to describe his title give him away.

By the end of the quotation, everyone must feel very sure that all the ladies do *not* fall in love with the speaker and that, in fact, most of his claims about himself will prove false. In short, *that* the passage is ironic is unmistakably revealed through violations of stylistic norms that the reader shares with Poe. Though the process of inferring Poe's own home ground is intricate enough, it is hard to imagine readers failing to manage the first steps.

But why, then, do we not reject *everything* that this liar and braggart tells us? Why do we believe him when he tells us that he has inherited a baronetcy? Why are we not *sure* he is lying when, in the next sentence after the quotation above, he says that he is six feet three inches tall? And why do we then refuse to believe him when he goes on to describe his rival in love, the "little Frenchman," as only "three fut and a bit"? Such questions can never, I believe, be answered by looking at style alone.

Another of Poe's tales, "The Man That Was Used Up," begins this way:

> I cannot just now remember when or where I first made the acquaintance of that truly fine-looking fellow, Brevet Brigadier-General John A. B. C. Smith. Some one *did* introduce me to the gentleman, I am sure—at some public meeting, I know very well —held about something of great importance, no doubt—at some place or other, I feel convinced—whose name I have unaccountably forgotten. The truth is—that the introduction was attended, upon my part, with a degree of anxious embarrassment which operated to prevent any definite impressions of either time or place. I am constitutionally nervous—this, with me, is a family failing, and I can't help it. In especial, the slightest appearance of mystery—of any point I cannot exactly comprehend—puts me at once into a pitiable state of agitation.

You do not write that way; I do not write that way; Poe does not —in his own voice—write that way. Only Poe's narrator writes that way, and everything in his tale is thus colored toward comic effects and away from the effects of horror that Poe might have achieved with the same materials. But if anyone asked us to prove it, we would perhaps be in difficulty. We should certainly have to take at least one more step than with the passage by E. B. White, pointing to this, this, and this piece by Poe in radically different styles. But if our questioner persisted, asking "How do you know that Poe has not here, for once and once only, written in the style that he finds most admirable?" we might fall back on a line of argument that in some circles would seem completely disreputable: "My experience of life and literature makes it impossible for me to doubt that Poe intends us to see the 'nervous' style, with its dashes and piling up of qualifications and assurances, as characteristic of the absurd nervousness of this agitated speaker." Not entirely convincing, and it is fortunate that when the critical pressure gets really high, we can turn for a further defense to the arguments we meet in the next chapter.

The most obvious use of stylistic clues in stable irony is found in parody, the mocking imitation by one author of another author's style. No kind of irony dramatizes more painfully the difference between experienced and inexperienced readers. The contrasts between an original and a really skillful parody can be so slight that efforts to explain them can seem even less adequate to the true subtleties than explanations of other ironies. Though parody is not ordinarily thought of as "irony," it is ironic in our definition: the surface meaning must be rejected, and another, incongruous, and "higher" meaning must be found by reconstruction. The foundations on which the reconstruction rests need not be only stylistic; good parodies usually parody beliefs as well as style, as do Max Beerbohm's of Kipling and James:[25]

P.C.,X,36
By R*d**rd K*pl*ng

> Then it's collar 'im tight,
>   In the name o' the Lawd!
> 'Ustle 'im, shake 'im till 'e's sick!
>   Wot, 'e *would,* would 'e? Well,
>   Then yer've got ter give 'im 'Ell,
> An' it's trunch, trunch, truncheon does the trick!

POLICE STATION DITTIES.

I had spent Christmas Eve at the Club listening to a grand pow-wow between certain of the choicer sons of Adam. Then Slushby had cut in. Slushby is one who writes to newspapers and is theirs obediently "HUMANITARIAN." When Slushby cuts in, men remember they have to be up early next morning.

Sharp round a corner on the way home, I collided with something firmer than the regulation pillar-box. I righted myself after the recoil and saw some stars that were very pretty indeed. Then I perceived the nature of the obstruction.

"Evening, Judlip," I said sweetly, when I had collected my hat from the gutter. "Have I broken the law, Judlip? If so, I'll go quiet."

"Time yer was in bed," grunted X,36. "Yer Ma'll be lookin' out for yer."

This from the friend of my bosom! It hurt . . .

THE MOTE IN THE MIDDLE DISTANCE
by H*nry J*m*s

It was with the sense of a, for him, very memorable something that he peered now into the immediate future, and tried, not without compunction, to take that period up where he had, prospec-

---

25. Both parodies are by Max Beerbohm, from *A Christmas Garland* (London, 1912), pp. 3–4, 13–14.

tively, left it. But just where the duce *had* he left it? The consciousness of dubiety was, for our friend, not, this morning,
quite yet clean-cut enough to outline the figures on what she had
called his "horizon," between which and himself the twilight was
indeed of a quality somewhat intimidating. He had run up, in the
course of time, against a good number of "teasers"; and the function of teasing them back—of, as it were, giving them, every
now and then, "what for"—was in him so much a habit that he
would have been at a loss had there been, on the face of it, nothing
to lose. Oh, he always had offered rewards, of course—had ever
so liberally pasted the windows of his soul with staring appeals,
minute descriptions, promises that knew no bounds. But the
actual recovery of the article—the business of drawing and cross-
ing the cheque, blotched though this were with tears of joy—had
blankly appeared to him rather in the light of a sacrilege, casting,
he someimes felt, a palpable chill on the fervour of the next
guest . . .

There is no problem here in recognizing that irony is present.
Beerbohm provides an explicit acknowledgment, in the titles, that
each of these passages is a parody. A reader who has never read any
Kipling or James will enjoy some of the fun translating the ostensible
subject into the real subject by inferring what the originals must be
like. But the full pleasure depends on our having read the two victims
in the original; only if we know how close Beerbohm comes to an
accurate imitation can we recognize what fine strokes he is taking with
his battle axe and thus enjoy the slaughter to the full.

In relying on our knowledge as insiders, parody is like most irony
that is revealed through style. We can be sure of ourselves only when
we have good reason to believe that the author's conception of how to
write would exclude his speaker's way of writing—as in the two examples from Poe. And even when we are certain of mockery, as in the
Beerbohm parodies, we must still rely on special experience if we are
to catch such precise shadings. This is another way of saying that only
by reading widely can we prepare ourselves for these special pleasures.
It is scarcely surprising, then, that like other ironies, parody has often
been attacked as immorally elitist, a game for snobs. The circle of those
who know is often very small and very elevated indeed.

## 5. Conflicts of Belief

Finally, we are alerted whenever we notice an unmistakable conflict
between the beliefs expressed and the beliefs we hold *and suspect the
author of holding*. We can see the resulting ironies most clearly when
there is an incredible passage in the midst of straightforward writing. In

the next passage, Bertrand Russell is writing about "The Sense of Sin," and he has employed no irony for many paragraphs.

> The word "conscience" covers as a matter of fact several different feelings; the simplest of these is the fear of being found out. You, reader, have, I am sure, lived a completely blameless life, but if you will ask some one who has at some time acted in a manner for which he would be punished if it became known, you will find that when discovery seemed imminent, the person in question repented of his crime. I do not say that this would apply to the professional thief. . . .[26]

How do we know that Russell is ironic in the second sentence? The sudden shift to the jerky, comma-ridden style is no real help (try inserting "not" after "have" in the second sentence). It would prove nothing if the sentence did not flatly violate our conviction that nobody is blameless, and that nobody but a fool could believe that his readers believed themselves blameless. Unless Russell is a fool, or unless he believes all of his readers are fools, he is fooling here: I am talking about you, reader, while pretending to exempt you.

The structure of inference is identical with that we found in analyzing conflicts of knowledge and conflicts of style. There is a literal statement which rests on assumptions (readers are likely to be blameless, and to think themselves blameless) that the reader is expected to reject; he then must shift to firmer ground (all men are blameworthy, and probably believe themselves to be blameworthy). On that ground the revised statement with its various nuances can be constructed—something like: "You and I both know, wise men of the world that we are, that you have done things—just as I have done things—which were punishable." This is not the first time that we have discovered a reconstruction which simply could not have been given in direct language; if Russell has said all this openly, we would be annoyed at his assumption of his own cleverness, and we might even accuse him of accusing us of cynicism. But in ironic form, the statement unites us with the author against those implied prigs who claim that they have led blameless lives.

The difference between this kind of reconstruction and what we have seen earlier is not then in the process but in the degree of sureness one feels about the conflicting grounds on which the conflicting conclusions are built. Though most of what we called facts or knowledge

---

26. *The Conquest of Happiness* (London, 1930), chap. 7. Signet Key Books (New York, 1951), p. 58.

could be reduced to "belief" by an aggressive Socratic questioner, we were in general dealing there with what most men would agree to without argument. Now we have come to what men dispute about, and we are thus more likely to find ironies that are overlooked, or interpreted differently when found. If someone disputes our reading, we are faced with a question that is clearly both critical and historical: what is a convincing reading of this line in this context (the question we turn to in chapter 4), and what was a given man likely to believe at a given time? Pressed for proof on the historical question, we might find, after hard search, that Russell nowhere flatly contradicts his assertion, and we would thus have to fall back on its general implausibility. In practice, the search for agreement about what a given author probably believed may be easy, as it is here, or it may remain unsuccessful after generations of scholarly research, as in some current controversies about Chaucer's irony.

*Illogicality*. Every reader knows, or thinks he knows, what is "logical." Violations of normal reasoning processes will be subject to exactly the same manipulations as violations of other beliefs or knowledge.

" 'Don't be silly,' answered St. John. 'Nobody ever gets raped in the United States. What do you think this is, a barbarous, medieval country?' "[27] There is of course a violation of known fact here: "everyone knows" that there are rapes in the United States. But more striking is the reversal of normal ways of deciding whether a given thing exists. The overt reasoning which moves from abstract notions about the advanced nation to conclusions about what in fact goes on in it is exactly the reverse of what the speaker intends, and the impossibility of his really believing that what he "says" makes sense is what reveals the irony.

"I know that he could [talk with animals] because he told me so himself." Any illogical inference dramatized like this will wrench us into an act of reconstruction. The reconstruction, like any local interpretation, may or may not prove stable. A deliberate illogicality can, of course, be either a clue to a character's fallacious thoughts or an invitation to join the author in denouncing the absurdity of things. Samuel Beckett's *Watt* begins like this:

Mr. Hackett turned the corner and saw, in the failing light, at some little distance, his seat. . . . This seat, the property very likely of the municipality, or of the public, was of course not his, but he

27. Calder Willingham, *Geraldine Bradshaw* (London, 1964), p. 98.

75

thought of it as his. This was Mr. Hackett's attitude toward things that pleased him. He knew they were not his, but he thought of them as his. He knew were not his, because they pleased him.[28]

Whether or not the grammatical breakdown of the final sentence is deliberate (the lost "they" reappears in the author's French version), we see here the plain unreasonableness of deciding a property question with affective evidence. But we cannot know without a good deal of probing—and perhaps not even then—whether the author intends the illogicality as error or insight. Could it not be that Mr. Hackett has discovered a universal truth? "A sure sign, in this world of ours, that we will lose our hold on something is our wanting to keep it—it is not, in fact *cannot* be, 'ours,' *because* it pleases us." The process in unstable ironies thus begins precisely as in Russell or Mark Twain, but where does it end?

## Toward Genre: Clues in Context

Since ironic attacks are usually directed against positions that are actually held by some possible readers (otherwise, why bother to attack?), and since authors often do actually advocate in all seriousness what the ironist is pretending to advocate, it is scarcely surprising that though irony cannot take in all readers all the time, nobody escapes troubles with it.

How can we explain those readers who saw no irony in William H. Whyte's "Case for the Universal Card," an ironic argument first published in *Fortune Magazine*?[29] Carelessness had a good deal to do with it, no doubt; it is hard to see how anyone taking in all the words would not grow suspicious from the beginning:

### THE CASE FOR THE UNIVERSAL CARD
### by Otis Binet Stanford

I am glad to have this opportunity to clear up the misunderstandings over the Universal Card development. For one thing, my own part in it. I have been much flattered by the praise my modest contribution has attracted; at the outset, however, I must make plain that it is really my colleagues in corporation personnel work who deserve the credit. All I have done, essentially, is to bring together the techniques that they are already using and extend them to their logical development.

The very boldness of the plan has disturbed some people. In American business, unfortunately, there are still many person-

28. *Watt* (London, 1953), p. 5.
29. April 1954.

nel men who have a laissez-faire attitude toward human relations, who argue that there is a large part of the employee's life and personality that is not of concern to the corporation. (This is an attitude, if it is not too ungracious for me to say so, that often marks the pages of FORTUNE.) These gentlemen, I am afraid, are guilty of a semantic error. The Universal Card system is just as "democratic," for example, as the managerial selection and training programs now in use in business. I intend no criticism by this; of necessity corporations have had to screen from their cadres non-college men and those whom psychological tests show to be unfitted for corporation life. But progress will be better served, I think, if, rather than gloss over these facts, we acknowledge them openly and thereby build more wisely for the future. The Universal Card plan may be bold, but there is no sloppy sentimentality about it.

### A Sudden Insight

The seminal idea hit me, not unlike Newton's apple, through an apparently humdrum incident.

Unless we happen to know already that it is Whyte who is writing—and that fact is not given until the end, in an unobtrusive footnote—we will probably catch no stylistic clues here, and there are no violations of fact. (It is of course unlikely that any author's name piles up IQ tests quite as deep as "Otis Binet Stanford," but for all anyone knows there could be such a man.) Everything thus depends on belief. The author strongly approves of the techniques that "my colleagues in personnel work" are already using; he thinks that every part of an employee's life and personality should be the "concern of the corporation," and that the present selection and training programs are "democratic." If the reader thinks the same, how can he detect irony? Whyte is of course deliberately saving his more extreme absurdities for later on, and he makes things even more interesting by turning to beliefs that most readers of *Fortune* will share:

I was returning from Washington in a Pennsylvania Railroad diner. Having just left a very stimulating personnel workshop, I was mulling over our unsolved problems when the waiter presented the check. Finding myself low in funds, I called the steward and, with a view to cashing a check, began showing him all the cards in my wallet.

I had never before realized quite how many I carried. As I took them out one by one, the inventory mounted. There was (1) operator's license, (2) car-registration certificate, (3) company identification card, with my laminated picture, (4) social-security card, (5) air-travel card, (6) automobile insurance policy card, (7) A.A.A. bail-bond certificate, (8) Kirkeby Hotels credit card, (9) Hilton Hotels credit card, (10) Sheraton Hotels credit card, (11) United Medical Service card, (12) blood donor's card.

Nonetheless I was in a fix. The steward's courtesy was up to the same high standard as the food, but he had to explain to me that no card I had with me would do. None meshed with the Pennsylvania's accounting system. At that instant the idea hit. Why not *one master, all-purpose card?*

Everything began to fall into place. For the more I thought, the more I came to realize that the least of the card's advantages would be its convenience to the individual. The real promise lay in another direction. In one fell stroke the Universal Card could solve all the major unfinished problems of organization life.

It is easy to see, then, how even fairly competent readers, if they are speeding along without much thought, could reach this point without serious misgivings. And once a momentum of agreement is established, it takes a fairly rude shock to break it. Yet to anyone reading the piece slowly, knowing the whole story, it would seem that such rude shocks are provided in delightful number. But the reader who takes Whyte literally must accept all the following:

> . . . the diversity of testing methods now used . . . keep the records from being interchangeable. Valuable as each method may be as a peephole into an applicant's character, the lack of standardization means each succeeding organization has to start on the man all over again . . .

> Under the Universal Card system . . . [employees] could not cut the cord with the organization. Physically, they might move to other jobs—I see no way to prohibit the movement—but wherever they went the card and its accumulation of years of scrutiny and testing would follow them and condition their attitudes. . . . They would be loyal to organization itself . . .

> As a result of this surveillance, and such encouragements as probationary fellowships, we would ensure a constantly replenishing reservoir of potential cardholders. Thus even though a parent might not be a cardholder himself, he could cherish the dream that one day one of his children could become one.

> At the same time we were bringing newcomers in we would be pruning the current membership. There would be nothing static about the system, and if a man fell beneath an acceptable rating, we would revoke his card. This would be hard on the

people concerned, but they would be the lone-persons, the mystics, the intellectual agitators—which is to say, the kind of people that the modern organization doesn't really want anyway.

Finally, after building his authoritarian version of Big Brother, Whyte gives what would seem an almost too obvious demurrer:

> More than anything else, the Universal Card system would protect us from authoritarianism. Those who are working with me do not relish 1984 and the prospect of Big Brother and dictators like him taking over. . . . People like Big Brother can succeed only where they find society fragmented, unorganized, and leaderless. But if the Universal Card is adopted, Big Brother and his henchmen could not get into the positions of authority. We would be there already.

We can see that the internal clues here will operate only for the reader whose beliefs do not correspond point for point with those of "Otis Binet Stanford." Those readers who wrote Whyte asking him to help develop the details so that they could implement his plan in their businesses could not be told that they had overlooked direct clues, except perhaps for the footnote at the very end explaining that "Otis Binet Stanford is a pseudonym for the author of this essay, *Fortune* Editor William H. Whyte Jr." But even that does not explicitly repudiate the content. And there is no violation of generally accessible knowledge. (Whyte later learned, in fact, that Westinghouse Electric had already developed a card not so very different from the one he proposed.) There were no obvious stylistic absurdities, though there are many fine ironic imitations of business jargon. What could a reader have done?

Clearly he was expected to rely on something like the two following tests:

*a*) What has been my past experience with this moral or intellectual position? Do many people I respect seriously hold what is being argued here? If so, the likelihood of irony is diminished, though by no means removed. But if almost everyone I know would reject either the main point or the arguments advanced for it, then the likelihood of irony is greatly increased. Surely this is a very shaky test, depending on the accidents of my time and class.

Whyte's mock argument yields conflicting results when this test is applied. In itself, the card is a thoroughly "rational" extension, entirely believable, of practices to be found everywhere. The objections to the card are not self-evident to all reasonable men, obvious as they may seem to some of us; in fact, Whyte finds himself having to argue at length, in *The Organization Man,* to show that such a card and the tests on which it is based could not accomplish what is claimed for them.[30]

On the other hand, the *reasons* advanced for the card's usefulness ought to have alerted every attentive reader. How many acquaintances do I have who really believe that "people who question things" are *always* dangerous and *should be silenced*? And of these, how many are likely to state their belief in print? A moment's thought about either of these beliefs should have alerted any reader to suspect irony. But obviously those who bit did not give even a moment's thought to the norms they were accepting.

Though this first test, then, is not here as decisive as it often can be, it should have made readers suspicious, even without stylistic and factual conflicts.

*b*) What do I know about the beliefs of the man signing his name to this piece? Assuming that I have read closely enough to discover that Whyte wrote it—not a very demanding exercise, since it is stated in so many words—I can then ask whether it is probable that he supports the ideas he claims to support. And of course anyone who had read anything else by Whyte on the subject of organization would suspect that he was not serious in this essay. Is he, secondly, likely to use irony? The readers of Whyte's piece were at a disadvantage here. Most of his writing is serious social analysis, and this ironic bit was sandwiched between hundreds of thoroughly trustworthy pieces in *Fortune,* a magazine not ordinarily thought of as the mother of conscious ironies. According to this second criterion, then, the reader would have been justified only in assuming that the piece *might* be ironic, since Whyte in his other writings contradicts the point he seems to make here; the other signs suggest that he would write without irony.

Ordinarily this test is more useful. If I have read one ironic essay by Mark Twain (or even if I have only seen him described, in my desk dictionary, as a "humorist") I should be alerted. Such probabilities are always fairly weak, however, and it is easy to use them destructively. Ronald S. Crane argued that they can never settle interpretations.[31] To know that many medievalists have used Christian allegory cannot teach us that *this* medieval text is allegorical; to know that Twain is often

30. *The Organization Man* (New York, 1956), chaps. 14 and 15. I don't know what we can do about the writer in *Punch* who took Whyte's card seriously, "as one more evidence of Yankee boorishness" (*The Organization Man,* p. 176). Perhaps figure 4, p. 223 below, would be helpful here.

31. "On Hypotheses in 'Historical Criticism': Apropos of Certain Contemporary Medievalists," *The Idea of the Humanities* (Chicago, 1967), 2: 236–60.

ironic cannot in itself settle whether he is ironic *here*. Crane's point is sound, so long as we are looking for decisive proof. But in practice we look for clues, for circumstantial evidence, as it were, and weak probabilities can sometimes provide an intuitive click of recognition which enables other evidence to fall into place. The on-off switch of irony is especially subject to such subtle leadings. A text, let us say, bores me when read straight; I learn that its pseudonymous author is really a famous ironist, or for some other reason I suspect irony. The text suddenly becomes interesting again, and my new interest feels like confirmation of the hunch. The dull becomes clever, the stupid brilliant. (The process can of course work in reverse. *The Report from Iron Mountain* is in some ways more interesting as a possibly true exposé than as an ironic hoax.)[32]

Every reader will have greatest difficulty detecting irony that mocks his own beliefs or characteristics. If an author invents a speaker whose stupidities strike me as gems of wisdom, how am I to know that he is not a prophet? If his mock style seems like good writing to me, what am I to do? And if his incongruities of fact and logic are such as I might commit, I am doomed. None of us can tell how many ironies we have missed in our lives because we share ignorance, stylistic naiveté, or outlandish beliefs with the ridiculed mask. For this reason all of the tests I have described are highly fallible. No complex piece of irony can be read merely with tests or devices or rules, and it would be a foolish man who felt sure that he could never mistake irony for straight talk.

The opposite mistake, taking straight talk for irony, is most probable where an author's beliefs differ most from the reader's. I once decided that a piece in a professional journal was ironic, because the author's proposal for a "multiple response device in the teaching of remedial English" was on the face of it absurd; he had provided each student with an electric switch, underneath each desk, connected to a panel of lights and switches at the teacher's desk. "The teacher can ask students to choose a response to a multiple choice or true and false question and then the student may indicate his choice by turning his switch to one of four positions. When the students have made their

---

32. Leonard C. Lewin, *The Report from Iron Mountain* (New York, 1967).

See *Trans-Action* (January–February 1968) for reviews (straight and ironic) and an editorial about the book. For an example of literal reading, see the piece by Fernand Gigon in *Atlas* (September 1968), originally published in *Le Figaro littéraire*. I am grateful to Mr. Lewin for correspondence and references concerning straight readings, and for his insistence that he does not now and has not ever conceded that his book is an ironic satire.

choice, the teacher depresses one of four switches which designates the correct response. If the student's choice is correct, his individual light turns on in the panel of lights at the front of the room. . . . Consequently, each student knows immediately whether or not his response is correct." And so on. The arguments for what the author called MIRD (for Multiple Integrated Response Device) left me puzzled but on balance fairly sure that the whole thing was a spoof. But the editor replied to my inquiry saying that I was wrong as wrong could be; I had been misled by my own beliefs and by previous ironic essays in the same section of the same journal.

I take that case as representative of a good deal of literary controversy today in which critics, unable to believe that an author could really contradict their own beliefs, conclude that he is being ironic. Pious authors cannot possibly have meant their piety, defenders of authority must have been kidding. In the fourth book of *Gulliver's Travels,* Swift cannot possibly have approved of the rationality of the Houyhnhnms because it is so obviously—by some standards of this century—absurd. Jane Austen must have been ironic in her treatment of Fanny Price in *Mansfield Park* because—well, because the Crawfords whom she takes to be so deficient morally are really—to us—so much more *interesting.* Goldsmith cannot have meant all that sentiment in *The Vicar of Wakefield.* I shall be considering some cases of over-reading later on. For now these examples serve only to show just how hard it is to apply tests of belief.

But difficult or unsolved cases should not lead any reader to throw up his hands in despair or indifference. Rather we should marvel, in a time when everyone talks so much about the breakdown of values and the widening of communication gaps, at the astonishing agreements that stable ironies can produce among us. To dramatize this point one more time and to summarize, I conclude with a famous piece of irony—the beginning of Huxley's *Brave New World* (1932). My reading will I hope seem obvious to most readers. In being so, it should underline the remarkable feat we perform in following ironic blueprints accurately together.

To some readers some of my points may, on the other hand, seem wrongly taken; that will not matter, too much, so long as we can be clear about how we might argue in settling our differences. I can think of two other kinds of readers who may want to skip the following details: those who think all this unimportant and pedestrian, because meanwhile those wonderfully juicy ambiguous unstable ironies lie uninterpreted; and those who think that polemical novels-of-ideas like *Brave New World* are not worth our attention because they are not "true novels" or "really literature." I hope they will resist, not because of any wisdom offered in my reading, but because if we can get together in these matters, it may help us when we later on take courage and look on Infinite Negativity bare.


A squat grey building of only thirty-four stories. Over the main entrance the words, CENTRAL LONDON HATCHERY AND CONDI-TIONING CENTRE, and, in a shield, the World State's motto, COM-MUNITY, IDENTITY, STABILITY.

The enormous room on the ground floor faced towards the north. Cold for all the summer beyond the panes, for all the tropical heat of the room itself, a harsh thin light glared through the windows, hungrily seeking some draped lay figure, some pallid shape of academic goose-flesh, but finding only the glass and nickel and bleakly shining porcelain of a laboratory. Wintriness responded to wintriness. The overalls of the workers were white, their hands gloved with a pale corpse-coloured rubber. The light was frozen, dead, a ghost. Only from the yellow barrels of the microscopes did it borrow a certain rich and living substance, lying along the polished tubes like butter, streak after luscious streak in long recession down the work tables.

"And this," said the Director opening the door, "is the Fertilizing Room."

Bent over their instruments, three hundred Fertilizers were plunged, as the Director of Hatcheries and Conditioning entered the room, in the scarcely breathing silence, the absent-minded, soliloquizing hum or whistle, of absorbed concentration. A troop of newly arrived students, very young, pink and callow, followed nervously, rather abjectly, at the Director's heels. Each of them carried a notebook, in which, whenever the great man spoke, he desperately scribbled. Straight from the horse's mouth. It was a rare privilege. The D.H.C. for Central London always made a point of personally conducting his new students round the various departments.

"Just to give you a general idea," he would explain to them. For of course some sort of general idea they must have, if they were to do their work intelligently—though as little of one, if they were to be good and happy members of society, as possible. For particulars, as everyone knows, make for virtue and happiness; generalities are intellectually necessary evils. Not philosophers but fret-sawyers and stamp collectors compose the backbone of society.

How does one know that the final sentence does not mean what it says, and that indeed the whole selection is riddled with ironies?

1. *Direct guidance from the author*
*a*) Title? Does not help much. In *The Tempest* Miranda sees the first group of young human beings she has ever seen, says, "O brave new world / That hath such people in't!" This bit of knowledge could fit either a literal or an ironic reading, depending perhaps on how one reads the play; the people Miranda sees are clearly less wonderful than she thinks.

But what about that word "Brave"? *Courageous* doesn't make sense in the Shakespeare. If necessary, we look it up: "Archaic: superior, excellent, fine."

*b*) Epigraph? Yes, an overlooked quotation from Berdiaeff, in French, which asks how we can manage to *avoid* the complete fulfillment of utopian dreams. "Utopias *can* be realized. . . . Perhaps we are coming into a century when intellectuals . . . will look for ways to avoid utopias and return to non-utopian society, less 'perfect' and with more freedom." Pay dirt here. Nothing could be more to the point. In opposition to "Brave," this sounds already like an anti-utopia.

*c*) Other direct clues? Note the obviously hostile description (par. 2) of the enormous building and the students. Squat, grey, cold, harsh, thin, glared, hunger for human figure, wintriness, pale, corpse-coloured, frozen, dead, ghost, callow, nervously, abjectly—this does not look like a superior world.

2 and 3. *Deliberate error*
"*Only* thirty-four stories"? Does *Huxley* use that word "only"? London had no skyscrapers in 1932. So "squat" and "only" could not be unqualified Huxley. "World State"? There is not, yet, a world state. Must be set in the future? That fits with the "new" of the title. The gloomy, frozen description seems to suggest that the new is not very "brave," which fits with the Berdiaeff. There is, so far as I know, no Central London Hatchery and Conditioning Centre. But that perhaps proves little.

4. *Disharmonies of style*
Many of them. There is simply no way of reconciling the goose-fleshy description of the room with the abstract affirmations about goodness and happiness in the final paragraph; the suspiciously cheerful author of the last paragraph could not easily be the same character as the sardonic, sharp-eyed narrator of paragraph 2.

But which of these "voices" wrote "Straight from the horse's mouth" and "It was a rare privilege"? The cheery one wrote about the privilege, obviously. But the other sentence could be either (*a*) sneering: "Straight from the horse's mouth" or (*b*) admiring: "Straight from the 'great man's' mouth."

We can be fairly sure by now that Huxley speaks directly in paragraph 2, then gradually moves behind a satiric mask in the "great man" paragraph and disappears totally by the end of the final paragraph. Note that Huxley's paragraph is full of particulars, while the mask's is all glittering generalities.

## 5. *Conflicts of belief*

Do *I* believe in Community, Identity, Stability? Not sure; it depends on what they mean, but in this context they arouse suspicion. Does Huxley believe in them? Can't be sure from the words themselves, but the other clues make me expect that they will turn out to be used ironically, for satire. The epigraph talked about fighting utopias in the name of freedom. All three of these terms *could* describe infringements of freedom.

Do I believe that "everyone knows" that particulars, not generalities, make for virtue and happiness, and that "good" and "happy" people are produced in this way? Obviously many people, including myself, do not. But does Huxley expect me to believe the opposite (as I do not)—that happiness is found only in universals? One can't tell from this passage, but anyone who knows about Huxley's aggressive pursuit of ideas—and especially of the truths behind mystical experiences—will be made doubly suspicious here.

Do I believe that fret-sawyers and stamp collectors compose the backbone of society? Absolutely not, and I cannot believe that Huxley does either. If I had no other clue this would be enough, because even stamp collectors, presumably, cannot believe that stamp collectors compose the backbone of society. The speaker in this paragraph is clearly Huxley's comic portrait of a misguided defender of this vile new world.

## *Decision*

I am now certain that Huxley is ironic whenever he uses a term of praise for the new world. In light of this decision, I look again at "Hatchery"—ah, of course, a clue to the dehumanization of this society; and "conditioning"—another one, an anti-freedom word. What about the life revealed at the end of the frozen paragraph? Clearly the only life is still mechanical, reflected (in the "Fertilizing Room" of the "Hatchery") only from a long row of microscopes.

By now Huxley has led us securely into a pattern of reconstructions that enables us to deal with a wide variety of voices or tones without hesitation. We inhabit with him a world in which freedom and independence and intelligence and variety and personal human warmth are important, and we "look down on" the *presented* world in which all that we care for is violated or—at best—simulated.

The extent of our education at Huxley's hands can be seen in our way of handling the phrase, "good and happy members of society." In many another context, we would share with the author an absolutely literal acceptance of this value—in reading Aristotle, for example, or Spinoza, or Kant. But here the phrase means something like "suppressed and mindlessly cheerful cogs in a supermachine."

But in talking of contexts in this way, I have already moved beyond the simple problem with which we began. Once I have read a few lines of *Brave New World,* I cannot resist forming hypotheses, however unconsciously, about its general nature. I simply could not write the account without using terms like "anti-utopia" and "satire," and once such terms have come to mind, each succeeding detail is inevitably taken as confirming or denying my hunches about the kind of voyage upon which Huxley is embarked. We can be alerted to suspect irony by the five kinds of clues discussed so far. But to come to the sureties that we enjoy after three pages of Huxley we have already moved into another kind of problem entirely: how do we recognize a genre when we meet one?

. . . Valid interpretation depends on a valid inference about the proprieties of the intrinsic genre. . . . The author and the interpreter are both constrained by genre proprieties, and . . . the author's meaning is determined by his willing of a particular intrinsic genre . . .

—E. D. Hirsch

Shakespeare . . . in no wise allows the substantial content to evaporate in an ever more volatile sublimation, and insofar as his lyricism sometimes culminates in madness there is in this madness nevertheless an extraordinary degree of objectivity. Accordingly, when Shakespeare relates himself ironically to his work, this is simply in order to let the objective prevail. Irony is now pervasive, ratifying each particular feature so there is neither too much nor too little, so that everything receives its due . . .

—Kierkegaard

As learned Commentators view
In Homer more than Homer knew . . .
—Swift

I design, in a short Time, to consider the Case of *Irony* and *Innuendoes* in a *judicial* Light; and how far a *forced, distant,* or *inverted* Construction of any Sentence is consistent with common *Equity* and the *Liberties* of this Nation, when a *plain, natural* and *obvious* Meaning is ready at Hand.

—*The Craftsman* (1731)

# PART II LEARNING WHERE TO STOP

Deride our weak forefathers' musty rule,
Who therefore smiled, because they saw a Fool;
Sublimer logic now adorns our isle,
We therefore see a Fool, because we smile.

—Pope

. . . resorting to that last expedient of a despairing commentator, the assumption of "sarcastic irony."

—Eduard Fraenkel

The family of Herod, at least after it had been favoured by fortune, was lineally descended from Cimon and Miltiades, Theseus and Cecrops, Aeacus and Jupiter.

—Gibbon

# FOUR | Essays, Satires, Parody

In this chapter we shall begin reading whole works, trying to discover how their embodied intentions lead us to go so far—and no farther —in seeing ironic meanings.[1]

Whether a given word or passage or work *is* ironic depends, in our present view, not on the ingenuity of the reader but on the intentions that constitute the creative act. And whether it is *seen* as ironic depends on the reader's catching the proper clues to those intentions. It has become conventional to say that the reader discovers these clues "in the context." This is a safe enough way of putting it, provided we remember that we cannot know in advance which of many possible contextual matters will be relevant—other parts of the work itself, knowledge about the author's life and times, or the reader's deepest convictions about what authors are likely to say in earnest. Even those of us who believe that "the text" is always in some sense final arbiter of meanings will find ourselves using many contexts that according to some critical theories are extrinsic.

In any given piece of stable irony, the central meaning of the words is fixed and univocal, regardless of how many peripheral and even contradictory significances different readers may add. And yet the same words can be used in other creative acts for widely different intentions, ironic and literal.

Consider once again the words, "Hail, King of the Jews!" We can easily imagine an early scene with a crowd of admirers shouting these

1. See Hirsch, *Validity in Interpretation*, for a good statement of the case for placing the author's intentions at the center of our interpretative act. I necessarily scant the philosophical issues that cluster about the notion of intentions. They vary, of course, from philosophy to philosophy. In the "analytical" mode, I have found most helpful Roy Lawrence's *Motive and Intention* (Evanston, 1972), G. E. M. Anscombe's *Intention* (Ithaca, 1957), and H. P. Grice's "Meaning," *Philosophical Review* 64 (1957), *"Utterer's Meaning and Intentions,"* ibid. 78 (1969), and "Utterer's Meaning, Sentence Meaning, and Word Meaning," *Foundations of Language* 4 (1968). Max Black sets out to refute Grice's reliance on intentions in "Meaning and Intention: An Examination of Grice's Views," *New Literary History* 4 (Winter 1973), but I note that when the chips are down, Black exempts irony from his claim: "In standard and unproblematic cases, where we are not dealing with some transposed form of speech such as irony, or a case of deception, the relevant speaker's intention is *constituted* by the meaning of what he says [and is not the court of appeal in determining that meaning]" (p. 276). Black gives an extensive bibliography of the controversy Grice's views have stimulated (p. 257).

words in absolute devotion. But when the busy little ironists conducting the crucifixion shouted the message, the words became ironic, not of course by virtue of any verbal change, but by a change in intentions. The new context, a religious, social, and political situation had to be seen for what it was by any bystander who hoped to understand the ironic meaning. Then, when Mark reported the words in his gospel account, *his* intentions, discovered in a totally new context (unlike the first two this one could be called "verbal" or literary) displayed a double irony.[2] And it would not be hard to imagine another literary work, written by a passionate anti-Christian, in which Mark's words would be once again reversed by the new satiric context into one more ironic message: poor misguided Mark, who thought that the man mocked for being called King of the Jews was in fact King of the Jews, when he was really a fanatical paranoid!

The last three of these four different "works of art," all using the same words, are all stable ironies. No one of them is in the slightest degree ambiguous; each of them judges us as right or wrong in our interpretation; there is no escape into cheerful talk about richly polysemous words. In each case we either catch the intention or we do not. And in each case we must make quite complicated decisions about which of many possibly relevant contexts actually determined, as intentions, what the words meant—and hence mean. That concentric circles of expanded context can be added indefinitely does not affect the fixity of interpretation within any one circle.

The instabilities of some modern irony have led many critics to overlook or deny the immense sureties of interpretation that can be given an ironic passage by a fully developed literary context like that provided by Mark. Morton Gurewitch, writing on the disorienting instabilities of European romantic irony, echoes many others in describing irony as only corrosive:

> Irony, unlike satire, does not work in the interests of stability. Irony entails hypersensitivity to a universe permanently out of joint and unfailingly grotesque. The ironist does not pretend to cure such a universe or to solve its mysteries. It is satire that solves. The images of vanity, for example, that litter the world's satire are always satisfactorily deflated in the end; but the vanity of vanities that informs the world's irony is beyond liquidation.[3]

2. See above, chap. 1, n. 21.
3. Morton Gurewitch, "European Romantic Irony," Ph.D. dissertation, University of Michigan, Ann Arbor, 1957, p. 13; quoted in Muecke, *Compass of Irony,* p. 27.

That this view of the world as "permanently" unstable (a curious oxymoron), as "unfailingly" failing, has been widespread needs no proof here. And if this is the universe we live in, what could be more absurd than the effort to talk of "stable ironies," or to search ironies for their stabilities? If irony is, as Kierkegaard and the German romantics taught the world, "absolute infinite negativity," and if, as many believe, the world or universe or creation provides at no point a hard and fast resistance to further ironic corrosion, then all meanings dissolve into the one supreme meaning: No meaning!

But theories of the universe and the nature of irony are one thing, our reading experience another. And the fact is that every reader climbs many ironic heights with great security, even when his primary attention is on how many dangers surround him. And the way in which literary contexts make such security possible is as interesting, inherently, as the more frequently stressed way in which they can throw us off balance.

It is sometimes said that conversational ironies are easier to interpret than literary ironies, because we have available such aids as rib-punching, eyebrow-raising, and ironic intonation—what the rhetorical tradition called "delivery." But our experience is often the other way around: conversational ironies go astray because they lack the clarifying, the "fixing" context that is developed by literary ironies.

Here is some talk I overheard between two students:

"Hi, bird brain."
Silence.
"What's the matter?"
"I get tired of you insulting me all the time."
"But I'm *not* insulting you. I was being ironic."
"*I* think you meant it."
"Do you think that if I really thought you had a bird brain I'd tease you like that about it?"
"Maybe not. But you *do* think you're smarter than me."
"But that's stupid. I . . ."
"There, you see, you think I'm stupid!"

Anyone who practices and savors irony has observed or taken part in this little drama many times. In a sense the discussion is an effort to provide a context as fully determining as is provided by a good literary work.[4] On the other hand, it is when what I have called stable

4. Conversational instabilities can become stable when put back into a literary context. The grotesque confusions among Tristram Shandy's relatives are for the most part quite clear to readers. Richard B. Wright makes the contrast explicit:

ironies are placed back in the context of "the whole of life," and when philosophies about it are divorced from literary intentions, that they seem to become ambiguous or unsure.

When T. S. Eliot wrote, in "The Hippopotamus,"

> The hippopotamus's day
> Is passed in sleep; at night he hunts;
> God works in a mysterious way—
> The Church can sleep and feed at once.

no reader could possibly mistake the irony and its satiric point against the church; the poem as a whole gave every stanza and every line a satiric thrust. Yet if the poem is placed into the context of Eliot's later conversion to Anglo-Catholicism, certainties begin to dissolve. Perhaps he was subtly satirizing the speaker, or was unconsciously getting out of his system all remaining hostility toward a church he was about to embrace. And if that new ironic step is then placed into a context of the convictions of men who think all religious belief absurd, we have a new world in which ironies can be piled on ironies indefinitely.

But note that what has really happened when we raise such doubts about Eliot's poem is that we have been playing with its significance, not its meaning. There is simply nothing in the poem or any of its contexts at the time of its construction to lead us to discount its ironies against the "true church." Eliot's later conversion adds a rich human significance to the poem, but the satiric force of its ironies remains constant.

## CONTEXTS AND THE GROOVES OF GENRE

Here are two words, written by the same author in two different short pieces for *X* magazine: *delighted* and *miracle*. If anyone were foolish enough to ask whether these words are in themselves ironic, one could

---

" 'Who is this fellow Pendle?'

" 'He teaches at Union Place Secondary.'

" 'One of Dunc MacCauley's men?'

" 'Yes.'

" 'Well . . . it looks promising.'

" 'No kidding.'

"I mean my innocent American-sounding phrase to convey genuine wonder but perhaps I don't give it the proper rising inflection. And Cecil still seems to think that I'm transmitting on our own special ironic wave-length. So he springs the door open and smiles faintly with the air of a diffident man who has already disclosed too much" (*The Weekend Man* [New York, 1970] p. 113).

94

only tell him that without a context their possible meanings range almost without limit. "Delighted" could range in meaning from disgusted to any one of dozens of different shades of pleasure. "Miracle" could be a term of praise or ridicule, in innumerable different dosages.

But of course one does not ordinarily face words in complete isolation. Instead, one picks up an old magazine in the doctor's office, say *The New Yorker,* opens to the first page of text, sees "The Talk of the Town," and begins to read: "We are delighted with the recent censorship ruling in the matter of motion-picture harems." No matter how much the reader knows about current attitudes toward censorship, or about *The New Yorker's* general position, he still cannot know for certain whether delighted means delighted, disgusted, or something in between. Even if he learns that E. B. White wrote the piece, he still cannot tell, though his suspicions of irony may be aroused. Only if he happens to know precisely what the ruling was—in short, only if he can provide an external context—can he infer, with some degree of surety, what the sentence means without seeing it as part of some other larger whole.

Before looking at the literary context of "delighted," consider the other word, "miracle," found in another opening sentence written also by White for the same magazine: "A bird sitting on eggs is all eye and tail, a miracle of silent radiation and patience." Is "miracle" ironic? We certainly cannot tell for sure, without further evidence. And note again how it is impossible to resist calling into play contexts quite external to whatever the particular work will turn out to be. As soon as I did not say "X magazine" but *The New Yorker,* many readers' expectations of irony rose dramatically. When I added "The Talk of the Town" and "E. B. White," they rose further. What is more, the particular words are laden with delicate but real and special expectations depending on our experience with their place and time: "miracle" is not likely to prove literal, since it is a commonplace that nobody believes in miracles these days (least of all writers for magazines like *The New Yorker*).

Now that we have one sentence, it begins to sharpen these general expectations derived from what some contextualist critics have called extrinsic sources: the sitting of that hen will not turn out to be a literal miracle, surely, but it may very easily become either a metaphorical miracle or a trivial event to be scoffed at. Like the other single sentence, this one still does not mean much, in isolation.

Observe now what happens to the two words when we see them in the complete (though short) works from which they came:

## Censorship

We are delighted with the recent censorship ruling in the matter of motion-picture harems. Some scenes in a Paramount picture now in production are set in a harem, and after careful deliberation the censors have decided to allow this type of poly-form allure *provided* the boudoir does not contain the sultan. The girls can mill about among the pillows, back and side having gone bare, but no male eye must gaze upon them—save, of course, yours, lucky reader. This harem-but-no-sultan decision belongs in the truly great body of opinion interpreting the American moral law. It takes its place alongside the celebrated 1939 ruling on the exposure of female breasts in the Flushing World of Tomorrow, which provided that one breast could be presented publicly but not two, and thereby satisfied the two seemingly irreconcilable groups: the art-lovers, who demanded breasts but were willing to admit that if you'd seen one you'd seen them both, and the decency clique, who held out for concealment but were agreed that the fact of concealing one breast established the essential reticence of the owner and thereby covered the whole situation, or chest. That subtle and far-reaching ruling carried the Fair, as we know, safely through two difficult seasons, and we imagine that the aseptic harem will do as much for Hollywood.[5]

## Incubation

A bird sitting on eggs is all eye and tail, a miracle of silent radiation and patience. It is almost impossible to meet, squarely, the accusing gaze of a broody bird, however unjust the accusation may seem. Perhaps this is because the bird's dedication is pure—untainted by expectations of a hatch. (Nobody is more surprised than a hen bird when a shell opens and a chick comes out.) This classic pose of a bird is the despair of creative people: we have never seen a broody artist sitting on an egg except knowingly, in an attitude of sly expectancy.[6]

How do we decide that "delighted" in the first passage means something like "amused by the silly decision" rather than "pleased by the 'truly great' decision"? How do we know, in contrast, that "miracle" in the second means what it says, or something very close to it? The censorship ruling delights White not, except, of course, as an object of fun, while the bird is to him a genuine wonder. But how do we know?

On the one hand we use the literary context, the form that we reconstruct as we read, referring part to part and parts to whole; on

5. As reprinted in E. B. White, *The Second Tree from the Corner* (New York, 1962), pp. 112–13.
6. Ibid., p. 170.

the other is the historical context—personal and social—in which the piece was written and printed and read, and to which we may or may not need to refer explicitly in reconstructing its meanings. In effect, the first context is what we finally arrive at, in our total act of successful reading: it does not exist for us until the passage clicks into place as a kind of completed whole. The second exists before, during, and after this reading, available to be referred to as an aid in our reconstruction—and also available as a possible distraction from a sound reading.

We can see more clearly how this reciprocity of form and history works if we look at both pieces in detail. In a way, "Incubation" is the more interesting problem, because it presents a kind of battle, in a very short space, among various expectations of the reader. As I have said, readers of "The Talk of the Town" have reason to expect irony, and the subject is not in itself likely to change their expectations; a brooding bird, thoughtless, overprotective, nervous, stubborn, or sluggish, is at least as well suited to a comic attack as to a hymn of praise. On the other hand, readers of the column during White's tenure came to expect that animals would be treated with sympathy or admiration, and that they would be used as a source of metaphoric illumination of the life around them in the cities.

Neither of these two general probabilities is strong enough to settle any questions for us, but they do provide a very broad band of expectations within which we find ourselves working; if White had decided to give serious instructions to poultry raisers in "The Talk of the Town," he would have had to take extra pains to prevent readers from seeing some hidden metaphoric or ironic meaning in his words, just as the writer of an ironic piece for any characteristically literal journal— the *New York Times* financial page, the *Wall Street Journal,* the *Congressional Record*—must be willing to offer special clues to overcome habits of literal-mindedness.

The curious thing is that within the extremely broad band of expectations established by these probabilities, we so quickly find our way, using what seem such slight clues. By the end of the second sentence, we feel confident that "miracle of silent radiation and patience" means what it says—the humor of the shamefaced human being unable to stare down the accusing hen has somehow ruled out once and for all any possibility that "miracle" will turn out to be a term of abuse. The further personification of the hen with "dedication" and "pure" and "untainted" is not really needed for clarity, but by bringing us to the point about dedication, it prepares us for the shift to direct satire of "creative people" with their impure dedication and sly expectancy.

97

If the paragraph did not take this rapid movement toward a strong satiric point, our decision that "miracle" was not ironic would not prevent our being baffled, unless some *other* recognizable literary genre were completed. A simple piece praising the pure dedication of the bird would strike everyone as a feeble bit of sentimentality about nature—sentimental outbursts about nature being another recognizable, and therefore expectable, literary genre. In the context, one might in fact go back and reconsider the earlier decision: surely White and *The New Yorker* have more of a point in mind than this! But in this paragraph everything works quickly and efficiently for the greatest amount of what I must call, for want of a standard term for this literary genre, amiable pastoral satire. We are made to expect, very early, that there will be no serious undercutting of "miracle." The expectation becomes practical certainty, not necessarily as we read the final word, but rather at any point in our reading when the whole work comes into focus, with every detail seen as playing a forceful and economical—or at least harmonious—part in the satire. At the instant of recognition, we are led to forget all the irrelevant things we might know about brooding hens and all the cute reversals of "miracle" that might have been made; we remember only the tendency of artists to corrupt their work by having one eye on future reward. It *is* a miracle indeed when any creature can give himself fully to an important task, with silent radiation and patience, without the sly expectancy that spoils the purity of creation.

As I have said, many critics have defined irony broadly enough to include such a passage, since it packs so much meaning into so few words and contrasts the bird "ironically" with the artist. It is also true that we have had to "read between the lines"—another presumed clue to irony. But no word has been inverted or radically twisted by its context: miracle is miracle, patience is patience, pure dedication is pure dedication, despair is (amused) despair. The meaning is thus much closer to traditional "stable metaphor" or simile ("a brooding hen is *like* what a true artist should be") than to stable irony.

Contrast all of this with "Censorship." We approach it, of course, with the same broad range of probabilities in mind; we do not expect pornography, or a detective story, or an account of censorship in the Ottoman empire; if we have read much by this author, we expect to be amused by some sort of serious point about censorship, and we are prepared for irony if it should be present. We also expect—and this is important—that *The New Yorker* will be against censorship.

The first sentence certainly does not change our expectations, except to increase the likelihood of irony, with the slight anticlimax of "motion-picture harems" and the possible air of parody in the style (especially "in the matter of"). As soon as we learn from the second sentence what the ruling was, our knowledge about *The New Yorker* and White become really useful. It is unlikely to the point of absurdity that White is genuinely pleased by the ruling except as an object of ridicule: "polyform allure" (clearly he doesn't care a pin about harems as such); "careful deliberation" (about boudoirs and sultans?)—we now know where we stand. The inverted meaning of "delighted" is now fixed, but each new bit of mockery continues to teach us in what sense White is delighted with (that is, contemptuously amused by) the truly great (that is, petty) interpreters of the moral (that is, immoral and foolish) law.

The "context," then, is not just the words but the words as they relate to our total view of the subject, to our range of inferences about what the author would most probably mean by each stroke, and to our range of possible genres. By now it has become a fixed and precisely determinate thing; if someone tried to get me to believe that White was really in favor of the decision, and was not being ironic, I could no more believe him than I could believe that this sentence I am now writing is intended ironically. Even if I have not yet read the complete work, I am now firmly located in a fairly narrow groove—a created form in a recognizable literary genre that makes sense of everything I have read so far; let us call this one "satire through pretended praise"—a name that immediately reminds us of how many members of this genre we have met before.

White's second example, the 1939 ruling, does not—and I suspect it could not no matter how hard the author tried—contradict our ironic picture of the first, but it does serve to broaden White's message. He is not simply saying, as the first half might have suggested, "Repeal this ridiculous ruling," but rather something like: "Let's laugh the stupid censors—*all* of them—out of business." Thus the ironic freight continues to be loaded on "delighted" until the very end—from "celebrated," down through "subtle and far-reaching," as well as the less direct but equally effective puncturings given by "art-lovers" and "chest."

What do we mean, then, by the "context" of these two words? What determines the *relevant* context out of the infinite number of surrounding details are the author's choices and the reader's inferences about those choices: the relevant context becomes the picture of a coherent whole, with every detail referring reciprocally to every other in the work. But at the same time, it is impossible to say that only what is "in the work" is relevant context, because at every point the author depends on inferences about what his reader will likely assume or know—about both his factual knowledge and his experience of literature. And the reader depends on inferences about what the author could assume. Is the author's allusion, for example, to an English drinking song—"Back and side go bare, go bare"—internal?

Thus the whole engagement between author and reader depends on a world they never made, and it depends, in summary, on at least three kinds of agreement: (*a*) their common experience of the vocabulary and grammar of English—the dictionary meanings of breast and chest, of harem and censorship, along with understanding of rules which allow for and control verbal inventions, like "polyform allure"; (*b*) their common cultural experience and their agreement about its meaning and value—Hollywood harems are inherently ridiculous, the safety of Hollywood is not of major importance, nudity shouldn't matter much to anyone, compromises between prudery and license are not part of important "moral law" but are instead comic, and so on; (*c*) their common experience of literary genres, a potentially large (but almost certainly finite) number of shared grooves or tracks into which reading experience can be directed.

The first two of these are indispensable, but it is the third that finally determines the precise fixing of ironies and non-ironies that we have seen. No matter how much biographical or historical information we need or use in making our reconstructions, they are finally built into patterns of shared literary expectations—the grooves of genre, the trajectories of aroused expectations and gratifications.[7]

7. Some critics believe that the grooves of genre are in some sense innate—that men are *by nature* inclined to fit their experiences into comic and tragic and satirical and farcical patterns, to say nothing of pastoral-comical, historical-pastoral, tragical-historical, and tragical-comical-historical-pastoral. Others believe that the grooves are entirely dependent on experience, learned and then imitated. The debate is closely related to the one among linguists about whether there are such things as innate linguistic "ideas," predetermining all languages into forms that in a sense constitute a kind of universal grammar. Fortunately for our purposes we need not take sides in this debate; it is, in any case, probably not resolvable when put this way. We need only recognize that there seems to be no predeterminable limit to the number of possible genres (new ones are invented from time to time) and that at the same time a surprisingly large share of our literary experience falls into a small number of patterns.

The attempt by Northrop Frye, in the *Anatomy of Criticism* (Princeton, 1957), to provide a "scientific" schema of all possible literary genres, by tracing the possible ways in which certain ideas like "successful quest" and "romantic view of reality" can interrelate, seems to me destined from the outset both to succeed and to fail. It cannot help succeeding, since like any other logical slicing of the whole world it will inevitably *cover* the whole world. And it cannot help failing, because literary forms are too precise to be caught in even a highly

There is a sense in which stable irony is in itself a literary kind: we often find that everything in a passage or situation suddenly makes sense if and only if we see it as irony, and one could argue that we are either made or "programmed" to enjoy and use this particular kind of inversion whenever possible or appropriate. There may even be an ironic literary genre in a further sense: works written *for the sake of the irony,* not works using irony for tragic or comic or satiric or eulogistic ends. I cannot think of any significant candidates until the twentieth century, and even those ironic novels and plays which some critics might suggest—Musil's *Man without Qualities,* Ionesco's and Beckett's plays, Kafka's stories—I would be inclined to describe as using pervasive ironies for a variety of literary effects not really illuminated by the word "irony."

In any case it is clear that stable irony can be used in the service of the most diverse literary effects. Not all effects. It may be safe to use it when you pray to Jehovah, himself a great ironist.[8] But be cautious about it when you write the governor asking him to grant pardon for murder, or when you call the police to report a burglary. You can heighten your tragedies with it—"A little water clears us of this deed" —and your comedies: "I wish your Grace would take me with you. Whom means your Grace?" And as we have seen, it will strengthen your satires and even your love songs. But do not make the mistake of thinking that the effect of anything you write will be *simply* heightened by an ironic infusion: it will be changed, slightly or greatly, into a different thing.

### COMPLEXITY ILLUSTRATED

Here is another short complete work which will help to clarify the reciprocal effect of irony on its context and context on perception of irony. It is a letter from Lord Bathurst to Jonathan Swift,[9] and its genre is utterly unlike anything we have seen so far:

> I receive so much pleasure in reading your letters, that, according to the usual good-nature and justice of mankind, I can dispense

---

articulated grid—or to put it another way, because authors are always inventing new forms out of old. But even Frye's enormous lumpings can serve to explain how genre-as-context provides readers with a firm and reliable control over their patterns of inference.

Probably the most influential discussion of the determinative power of genre is that by Hirsch, *Validity,* esp. chap. 3.

8. See Edwin M. Good, *Irony in the Old Testament* (London, 1965).

9. 9 September 1730, from Norman Knox, *The Word "Irony" and Its Context: 1500 to 1755,* pp. 57–58.

with the trouble I give you in reading mine. But if you grow obstinate, and will not answer me, I will plague and pester you, and do all I can to vex you. I will take your works to pieces, and show you that they are all borrowed or stolen. Have you not stolen the sweetness of your numbers from Dryden and Waller? Have not you borrowed thoughts from Virgil and Horace? At least, I am sure I have seen something like them in those books. And in your prose writings, which they make such a noise about, they are only some little improvements upon the humour you have stolen from Miguel de Cervantes and Rabelais. Well, but the style—a great matter indeed, for an Englishman to value himself upon, that he can write English; why, I write English too, but it is in another style.

But I will not forget your political tracts. You may say, that you have ventured your ears at one time, and your neck at another, for the good of your country. Why, that other people have done in another manner, upon less occasion, and are not at all proud of it. You have overturned and supported Ministers; you have set kingdoms in a flame by your pen. Pray, what is there in that, but having the knack of hitting the passions of mankind? With that alone, and a little knowledge of ancient and modern history, and seeing a little farther into the inside of things than the generality of men, you have made this bustle. There is no wit in any of them: I have read them all over, and do not remember any of those pretty flowers, those just antitheses, which one meets with so frequently in the French writers; none of those clever turns upon words, nor those apt quotations out of Latin authors, which the writers of the last age among us abounded in; none of those pretty similes, which some of our modern authors adorn their works with, that are not only a little like the thing they would illustrate, but are also like twenty other things. In short as often as I have read any of your tracts, I have been so tired with them, that I have never been easy till I got to the end of them. I have found my brain heated, my imagination fired, just as if I was drunk. A pretty thing, indeed, for one of your gown to value himself upon, that with sitting still an hour in his study, he has often made three kingdoms drunk at once.

Taken out of context, some parts of this letter could seem almost identical in effect with E. B. White's attack on censorship. Bathurst uses pretended praise to attack the ornateness of the French writers, the heavy learnedness of the previous generation of English writers, the banality and imprecision of Swift's contemporaries. But few readers, having recognized this, could ever make the mistake of pursuing this form of reconstruction further, to include Cervantes and Rabelais and

102

Dryden in the indictment, to say nothing of Swift himself. Though the genre of epistolary-praise-through-pretended-blame is so rare that some readers may be meeting it for the first time, the grooves of genre are here plainly laid out almost from the opening words. Certainly for Swift the letter would be quite clear from the beginning, though for us who listen in, unless we have some facts in hand about Swift's relation to Bathurst, the precise tone may not be clear for a line or so. One can imagine that an intelligent but ill-informed reader who knew nothing about any of the proper names mentioned might have difficulty for a while longer. But even for the most ignorant, when Bathurst concedes explicitly "the knack of hitting the passions of mankind" and "seeing a little farther in the inside of things than the generality of men," it becomes impossible to make sense of what has gone before except by turning it, through our four-step process, into delightfully extravagant praise. For most readers there will be at least some slight aura of greatness about the mentioned names, and even if we do not know that the authors cited were among Swift's favorites, we know that to have "improved on" Cervantes and Rabelais is high praise indeed.

So once again the reconstruction is not especially difficult, but it is perhaps less predictable than anything we have seen before: an elaborate ironic work designed to praise one man through seeming to blame him, and to do so by seeming to praise other men while in fact damning them.

But the full picture is even more complex than that, since it depends on our inferring a precise and varying judgment on every detail mentioned. Suppose we list some of the more important shared values and opinions taken from only seven sentences in the second paragraph: the building materials that go into the elevated edifice in which Swift and Bathurst and you and I finally dwell together.

| *Conclusions* | | *Evidence offered, or unspoken assumptions* |
|---|---|---|
| 1. You (Swift) will not say, but I will, that you have risked yourself for the good of your country, | because | "those of us who know" know about your bold pamphleteering. |
| 2. Unlike the "patriotic" risks taken by some men, which are bad, | because | "we know" they have been in a bad cause and for selfish motives, |
| 3. . . . your risks have been good, | because | we know them to have been taken in a good cause, selflessly. |

| | | |
|---|---|---|
| 4. You have produced great effects, | because | we know the true valuation of the ministers you have overturned and supported and the flames you have ignited (Swift and Bathurst would share a large supply of bits of information supporting this "knowledge"). |
| 5. You have rare genius, | because | you have the rare knack of hitting the passions of mankind; |
| 6. | because | you are unusually learned in ancient and modern history; |
| 7. | because | you see more profoundly than other men. |
| 8. Your works are works of greatness, not only | because | they rival the great authors mentioned in paragraph 1, whose works "we know" to be greatest in your kind of thing, |
| 9. | but also because | they lack the faults of authors "we know" to be inferior: the ugly over-ornamentation (pretty flowers); pedantry (apt quotations); vague and irrelevant similes. |

Think for a moment of the innumerable details of information shared by the author and reader of this letter under inference 9 alone—the lists of authors and works that would come to Swift's mind in reading this flood of condemnation. Presumably even the scholar who is expert in Swift, his circle of friends, and their reading would overlook some of the data on which the full reconstruction available to Swift himself would depend. And every detail lost is a pleasure lost, though perhaps after a time the lost pleasures become sufficiently trivial to allow us to insert, as I have done, an etcetera or two.

The point of such unpacking, by no means exhaustive, is that the complex mental operations irony demands of us make possible a density and economy impossible in any literal mode. Many pages would be required to state the sheer information Bathurst packs into these few lines. But the information is only a part of what is communicated: the pleasures of the ironic dance itself simply disappear in any paraphrase, however complete.

## "A MODEST PROPOSAL" AND THE IRONIC SUBLIME

But it is now time to turn to the difficulties offered by even more intricate contexts. For greatest speculative interest, I perhaps ought now to tackle one of the sources of famous critical disagreement—say, Swift's *A Tale of a Tub,* or the fourth book of *Gulliver's Travels,* or Melville's *Billy Budd.* But for the purpose of understanding, it is still important to stress the sources of our agreement. And so I choose "A Modest Proposal," to me the finest of all ironic satires. In spite of its intricacies it has produced enough critical consensus to justify my calling it stable, not only in intent but in effect.

The consensus is of course not universal. Though no publishing critic, so far as I know, has ever attributed to Swift himself the cruelty of his speaker's proposal that young children be bred, slaughtered, and sold as meat for human consumption, some inexperienced readers do so. I have met the bizarre reading only in teaching college freshmen— perhaps half a dozen out of hundreds who have read it with me. High school teachers report a higher incidence. It seems an incredible kind of misreading, since so far as I can determine, these readers *always* condemn the proposal itself as outrageous. I have never heard of anyone who said, "Good idea, that. Why didn't I think of it myself, as a solution to the population explosion?" Unlike Whyte's modest proposal for the Universal Personnel Card, Swift's plan is, even the bad readers say, obviously "crazy," or "criminal."

It is frequently said that irony always presupposes such victims, or even that it is written with the intent to deliberately deceive them.

> To write ironically with success a writer needs to be alert to two audiences: those who will recognize the ironic intention and enjoy the joke, and those who are the object of the satire and are deceived by it. This implies that the ironist has ranged himself with those of his readers who share his superior values, intelligence and literary sensibility; together they look down on the benighted mob.

So writes James T. Boulton, attempting to show that Defoe's style "makes no provision for irony," since all readers of "normal intelligence should respond in the same manner with one another."[10]

10. As quoted in "Defoe's Use of Irony" by Maximillian E. Novak, *Irony in Defoe and Swift* (Los Angeles, 1966), p. 7. Critical debate about Swift's satire and irony runs by now to what must be thousands of books and articles. The central issues are incisively analyzed by Edward W. Rosenheim, Jr., in *Swift and the Satirist's Art* (Chicago, 1963), chap. 1, a book to which I owe a great deal here. Mr. Rosenheim rightly notes that to call a work by Swift "ironic" says practically nothing about it, given the grotesque looseness of the term; he

But it is clear that Swift wrote with an absolute and justified expectation that every proper reader would, as an essential part of his reconstruction of the essay, "respond in the same manner" and repudiate the proposal as mad. The essential structure of this irony is not designed to "deceive some readers and allow others to see the secret message" but to deceive *all* readers for a time and then require *all* readers to recognize and cope with their deception. There has been so much written about the "marvelous consistency" of this work that a close look at its controlled inconsistencies should be justified.

A Modest
## PROPOSAL
For

*Preventing the Children of poor People in* Ireland, *from being a Burden to their Parents or Country; and for making them beneficial to the Publick.*

[1] It is a melancholly Object to those, who walk through this great Town, or travel in the Country; when they see the *Streets,* the *Roads,* and *Cabbin-doors* crowded with *Beggars* of the Female Sex, followed by three, four, or six Children, *all in Rags,* and importuning every Passenger for an Alms. These *Mothers,* instead of being able to work for their honest Livelyhood, are forced to employ all their Time in stroling to beg Sustenance for their *helpless Infants*; who, as they grow up, either turn *Thieves* for want of Work; or leave their *dear Native Country, to fight for the Pretender in* Spain, or sell themselves to the *Barbadoes.*

[2] I think it is agreed by all Parties, that this prodigious Number of Children in the Arms, or on the Backs, or at the *Heels* of their *Mothers,* and frequently of their *Fathers,* is *in the present deplorable State of the Kingdom,* a very great additional Grievance; and therefore, whoever could find out a fair, cheap, and easy Method of making these Children sound and useful Members of the Commonwealth, would deserve so well of the Publick, as to have his Statue set up for a Preserver of the Nation.

---

then in effect puts irony to one side and discusses what I call stable ironies under other critical terms. It is a good strategy, given the world's habit of equating irony with ambiguity, and given his intent, which I share, to show Swift's passion for clarity through devices of indirection—his "concern for total intelligibility" (see esp. pp. 236–38). Of the works appearing since Mr. Rosenheim's critical survey, I have found Denis Donoghue's *Jonathan Swift: A Critical Introduction* (Cambridge, 1969) most helpful.

[3] But my Intention is very far from being confined to provide only for the Children of *professed Beggars*: It is of a much greater Extent, and shall take in the whole Number of Infants at a certain Age, who are born of Parents, in effect as little able to support them, as those who demand our Charity in the Streets.

[4] As to my own Part, having turned my Thoughts for many Years, upon this important Subject, and maturely weighed the several *Schemes of other Projectors,* I have always found them grosly mistaken in their Computation. It is true a Child, *just dropt from its Dam,* may be supported by her Milk, for a Solar Year with little other Nourishment; at most not above the Value of two Shillings; which the Mother may certainly get, or the Value in *Scraps,* by her lawful Occupation of *Begging*: And, it is exactly at one Year old, that I propose to provide for them in such a Manner, as, instead of being a Charge upon their *Parents,* or the *Parish,* or *wanting Food and Raiment* for the rest of their Lives; they shall, on the contrary, contribute to the Feeding, and partly to the Cloathing, of many Thousands.

[5] There is likewise another great Advantage in my *Scheme,* that it will prevent those *voluntary Abortions,* and that horrid Practice of *Women murdering their Bastard Children*; alas! too frequent among us; sacrificing the *poor innocent Babes,* I doubt, more to avoid the Expence than the Shame; which would move Tears and Pity in the most Savage and inhuman Breast.

[6] The Number of Souls in *Ireland* being usually reckoned one Million and a half; of these I calculate there may be about Two hundred Thousand Couple whose Wives are Breeders; from which Number I subtract thirty thousand Couples, who are able to maintain their own Children; although I apprehend there cannot be so many, under *the present Distresses of the Kingdom*; but this being granted, there will remain an Hundred and Seventy Thousand Breeders. I again subtract Fifty Thousand, for those Women who miscarry, or whose Children die by Accident, or Disease, within the Year. There only remain an Hundred and Twenty Thousand Children of poor Parents, annually born: The Question therefore is, How this Number shall be reared, and provided for? Which, as I have already said, under the present Situation of Affairs, is utterly impossible, by all the Methods hitherto proposed: For we can *neither employ them in Handicraft* or *Agriculture*; we neither build Houses, (I mean in the Country) nor cultivate Land: They can very seldom pick up a Livelyhood *by Stealing* until they arrive at six Years old; except where they are of towardly Parts; although, I confess, they learn the Rudiments much earlier; during which Time, they can, however, be properly looked upon only as *Probationers*; as I have been informed by a principal Gentleman in the County of *Cavan,* who protested to me, that he never knew above one or two Instances under the Age of six, even in a Part of the Kingdom *so renowned for the quickest Proficiency in that Art.*

[7] I am assured by our Merchants, that a Boy or a Girl before twelve Years old, is no saleable Commodity; and even when they come to this Age, they will not yield above Three Pounds, or Three Pounds and half a Crown at most, on the Exchange; which cannot turn to Account either to the Parents or the Kingdom; the Charge of Nutriment and Rags, having been at least four Times that Value.

[8] I shall now therefore humbly propose my own Thoughts; which I hope will not be liable to the least Objection.

[9] I have been assured by a very knowing *American* of my Acquaintance in *London;* that a young healthy Child, well nursed, is, at a Year old, a most delicious, nourishing, and wholesome Food; whether *Stewed, Roasted, Baked,* or *Broiled*; and, I make no doubt, that it will equally serve in a *Fricasie,* or *Ragoust*.

[10] I do therefore humbly offer it to *publick Consideration,* that of the Hundred and Twenty Thousand Children, already computed, Twenty thousand may be reserved for Breed; whereof only one Fourth Part to be Males; which is more than we allow to *Sheep, black Cattle,* or *Swine*; and my Reason is, that these Children are seldom the Fruits of Marriage, *a Circumstance not much regarded by our Savages*; therefore, *one Male* will be sufficient to serve *four Females.* That the remaining Hundred thousand, may, at a Year old, be offered in Sale to the *Persons of Quality* and *Fortune,* through the Kingdom; always advising the Mother to let them suck plentifully in the last Month, so as to render them plump, and fat for a good Table. A Child will make two Dishes at an Entertainment for Friends; and when the Family dines alone, the fore or hind Quarter will make a reasonable Dish; and seasoned with a little Pepper or Salt, will be very good Boiled on the fourth Day, especially in *Winter*.

[11] I have reckoned upon a Medium, that a Child just born will weigh Twelve Pounds; and in a solar Year, if tolerably nursed, encreaseth to twenty eight Pounds.

[12] I grant this Food will be somewhat dear, and therefore very *proper for Landlords*; who, as they have already devoured most of the Parents, seem to have the best Title to the Children.

And so the full picture of the brutal proposal is developed. Different readers will become suspicious at different points. Some will begin to wonder with the phrase "just dropt from its Dam," in the fourth paragraph, because of the curious barnyard terminology; some may wince at "Breeders" in the first sentence of paragraph 6. (On second reading we may wonder how we missed earlier clues, like the style of the first sentence in the second paragraph.) Some will feel sure of themselves only when they come to the talk of training pickpockets at the end of paragraph 6. But most will have had their suspicions fully aroused by paragraph 7, and every reader should know, by paragraph

9, that the most wrenching kind of irony is at work. Every reader has thus to some degree been duped—not simply for a fleeting moment of shock and reconstruction that is produced by essays that are ironic from the first word, but for several paragraphs. And every reader has thus been drawn into an engagement of the most active kind: having been driven to suspect, and finally to admit that the voice is speaking a kind of mad reasonableness, one is tricked into an intensely active state, mind and heart fully engaged—indeed apprehensive—about what is to come.

For one thing, no reader can possibly predict what it will be: too much of what the speaker has said has made sense. Nothing here can be simply reversed, once the irony is discovered. If the speaker's position is that he will save the children and the kingdom by butchering the children, *Swift's* position cannot be simply that "we should *not* butcher them"; nobody, not even the worst exploiter, had ever proposed that we should, and to write an essay attacking such a position would be absurd. How is the reader to reconstruct a sound version of Swift's intentions behind the speaker's double claim that the landlords "have already devoured most of the Parents," and thus "seem to have the best Title to the Children"? No amount of simple inversion to contraries, or substitution of one speaker's voice for another, can yield the reconstruction of such a mixture of truth and madness. I do not want to manufacture difficulties—most readers no doubt manage to decide that Swift stands fully behind the first half of it (though the "devoured" is metaphorical, the clause is not ironic in our sense), and that he stands behind neither the literal sense nor any easily formulated "reversal" of the second half: to reconstruct it as "the landlords do *not* have the best Title to the Children" lands us in another absurdity. And so we move along, accepting, rejecting, partially rejecting. But the question is, how?

As we move through the essay, we in fact distinguish at least three completely different kinds of statement. The first two are primarily important in determining the emotional power and the direction of the attack. The third, which I shall hold to one side for a moment, is useful in filling out our conception of the details of Swift's implicit affirmative position. All three are in one sense in the same tone of voice, we might say; except for the radical differences in moral content, I think that no one could say that the style or tone is verbally inconsistent. But the meaning conveyed, the moral tone, is an almost incredibly complex mixture of the three; the skill of it can hardly be appreciated except in uninterrupted reading:

[13] Infants Flesh will be in Season throughout the Year; but more plentiful in *March,* and a little before and after: For we are told by a

grave\* Author, an eminent *French* Physician, that *Fish being a pro-
lifick Dyet,* there are more Children born in *Roman Catholick Countries*
about Nine Months after *Lent,* than at any other Season: Therefore
reckoning a Year after *Lent,* the Markets will be more glutted than
usual; because the Number of *Popish Infants,* is, at least, three to one
in this Kingdom; and therefore it will have one other Collateral Advantage, by lessening the Number of *Papists* among us.

[14] I have already computed the Charge of nursing a Beggar's Child
(in which List I reckon all *Cottagers, Labourers,* and Four fifths of the
*Farmers*) to be about two Shillings *per Annum,* Rags included; and I
believe, no Gentleman would repine to give Ten Shillings for the *Carcase of a good fat Child*; which, as I have said, will make four Dishes
of excellent nutritive Meat, when he hath only some particular Friend,
or his own Family, to dine with him. Thus the Squire will learn to be a
good Landlord, and grow popular among his Tenants; the Mother will
have Eight Shillings net Profit, and be fit for Work until she produceth
another Child.

[15] Those who are more thrifty (*as I must confess the Times require*)
may flay the Carcase; the Skin of which, artificially dressed, will make
admirable *Gloves for Ladies,* and *Summer Boots for fine Gentlemen.*

[16] As to our City of *Dublin*; Shambles may be appointed for this
Purpose, in the most convenient Parts of it; and Butchers we may be
assured will not be wanting; although I rather recommend buying the
Children alive, and dressing them hot from the Knife, as we do *roasting
Pigs.*

[17] A very worthy Person, *a true Lover of his Country,* and whose
Virtues I highly esteem, was lately pleased, in discoursing on this
Matter, to offer a Refinement upon my Scheme. He said, that many
Gentlemen of this Kingdom, having of late destroyed their Deer; he
conceived, that the Want of Venison might be well supplied by the
Bodies of young Lads and Maidens, not exceeding fourteen Years of
Age, nor under twelve; so great a Number of both Sexes in every
County being now ready to starve, for Want of Work and Service: And
these to be disposed of by their Parents, if alive, or otherwise by their
nearest Relations. But with due Deference to so excellent a Friend, and
so deserving a Patriot, I cannot be altogether in his Sentiments. For as
to the Males, my *American* Acquaintance assured me from frequent
Experience, that their Flesh was generally tough and lean, like that of
our School-boys, by continual Exercise, and their Taste disagreeable;
and to fatten them would not answer the Charge. Then, as to the Females, it would, I think, with humble Submission, *be a Loss to the
Publick,* because they soon would become Breeders themselves: And
besides it is not improbable, that some scrupulous People might be apt
to censure such a Practice (although indeed very unjustly) as a little

\* Rabelais.

bordering upon Cruelty; which, I confess, hath always been with me the strongest Objection against any Project, how well soever intended. [18] But in order to justify my Friend; he confessed, that this Expedient was put into his Head by the famous *Salmanaazor*, a Native of the Island *Formosa*, who came from thence to *London*, above twenty Years ago, and in Conversation told my Friend, that in his Country, when any young Person happened to be put to Death, the Executioner sold the Carcase to *Persons of Quality*, as a prime Dainty; and that, in his Time, the Body of a plump Girl of fifteen, who was crucified for an Attempt to poison the Emperor, was sold to his Imperial *Majesty's prime Minister of State*, and other great *Mandarins* of the Court, *in Joints from the Gibbet*, at Four hundred Crowns. Neither indeed can I deny, that if the same Use were made of several plump young girls in this Town, who, without one single Groat to their Fortunes, cannot stir Abroad without a Chair, and appear at the *Play-house*, and *Assemblies* in foreign Fineries, which they never will pay for; the Kingdom would not be the worse.

[19] Some Persons of a desponding Spirit are in great Concern about that vast Number of poor People, who are Aged, Diseased, or Maimed; and I have been desired to employ my Thoughts what Course may be taken, to ease the Nation of so grievous an Incumbrance. But I am not in the least Pain upon that Matter; because it is very well known, that they are every Day *dying*, and *rotting*, by *Cold* and *Famine*, and *Filth*, and *Vermin*, as fast as can be reasonably expected. And as to the younger Labourers, they are now in almost as hopeful a Condition: They cannot get Work, and consequently pine away for Want of Nourishment, to a Degree, that if at any Time they are accidentally hired to common Labour, they have not Strength to perform it; and thus the Country, and themselves, are in a fair Way of being soon delivered from the Evils to come.

[20] I have too long digressed; and therefore shall return to my Subject. I think the Advantages by the Proposal which I have made, are obvious, and many, as well as of the highest Importance.

[21] For, *First*, as I have already observed, it would greatly lessen the *Number of Papists*, with whom we are yearly overrun; being the principal Breeders of the Nation, as well as our most dangerous Enemies; and who stay at home on Purpose, with a Design to *deliver the Kingdom to the Pretender*; hoping to take their Advantage by the Absence *of so many good Protestants*, who have chosen rather to leave their Country, than stay at home, and pay Tithes against their Conscience, to an idolatrous *Episcopal Curate*.

[22] Secondly, The poorer Tenants will have something valuable of their own, which, by Law, may be made liable to Distress, and help to pay their Landlord's Rent; their Corn and Cattle being already seized, and *Money a Thing unknown.*

[23] Thirdly, Whereas the Maintenance of an Hundred Thousand Chil-

dren, from two Years old, and upwards, cannot be computed at less than ten Shillings a Piece *per Annum,* the Nation's Stock will be thereby encreased Fifty Thousand Pounds *per Annum*; besides the Profit of a new Dish, introduced to the Tables of all *Gentlemen of Fortune* in the Kingdom, who have any Refinement in Taste; and the Money will circulate among ourselves, the Goods being entirely of our own Growth and Manufacture.

[24] Fourthly, The constant Breeders, besides the Gain of Eight Shillings *Sterling per Annum,* by the Sale of their Children, will be rid of the Charge of maintaining them after the first Year.

[25] Fifthly, This Food would likewise bring great *Custom to Taverns,* where the Vintners will certainly be so prudent, as to procure the best Receipts for dressing it to Perfection; and consequently, have their Houses frequented by all the *fine Gentlemen,* who justly value themselves upon their Knowledge in good Eating; and a skilful Cook, who understands how to oblige his Guests, will contrive to make it as expensive as they please.

[26] Sixthly, This would be a great Inducement to Marriage, which all wise Nations have either encouraged by Rewards, or enforced by Laws and Penalties. It would encrease the Care and Tenderness of Mothers towards their Children, when they were sure of a Settlement for Life, to the poor Babes, provided in some Sort by the Publick, to their annual Profit instead of Expence. We should soon see an honest Emulation among the married Women, *which of them could bring the fattest Child to the Market.* Men would become as *fond* of their Wives, during the Time of their Pregnancy, as they are now of their *Mares* in Foal, their *Cows* in Calf, or *Sows* when they are ready to farrow; nor offer to beat or kick them, (as it is too *frequent* a Practice) for fear of a Miscarriage.

[27] Many other Advantages might be enumerated. For instance, the Addition of some Thousand Carcasses in our Exportation of barrelled Beef: The Propagation of *Swines Flesh,* and Improvement in the Art of making good *Bacon*; so much wanted among us by the great Destruction of *Pigs,* too frequent at our Tables, and are no way comparable in Taste, or Magnificence, to a well-grown fat yearling Child; which, roasted whole, will make a considerable Figure at a *Lord Mayor's Feast,* or any other publick Entertainment. But this, and many others, I omit; being studious of Brevity.

[28] Supposing that one Thousand Families in this City, would be constant Customers for Infants Flesh; besides others who might have it at *merry Meetings,* particularly *Weddings* and *Christenings*; I compute that *Dublin* would take off, annually, about Twenty Thousand Carcasses; and the rest of the Kingdom (where probably they will be sold somewhat cheaper) the remaining Eighty Thousand.

[29] I can think of no one Objection, that will possibly be raised against this Proposal; unless it should be urged, that the Number of People will

be thereby much lessened in the Kingdom. This I freely own; and it was indeed one principal Design in offering it to the World. I desire the Reader will observe, that I calculate my Remedy *for this one individual Kingdom of* IRELAND, *and for no other that ever was, is, or I think ever can be upon Earth.*

The first voice, simply an extension of the one we hear when the essay opens, is that of a calm but indignant man trying to deal rationally with the admitted miseries of Ireland. If we had only this voice, we would probably make the mistake of saying that Jonathan Swift speaks directly to us throughout the essay: "The Landlords have already devoured"—"the present Distresses of the Kingdom"—"which is more than we allow to Sheep, black Cattle, or Swine"—"their Corn and Cattle being already seized, and Money a Thing unknown"—"I calculate my Remedy for this one individual Kingdom of Ireland, and for no other that ever was, is, or, I think, ever can be upon Earth"—and so on.

The second voice utters the mad proposals of cannibalism: "I recommend . . . dressing them hot from the Knife." The whole essay could have been made up of such extreme departures from the author's and reader's values and opinions. A speaker unwaveringly arguing his case would have made a very ironic work of it indeed, as consistent as "The Shortest Way with the Dissenters," and it would have become either obvious and less interesting (to most of us) or totally deceptive (to any mad landlords who happened to read it). Most of paragraphs 7 through 16 are made up of this mad reasoning—thoroughly rational if one agrees to discard all humane motives and view children as material assets.

It is true that the rationality is elegantly tainted with moments that seem to betray, like an uncontrollable nervous tic, a sadistic delight in the physical prospect of all that flesh: "Hot from the Knife," "plump and fat," "prime dainty," etc. But if we think of how easily Swift could have increased such signs of the madness, we see just how restrained the *style* is. If Swift had been interested mainly in a clever display of irony, he could have lingered over the succulence, the rich juices, as one might imagine the Poe of "A Cask of Amontillado" doing. Instead, this speaker is denied full license in order to maintain control of the main satiric point.

Any careful rereading of the shifts between these two radically different kinds of statement will show that it is in the mastery of the clashes between them, the very "inconsistency" of tone, that much of the essay's brilliance is found. Some critics have talked of the essay as marvelous in its "sustained irony," but though the quality of the work is marvelously sustained, and one must certainly call the whole piece ironic, the marvel is in the clarity and power achieved against the obstacles, as it were, of the shifting surface; there is a continuous, intense pressure upon us as we move back and forth from the true, angry but rational voice describing Ireland's woes and the mad, almost cheerfully "rational" voice describing the remedy.

But it is misleading, I repeat, to talk of voices here, because in *style* the voices are practically indistinguishable. We are given very little stylistic assistance in turning our innumerable somersaults: they all depend on inferences about the beliefs of Swift as they relate to the reasonable indignation of one voice and the mad reason of the other. If we did not find it possible to construct a solid and convincing "Swift" through the inferences we make about his agreement with many statements ("that horrid Practice of Women murdering their Bastard Children"; the spectacle of mothers murdering their "innocent Babes" should "move Tears and Pity in the most Savage and inhuman Breast"), we could never make our way through all of the non-sense with the kind of sure and strangely delightful confidence that the essay builds.

I doubt that any reader could trace fully how he manages to reconstruct his picture of what Swift intends behind all the complex interweavings. But it is surely in part a matter of the emotional intensity we sense, and share, at those moments when the speaker moves closest to Swift's views of Ireland's woes. When the speaker questions whether there are as many as thirty thousand couples who can maintain their own children, "under the present Distresses of the Kingdom," the reader cannot resist joining in the melancholy lament and inferring that Swift does too—it is a note that has been struck from the very beginning, with the description of Ireland's begging mothers; every detail of the piece (including the desperation of the remedy proposed) supports the inference that the woes of Ireland make, indeed, a "melancholy Object." It becomes, very early, impossible to doubt that Swift concurs with the speaker's distress about a country where the aged, diseased, and maimed are "every Day dying, and rotting, by Cold and Famine, and Filth, and Vermin. . . ." And it is this confidence that enables us to make that glorious ironic leap upward to the ironic sublime when Swift's speaker, plunging into a moral abyss, goes on to say, "as fast as can reasonably be expected."

At every shift, then, our inferential involvement is as great as our emotional concern, and it serves to strengthen our active embrace of those truths we discern behind the horrible "falsehoods." After the first four paragraphs we are never allowed to forget that Swift hates the evil conditions more passionately than the speaker who describes them as hateful—it is as if we said to ourselves, "the conditions are so

114

bad that even a man with as little true humanity as this speaker is offended by them—how much more strongly must Swift feel."

It does not matter very much, I think, whether we account for our reconciliation of the surface inconsistencies as I have done by seeing a passionate conflict between the two voices, neither of them precisely Swift's, or, as some others have done, by trying to construct a coherent single voice, that of a madman who can reconcile, in his madness, the brutal scheme with the angry compassion. I do think that one cannot really reconcile, in one literary portrait, the extremes that we find here, except by postulating a completely capricious, unrealistic kind of madness that could encompass the sort of thing found, say, in paragraph 19. But even if we could reconstruct a clear literary portrait of a single confused voice, the point still remains: it is through shifting the tone back and forth between totally unacceptable statements of the first kind and totally acceptable statements of the second kind that the rich passion of the essay emerges.

Once we have turned our somersaults several times, landing with confidence on the right platform each time (we know we are right because we are rewarded—the higher platform is always there), we have a new and secure context for the resolution of any doubts that occur about particular points. What do we do, for example, with the traditional debate about whether Swift is primarily attacking the absentee English landlords or the Irish who collaborate with them? There is, of course, a great deal of anger here against the English, but it will hardly do to resolve the dispute by saying simply that he is attacking both. The focus of the inverted attack is provided by the speaker, an Irishman who, while deploring Ireland's sufferings, can offer as cure only a program that produces worse suffering and degradation. He is thus a kind of mad collaborator, and he draws most of the indignation toward his own kind—Irishmen. The anger against the English is used merely to heighten the denunciation of those who play along with them.

Thus we need not appeal to such external evidence as the fact that the essay was written for Irish readers—evidence which in any case would be ambiguous as applied to this question. All we need do is ask ourselves how Swift would have rewritten the essay if he had been primarily concerned with arousing the Irish *against the English*. The most obvious change would have been, it seems to me, to make the speaker an English landlord, proposing to the Irish that they solve their problems with this inhuman scheme. Then the ironic fire would have been aimed at the English; but as the essay stands, it is an Irishman, facing Irish woes with fake rationality and deep concern, who pro-

115

poses the ultimate act of collaboration: let us offer ourselves to be eaten, since it is the only measure open to us.

The third "tone of voice" introduces an even deeper, but hence less troublesome, contrast. Swift occasionally offers quite direct, precise proposals of what might be done to cure Ireland's ills. The most obvious shift comes as paragraph 29 continues:

> Therefore, let no man talk to me of other Expedients: *Of taxing our Absentees at five Shillings a Pound: Of using neither Cloaths, nor Houshold Furniture except what is of our own Growth and Manufacture: Of utterly rejecting the Materials and Instruments that promote foreign Luxury: Of curing the Expensiveness of Pride, Vanity, Idleness, and Gaming in our Women: Of introducing a Vein of Parsimony, Prudence and Temperance: Of learning to love our Country, wherein we differ even from* LAPLANDERS, *and the Inhabitants of* TOPINAMBOO: *Of quitting our Animosities, and Factions; nor act any longer like the* JEWS, *who were murdering one another at the very Moment their City was taken: Of being a little cautious not to sell our Country and Consciences for nothing: Of teaching Landlords to have, at least, one Degree of Mercy towards their Tenants.* Lastly, *Of putting a Spirit of Honesty, Industry, and Skill into our Shop-keepers; who, if a Resolution could now be taken to buy only our native Goods, would immediately unite to cheat and exact upon us in the Price, the Measure, and the Goodness; nor could ever yet be brought to make one fair Proposal of just Dealing, though often and earnestly invited to it.*
> [30] Therefore I repeat, let no Man talk to me of these and the like Expedients; till he hath, at least, a Glimpse of Hope, that there will ever be some hearty and sincere Attempt to put *them in Practice.*

If we ignore the first clause, "therefore, let no man talk to me of other Expedients," all that follows in the paragraph is absolute Swift, without a touch of irony. (It is of course "ironic" that the direct program seems hopeless to the speaker, but once we are wrenched on to the proper platform, we do no ironic reconstructions throughout this passage. The only possible exception is the understatement of "being a little cautious" and "at least, one Degree of Mercy.") As a result, it simply cannot be as "interesting" to any reader who goes to the essay only for ironic pleasure, and critics have sometimes argued that it is an artistic flaw. But we have long since been taught by this essay that it is of a kind that seeks a practical effect in the world; diminishments in "entertainment" are not necessarily flaws, if they strengthen our indignation. If we put ourselves in the shoes of the original Irish readers, we can see at once that such portions are in fact the most vital of all, though not ironic; here it is that the full argument reaches its most careful definition. There have been earlier promises of this final direct list of answers: "for we can neither employ them in Handicraft or Agriculture; we neither build Houses, (I mean in the Country) nor cultivate Land" (par. 6). But the final list gives us that part of Swift's message which can be given best in direct language. And it confirms beyond question our earlier inference about that argument: it is directed to the Irish about the Irish. Not a single proposal here is for action by the landlords; the only sentence about landlords concerns *our* teaching them. It is all centered on what the *Irish* might do, if they attended to Swift's message.

Perhaps this point can be made more clear by imagining an ironic revision of this section:

> Once we have begun to carry out my Proposal, I have other Projects which I should be glad to develop in aid of my Countrymen: Of offering our Absentees a special Subvention to encourage them to treat us more kindly; Of ingratiating ourselves with them by raising our Imports of English Goods; Of providing all our Wives and Daughters as a common Store of paid Companions, the Profits thereof to go to the Poor; Of deporting all those who in their grovelling Poverty are a *Burden* upon the Landlord's senses of Sight and Smell and who are an economic Burden on the Country . . .

And so on. One cannot doubt that Swift could have invented ironies upon ironies, each one more outlandish and—if what we seek is only irony—the whole more delightfully ironic than what he has written.

It is clear by now that a consistently inconsistent ironic mixture has proved here to be an especially useful tool for portraying Swift's savage indignation. A simple attack ("every Day dying, and rotting, by Cold and Famine, and Filth, and Vermin") could have been powerful, but it would be impossible to sustain its interest for more than a few pages. A straightforward essay arguing for certain needed reforms, in the third tone of voice (par. 29), would be informative and useful, but it would lack all fire. A sustained piece of Swiftian impersonation, entirely in the second tone of voice, would be splendid, no doubt, but it would of course lack the practical specifications and clarity supplied by the third voice. And more important, it would, I am convinced, be relatively feeble: a weaker intellectual exercise with much less emotional engagement. Without our active battle to reconstruct the genuine values from the grotesque mixture of sane, half-sane, and mad, and without the sense this gives of Swift's own passionate involvement, almost bursting through the frame he has himself built, much of the force would be lost.

One can see what this means by looking closely at the next two paragraphs:

[31] But, as to my self; having been wearied out for many Years with offering vain, idle, visionary Thoughts; and at length utterly despairing of Success, I fortunately fell upon this Proposal; which, as it is wholly new, so it hath something *solid* and *real,* of no Expence, and little Trouble, full in our own Power; and whereby we can incur no Danger in *disobliging* ENGLAND: For, this Kind of Commodity will not bear Exportation; the Flesh being of too tender a Consistence, to admit a long Continuance in Salt; *although, perhaps, I could name a Country, which would be glad to eat up our whole Nation without it.*
[32] After all, I am not so violently bent upon my own Opinion, as to reject any Offer proposed by wise Men, which shall be found equally innocent, cheap, easy, and effectual. But before something of that Kind shall be advanced, in Contradiction to my Scheme, and offering a better; I desire the Author, or Authors, will be pleased maturely to consider two Points. *First,* As Things now stand, how they will be able to find Food and Raiment, for a Hundred Thousand useless Mouths and Backs? And *secondly,* There being a round Million of Creatures in human Figure, throughout this Kingdom; whose whole Subsistence, put into a common Stock, would leave them in Debt two Millions of Pounds *Sterling*; adding those, who are Beggars by Profession, to the Bulk of Farmers, Cottagers, and Labourers, with their Wives and Children, who are Beggars in Effect; I desire those Politicians, who dislike my Overture, and may perhaps be so bold to attempt an Answer, that they will first ask the Parents of these Mortals, Whether they would not, at this Day, think it a great Happiness to have been sold for Food at a Year old, in the Manner I prescribe; and thereby have avoided such a perpetual Scene of Misfortunes, as they have since gone through; by the *Oppression of Landlords*; the Impossibility of paying Rent, without Money or Trade; the Want of common Sustenance, with neither House nor Cloaths, to cover them from the Inclemencies of Weather; and the most inevitable Prospect of intailing the like, or greater Miseries upon their Breed for ever.

No reader really laughs, I suspect, or even smiles, throughout these paragraphs. For a moment all comic disparities are dropped; Swift, his speaker, and we readers are all united in a despairing vision of just how bad conditions are—since they have been made to seem morally worse than the modest proposal.

The final touch is brilliantly surprising, returning once again to comic irony. Suddenly we are back in the madman's world, reminded of just how far we stand from home ground:

[33] I profess, in the Sincerity of my Heart, that I have not the least personal Interest, in endeavouring to promote this necessary Work; having no other Motive than the *publick Good of my Country, by advancing our Trade, providing for Infants, relieving the Poor, and giving some Pleasure to the Rich.* I have no Children, by which I can propose to get a single Penny; the youngest being nine Years old, and my Wife past Child-bearing.

There could be no greater distance than that we place between the bitter Swift, speaking more or less directly in the previous paragraph, and the ridiculous disinterested rhetorician caricatured in this ending. Early in the essay this contrast would have been unacceptable, even unintelligible. But by now Swift has schooled us to follow such shifts with ease. Each statement in each tone of voice has a clear context of precedents into which it can fit. We have our reconstruction, we have it in great detail and with a good deal of emotional investment in every part of it. When anyone challenges our reading of those details, we are annoyed, as the history of controversy about Swift's ironies shows; we have been working at the peak of our powers. The author has paid us the compliment of assuming that we can be trusted to work as a kind of assistant in building the final complex edifice.

The building materials are of course derived from all the innumerable assumptions we make about what Swift would himself believe about cruelty, about exploitation, about absentee landlords, about what makes sense and what sounds mad. Some of these assumptions are a kind of historical information which, if challenged, could be decisively confirmed or refuted: without the assumption, for example, that the Irish were in fact exploited by the landlords, that conditions were in fact intolerable in Ireland, the essay will lose much of its meaning and power. If someone said to us (as nobody ever would) that in fact Swift thought the Irish were in good shape, and he was ironically satirizing anyone who would be so radical as to write such an unjustified satire, most of us have at least a smattering of knowledge about the actual history of the two countries to support our reply; and this knowledge could be then eked out with an hour or two of reading in the encyclopedia or any history of the period. I suppose that nobody ever feels that he needs to do so, but that is not because the historical assumptions are not important; it is because they seem so obvious: "Swift *must* have assumed that *we* would assume . . ." But what if he didn't? But of course he *did*.

119

We are confident that *he* did, but it is clear that our confidence does not depend primarily on our picture of the historical Swift; the highly articulated literary work has made us far less dependent on specific historical knowledge than we often are in shorter works. Though we still must make inferences about the author, the work has yielded an immense improbability that he was not ironic. It makes a kind of finished sense as a whole, read in this ironic way, that fixes us immovably in a certain position; if someone came to me saying that he had found a document proving Swift to have been really on the side of the landlords, I would not believe it. I would simply not be able to change my reading of the essay. I would choose the tale and not the teller, as the modern commonplace has it (that is, I would choose the embodied "Swift" and not Dean Swift), because the final intuition I have of the kind of literary work before me, and of the precise service that stable irony performs in it, leaves me no choices. This does not mean that I feel this level of confidence about every detail, or that I feel it about many or most of my readings: you could shake me easily, for example, about many parts of *A Tale of a Tub*. Nor does it mean that such "absolute" assurance can never be mistaken: it is a curious fact that two readers can sometimes feel total confidence in contradictory readings, each reader convinced that every detail in the work confirms his reading, bolted into place by a self-evident interpretation of the literary context.

## INTENTIONS ONCE AGAIN

We have seen that in political or moral satire, the reconstruction of ironies depends both on a proper use of knowledge or inference about the author and his surroundings and on discovery of a literary form that realizes itself properly for us only in an ironic reading. To distinguish the literary context as "internal" from the extra-literary context is thus in satire always difficult, and it may finally be impossible: should anyone really insist on challenging our claim that "the *essay* is ironic" he can always push us finally to the claim that *Swift* must have been ironic, because a Swift so careless or inept as to write these words without irony is inconceivable. Critics working in certain non-rhetorical modes could of course take the route of saying that it is ironic for a variety of other reasons, intentions being irrelevant: there is simply no statement or thing that cannot be called ironic in some definition. But so long as we remain interested in whether the work as made requires ironic reconstruction, we cannot ignore some picture of the intending author, much as we might like to. These words could not have been put

120

together in this way except by a human being with such-and-such intentions.

I think that anyone who reads through as much controversy about irony as I have recently forced myself to do will be struck by how often the critic's final court of appeal is explicitly to what the author—being such-and-such kind of man—must have done or not done. Consider as one especially revealing example the strange case of Swift's "Verses on His Own Death." The poem has never been read as anything other than ironic, and when I saw that a critic had written an article called "The Ironic Intention of Swift's Verses on His Own Death," I was amused: what a pass we have come to, if *that* point has to be proved! But it turns out that Mr. Barry Slepian claims to have caught out a group of very shrewd readers in misreading parts of this subtle and delightful poem.[11] There is no problem with the early lines about how friends react to Swift's death:

> And, then their Tenderness appears,
> By adding largely to my Years:

but when we come to a section about Swift's own art, there is trouble indeed. Some of Swift's friends, including Pope, removed parts of the poem before publication, feeling that the lines were arrogant and inconsistent—which is to say, the friends had concluded that in not being ironic, Swift's praise for himself was too embarrassing for publication. And of course they could make the decision that the lines were not ironic only by assuming that Swift the man was capable of committing the faults of arrogance and inconsistency which they had spotted in his verses:

> Consider, for instance, this couplet, which Dr. King said Swift's friends thought "might be liable to some objection, and . . . not, strictly speaking, a just part of [Swift's] character":

> Yet, Malice never was his Aim;
> He lash'd the Vice but spar'd the Name. (459–60)

11. Barry Slepian, "The Ironic Intention of Swift's Verses on His Own Death," *Review of English Studies*, n.s. 14 (1963): 249–56. Until Mr. Slepian made his case, nobody had suggested irony in Swift's self-praise. But most of the discussions since 1963 have accepted his arguments. The fullest effort to show why the case for irony, plausible as it is, cannot finally be sustained is in James Woolley's unpublished dissertation, "Swift's Later Poems: Studies in Circumstances and Texts," University of Chicago, 1972, pp. 1–40, esp. pp. 19–33. What is important for my point is that Mr. Woolley like Mr. Slepian sees Swift's artistry as in question: what to him seems like rhetorical ineffectiveness (p. 23) seems to Mr. Slepian ironic subtlety. Both rely on a picture of Swift to make their case.

Pope cut it out, because, as Dr. King wrote, in Swift's other writings "several persons have been lashed by name. . . ." Actually, in addition to Francis Charteris and William Whitshed, the following persons are lashed by name or title in this poem: King George, Queen Caroline, Sir Robert Walpole, Edmund Curll, James Moore Smyth, Colley Cibber, Lewis Theobald, John Henley, Thomas Woolston, William Wood, and Sir William Scroggs. Middleton Murry quotes the line and writes: "Shades of the Duchess of Somerset! Presumably Swift now believed it; but it is almost incredible that he did."

I cannot repeat all of Mr. Slepian's interesting argument here, nor am I concerned about deciding whether it is sound. What is important is to notice how he proceeds in making it:

Shades of "The Shortest Way with the Dissenters"! Murry misses the point. Swift was hardly so absent-minded as to forget that he had just finished attacking thirteen people by name: the line must be meant as a joke.
  Swift wrote:

> To steal a Hint was never known,
> But what he writ was all his own. (317–8)

Pope solemnly removed the couplet. . . . But George Birkbeck Hill noticed that the second of these lines is itself stolen from Denham's elegy on Cowley.[12]

Swift was hardly so absent-minded that—Swift was not so stupid that—Swift was not so mad that—Swift was not so arrogant that . . . Yet of course Swift's friends and contemporaries had concluded that what Murry calls the "almost incredible" intellectual faults were indeed displayed by Swift and must be concealed from readers. Mr. Slepian's argument is finally based on probabilities about a man, and whether we take that man as the real Swift or as the Swift implied by the verses themselves, we finally ask: just how probable was it that *he* would crib a line which itself claims that he never cribbed a line, or that he would lash thirteen men by name and then a few lines later claim never to lash by name? Every reader has encountered authors who could be as careless or maladroit as that, without irony; but it is incredible, Mr. Slepian claims, that the Swift we know should be so. Unless, of course, he had deteriorated, was already turning mad? Slepian carefully faces that possible objection: the poem was in fact written long before it was published, and thus long before Swift's mental troubles, whatever they really were, set in. I cannot see how anyone could accuse Mr. Slepian

12. Slepian, pp. 254–55.

of critical irrelevancy in bringing Swift's madness into the argument. Swift's creative sanity is precisely what is at stake. What the poem really is, and consequently what my pleasure in it will be, is radically altered if I read those lines of self-praise without irony.

### INTENTIONS IN PARODY

We see then that the "external" reference in ironic satire is not simply to the objects of the satire but to the picture we build of the satirist as ironic man, and that will be derived largely from "internal" clues! The same can be said for that form of satire called parody, in which the victim's style is imitated and distorted. As we saw even in the brief examples in chapter 3, every parody refers at every point to historical knowledge that is in a sense "outside itself"—that is, previous literary works—and thus to more or less probable genres; in this it is like "A Modest Proposal," which refers at every point to what is satirized, or like Bathurst's letter, which refers at every point to something "outside itself" that is praised. In parody, however, we discover a curiously doubled external reference. In reading Bathurst's letter, we made use of external information about other authors in order to build our picture of praise for Swift; in reading parody, we make use of external reference to other authors in order to understand how the parody attacks those same authors: the thing referred to, externally, to assist in comprehension, is the same thing referred to, externally, as the object of ridicule.

> My mistress' eyes are nothing like the sun;
> Coral is far more red than her lips' red;
> If snow be white, why then her breasts are dun;
> If hairs be wires, black wires grow on her head.
> I have seen roses damask'd, red and white,
> But no such roses see I in her cheeks;
> And in some perfumes is there more delight
> Than in the breath that from my mistress reeks.
> I love to hear her speak,—yet well I know
> That musick hath a far more pleasing sound;
> I grant I never saw a goddess go,—
> My mistress, when she walks, treads on the
>     ground;
> And yet, by heaven, I think my love as rare
> As any she bely'd with false compare.

To readers unfamiliar with other love sonnets, Shakespeare's poem might at first appear as straightforward satire against the mistress's deficiencies—until the final couplet. Except for the ninth line

—I love to hear her speak—there is not a single word of direct praise for twelve lines, and even this praise is immediately qualified. But the couplet makes clear to even the least sophisticated reader that the chief point is to praise the mistress.

What, then, is going on in the first twelve lines? It is clear enough that every quality denied to the mistress is a "false compare," a clichéd metaphor or simile taken from conventional love poems. Once alerted, even a reader who knows none of the parodied poems should be able to reconstruct in part what they must have been like—something like this, perhaps:

> My mistress' eyes do glisten like the sun;
> Coral is far less red than her lips' red;
> . . . . . . . . . . . . . . . . . . . . . . . . . . .
> I have seen roses damask'd red and white,
> But none that match the roses in her cheeks.

What is not so clear is how the satirical thrusts at other poems serve the purposes of a love poem. Two points are made at once: "Other love poets are silly" and "My mistress is 'rarer' than the others." But how do they relate?

Here again I think that the metaphor of the translation of locations or dwelling places is helpful. But it is not as simple a case as others we have traced in detail, because it turns out that there are three possible elevations, each with its own foundations and conclusions. The rhetorical process of the poem can be described without too much distortion as that of transferring to the mistress the "earned elevation" achieved by the poet's parody.

There is first the conventional ground where the other poets and their incredible mistresses live. It is a world of pure hyperbole, internally consistent but of course quite unrelated to real people. In contrast to this, the poet at first seems to be taking up his stand in an entirely realistic and even lower world, in which his mistress is in fact less attractive than the other mistresses; one could infer, falsely, a tone almost of honest complaint: the real world is pretty drab, but it is the best we can manage, with its black wires and off-color breasts and reeking breath (though reek did not have quite so strong a negative connotation then as now). It is almost as if the poet pretended for a few lines to be a complainer dwelling in a place inferior to the conventional idealized world. But having put on that pose for a bit, he rapidly raises our suspicions about it, until, with the couplet, he establishes a third level which enables us to see the other two clearly for the first time:

the poet has a superior dwelling indeed, because he has demonstrated his superiority not only to the conventional love poets but to those who might speak seriously in the tone that he imitated for twelve lines.

But once this is said we can see why the praise of the mistress is so successful: from the beginning it has been clear that wherever he dwells, she dwells; if he has earned the right to look down upon the foolish poets and belied mistresses, and their dupes, even lower, obviously she deserves his praise and dwells in fact with him. And the reader has no choice but to climb up to join them; all the intellectual energy required by the climb, and all the resulting pleasure in making the secret journey successfully, are at the end transferred to the mistress's glory: there are, after all, a great many victims supplied for us, but only if we are willing to accept the poet's final words of praise.

With the couplet, Shakespeare makes his reference to the victims of his irony direct: "false compare" provides us with a non-ironic summary of his ironies. But how do we *know* that it is not in itself ironic? We face with this question exactly the same problem as is given by non-ironic warnings or statements in titles, epigraphs, or introductory explanations (pp. 55–57): in themselves they can never determine our final view with any security. All we can say is that when there is some degree of disparity between the overt message of earlier parts of a work and the final word, the final word will probably be less ironic than the rest. But obviously it could be just the other way around: a series of statements to be taken straight, followed by an inverted summary that is made "obviously false" through our knowledge of what has come before. In Shakespeare's sonnet, we come to know the validity of the couplet through the rising generic probabilities as the poem progresses. We are expected to know the absurdity of the conventional metaphors, and unless we can take as plausible the pose of envious comparison of the mistress with those metaphors, we are forced by the poem into the clear, though complex, ordering of possible positions.

One further point about the process of arriving at this "obvious" or "certain" reading: in one sense it is circular, enclosed within itself, referring for its proofs back and forth within the poem. Nothing outside the poem can justify ignoring or violating what is revealed from this internal view. Suppose someone discovered that Shakespeare himself had said, "No, no, I really am making fun of the speaker because he doesn't appreciate all those rich metaphors and is trying to compensate for having such an inadequate mistress." If we have done a really careful reading, such a statement can seldom (I won't say never) greatly alter our view of anything but the author; in this case one would be forced to say either that Shakespeare had forgotten what his own poem was doing or that the part of his mind that made statements about his poems was not in good touch with the part that wrote the poems.[13]

Thus, though the poem is in one sense self-enclosed, it has implied within it an author and a reader, and nobody can pretend to have understood the poem unless he has made himself into that implied reader, and in some sense found the implied author. Often we do not want to stop there: having understood what the poem really says and does, we may quite legitimately say that we wish it said or did something else, or that for us, three hundred and fifty years later, there are additional meanings or lost responses. The great classics in one sense "mean" something different to each generation, but in making so much of this point, critics have often forgotten that the most interesting or useful "new" interpretations are usually those that do justice to the firmly grounded interpretations that all good readers share.

I persist in dwelling on this matter because it is so easily overlooked or even denied when we are wrestling with complex and controversial ironies of the kind I shall discuss in Part III. We cannot take refuge, reading "My Mistress' Eyes," in claims about ambiguity: the poem cannot with full power both make fun of the conventional metaphors and not make fun of them; it cannot both praise the mistress's eyes and breasts and mock them—not, that is, if the poet (or the poem) intends the fullest possible delight in a particular direction.

13. Once again we worry about the intentional fallacy. Perhaps it is time that we got beyond this worry. In the first place, a careful reading of "The Intentional Fallacy," in which W. K. Wimsatt and Monroe C. Beardsley in a sense popularized the worry, shows that they do not clearly rule out intentions in any sense that matters to us here; they rule out only statements made by the author outside the work about his *motives* or *purposes* or *plans* or *hopes for value*. The essay did lead to dogmatic claims that the poem is "autonomous" or even "anonymous," freed of its author and therefore—something that Wimsatt and Beardsley never believed—amenable to any whimsical interpretation that a reader decided to find in it. Secondly, there is by now an enormous literature showing that we simply cannot get along without using inferences about intention, try as we will. It will be noticed that I do not seek quite so vigorously as E. D. Hirsch for the "real author" found in historical evidence outside the work, being more interested in the implied author—a historical being just as real and hard as any but likely to be a very different, idealized version of "the man himself"; it is in fact part of what the author creates *by* writing the poem. As Saul Bellow said once in a private conversation, it wouldn't be much of an artist who couldn't make a better version of himself with all that careful revision! For a vigorous attack on my distinction between the author and implied author, see John Ross Baker, "From Imitation to Rhetoric: The Chicago Critics, Wayne C. Booth, and *Tom Jones*," *Novel* 6 (Spring 1973): 197–217.

It is quite true, as critical commonplace has it, that poets often create deliberate ambiguities and that there can be great rewards in doubled vision. Many literary works, as we shall see later on, not only can be but should be read in several different and even contradictory ways. But am I entitled to use that word *should*? If so even these works rule out some readings—namely, the *un*ambiguous!

This point is so much out of the mode that it should be dwelt on. I am not denying the delights of ambiguity; I am simply saying that they are radically different from the delights of stable irony, and that when we confuse them we are likely to diminish the latter. It is a little like the perceptual problems presented by optical illusions. As many theorists of perception have insisted, drawings that can be seen in two contradictory ways tell us something about how the mind works. The famous figure used by Wittgenstein and Gombrich (see fig. 3) illustrates the problem simply. As Gombrich says, you can see the figure either as a

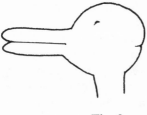

Fig. 3

rabbit or as a duck, but you can't *see* it as both at the same time. The figure clicks back and forth, visually, much as we have described our perception of ironic working as a click of recognition and reconstruction: what appeared as one figure suddenly appears as another figure.[14] If "My Mistress' Eyes" were truly ambiguous, it might be written both to praise and mock, depending on the reader's perception.

But consider further. Once our perception has played the double click with the figure, our minds no longer think of it as either a duck

14. E. H. Gombrich, *Art and Illusion: A Study in the Psychology of Pictorial Representation* (New York, 1960), Introduction, section II. Stable irony, I should perhaps add, is *like* optical illusions in that when we have seen both "partial views" we continue to use both as we rest in our final view: *this* is an illusion made of two views, *this* is an irony made of two (or many) views. But they are different in that the illusion maintains equality of the views even at the end, while irony requires all of the hierarchical placements I have described. It makes no sense to say that the figure looks a little like a duck but *is really* a rabbit-disguised-as-a-duck; but something like that is exactly what we are asked to do in reading stable ironies.

or a rabbit but *as an optical illusion*. Our *chief* pleasure now becomes our awareness of the duplicity. We can no longer concentrate entirely on the naive pleasure of seeing only one animal—our energies are concentrated on the trickiness of the process. All such illusions are likely to be deficient as art in either single perspective, because the artist has had to make a highly generalized, uninteresting rabbit in order to make a possible duck, but that duck will be equally generalized. Even an artist who works hard to improve the quality of each half-perception is inevitably constrained from anything like the perfection of ducks or rabbits that he could achieve if his intention were not to be an illusionist.[15]

(It might be objected that this argument holds only so long as we accept a naive criterion of realism, demanding "convincing" ducks or rabbits. But I intend the realistic example as illustrative of general limits: to do one thing well is to rule out the possibility of doing some other things. Regardless of one's criterion, success in duplicity flatly precludes success in single-mindedness—and vice versa.)

For both receiver and maker, then, the focusing of attention on duplicity inevitably makes each single effect peripheral and thus makes the full focusing on a single effect impossible. It may well be, as one modern commonplace has it, that double visions are inherently superior to single; I certainly do not believe that single sharp resolutions are inherently superior to ambiguities. But whatever we conclude about general values (I face them more directly in chapter 7), we must take into account how much we value clarities in a poem like Shakespeare's. Such stable irony is in the end rigidly disjunctive, even though its elements are intricate and not finally reducible to any simple list.

I spend a good deal of my professional life deploring "polar" thinking, reductive dichotomies, either-or disjunctions. And here I find myself saying that only in strict polar decisions can one kind of reading be properly performed. On the one hand, some of the greatest intellectual and artistic achievements seem to come when we learn how to say *both-and,* not *either-or,* when we see that people and works of art are too complex for simple true-false tests. Yet here I am saying that some of our most important literary experiences are designed precisely to demand flat and absolute choices, saying that in fact the sudden plain

15. M. C. Escher spent a lifetime painting pictures that are necessarily viewed in two conflicting perspectives. As "ambiguities" the results are brilliant, but neither perspective is ever as fully realized in itself as it might have been without the constraints of the other: the black ducks flying to the left must be highly generalized if their necks are at the same time to be the tails of white swans flying to the right. See *The World of M. C. Escher,* ed. J. L. Locher (New York, 1971).

irreducible "no" of the first step in ironic reconstruction is one of our most precious literary moments. I cannot pretend that even in Part III I find a full reconciliation of these two values. But I am sure that it is reconciliation, not an either-or choice that is needed: human beings somehow can *both* revel in sharp distinctions *and* swim in ambiguities.[16]

Usually in reading parodic literature we cannot count on explicit warnings or summaries of intent, even in the form of the playful labels provided by Beerbohm to his pieces on Kipling and James (pp. 72–73 above). Many mixtures of aesthetic praise and blame leave us, like the moral and intellectual mixtures we have already seen, depending on inference; with no direct help we construct our picture of more or less overt disparities, more or less covert communities of knowledge, sense of style, or belief.

Such effects are especially likely to be overlooked when they come in a context which readers think they understand. "Everyone knows," for example, that Jane Austen's *Northanger Abbey* is at least in part a parody of the "Gothic novel." The textbooks all say so, and what is more a reader would need to be blind indeed to overlook all the mockery of previous fiction. But if he is not to miss *some* of it, he must be willing to move at a slow pace, reconstructing and savoring each touch as it comes. One critic once complained (I wish I could believe ironically) that it took him eighteen hours to read *Emma*; I should think he ought to have rejoiced in an author who could provide him with such necessarily prolonged pleasures. Though *Northanger Abbey* is in many ways a simpler and easier novel than *Emma,* it similarly demands a play of mind over almost every phrase.

16. I am uneasily aware of how much current work in psychology, sociology, and anthropology—to say nothing of biology and information theory—relates to the problems I touch on here. Jean Piaget's wonderful explorations of how children deal with polarities and contradictions, for example, could illuminate how we deal with the non-linear *structures* of concepts and values and then choose among the structures. See, for example, "How the Child Reasons," in *Judgement and Reasoning in the Child* (London, 1928), esp. article 3. On the "unformalizable," "structural" nature of adult thought, see his *Logic and Psychology* (Manchester, 1957): ". . . axiomatic logic is atomistic in character and the order of its demonstrations necessarily linear. . . . Operational mechanisms, however, have a psychological existence, and are made up of *structured wholes,* the elements of which are connected in the form of a cyclical system irreducible to a linear deduction. In fact, we have here [and I would say also in all ironic choices] something that resembles more a system involving biological organization than a linear sequence of demonstrations. Thus in our investigation of mental life we must start from the operational structures themselves" (pp. 24–25).

No one who had ever seen Catherine Morland in her infancy, would have supposed her born to be an heroine. Her situation in life, the character of her father and mother, her own
person and disposition, were all equally against her. Her father
was a clergyman, without being neglected, or poor, and a very
respectable man, though his name was Richard—and he had
never been handsome. He had a considerable independence, besides two good livings—and he was not in the least addicted to
locking up his daughters. Her mother was a woman of useful
plain sense, with a good temper, and, what is more remarkable,
with a good constitution. She had three sons before Catherine was
born; and instead of dying in bringing the latter into the world, as
any body might expect, she still lived on—lived to have six children more—to see them growing up around her, and to enjoy
excellent health herself. A family of ten children will be always
called a fine family, where there are heads and arms and legs
enough for the number; but the Morlands had little other right
to the word, for they were in general very plain, and Catherine,
for many years of her life, as plain as any. She had a thin awkward
figure, a sallow skin without colour, dark lank hair, and strong
features;—so much for her person;—and not less unpropitious
for heroism seemed her mind. She was fond of all boys' plays,
and greatly preferred cricket not merely to dolls, but to the more
heroic enjoyments of infancy, nursing a dormouse, feeding a
canary-bird, or watering a rosebush. Indeed she had no taste for
a garden; and if she gathered flowers at all, it was chiefly for the
pleasure of mischief—at least so it was conjectured from her
always preferring those which she was forbidden to take.—Such
were her propensities—her abilities were quite as extraordinary.
She never could learn or understand any thing before she was
taught; and sometimes not even then, for she was often inatten-
tive, and occasionally stupid. . . .

The savoring of this "simple" passage is by no means a simple
matter. Once we have discovered, as we do in the third sentence, that
the first two sentences cannot be accepted as they stand, we have one
more complex task of constructing, first, what is in fact being said of
the heroine and her family, second, what is simultaneously being said
about some previous, presumably popular novels, and third, what is
being promised about *this* novel. What kind of work is its author offering us? No simple inversion of anything will quite do—for example, it
makes nonsense if one turns the first sentence upside down and says
that anyone who knew Catherine in her infancy would have thought
her destined *to be* a heroine. Yet one cannot accept it as it stands. And
in the second sentence, we finally arrive at a kind of "opposite"—

"were all equally against her"—but only if we have by now provided an inference: "*considered* as advantages or disadvantages for a *real* person, not for a heroine." And even then these words do not translate simply: presumably "not being handsome" is a disadvantage in a father for the silly kind of heroine, but not necessarily an advantage for a real girl. And what about for the heroine of this work, which is after all a novel, not a real history? It is true that the chief fun lies in reconstructing the conventional introductions to novels that Jane Austen is mocking here. But we simultaneously take care of that other essential matter, introducing the heroine and her family—by no means perfect and yet by no means entirely "real"—in the context of the author's emerging norms.

I have recorded for myself several pages of inferences from this first paragraph alone. Since they contain more extractions from the passage than anyone else will want to share, I suppress them here, but they are important to me as showing the variety of directions and degrees of security that such a "straightforward" piece of irony can produce. At one extreme we have virtually certain inferences, as when we read "and instead of dying in bringing the latter into the world, as anybody might expect" and add for ourselves "as silly readers of conventional fiction might expect." The strength of our conviction here, aside from the fact that probabilities rise with each additional thrust, comes from the great improbability that a novelist would really mean that the failure of a mother to die in childbirth is a disadvantage to a girl. With equal sureness we accept some stated facts about the family as facts, even though this author has already shown that she "cannot be trusted." Though we have already been undermined again and again, when we come to the "family of ten children" and the assertion that they are "plain," along with all the other negative judgments, we accept them literally. Nothing would be more surprising than for the author to say, as we turn the page: "No, as a matter of fact, there were seven children, and three of them were beautiful. Don't you know how to read irony?"

But how can we be so sure, in a context that has shown most propositions to be very unsure? It is because the pattern of ironic inference has been established on a base which *cannot be removed without removing the fun*: every additional "plain" detail asserted directly fits the pattern of playful attack on conventional romances and thus strengthens the base from which the next inference, ironic or direct, will be made. To doubt any one of the plain assertions would throw into question everything we have enjoyed up to that point. Yet we have no difficulty whatever in knowing, again with what amounts to certainty, that the word "heroic" must be overturned to be understood—again because *not* to reject it would violate the pattern of grounds and inference which is by now very firm.

Yet there are other inferences that are shaky indeed: "and a very respectable man, though his name was Richard." How do we read "respectable"? It is clearly a fact, like "plain," but is there further irony in it? And why the name *Richard*? Respectable *though* his name was Richard? Similarly, the precise weight put upon many of the judgments, both direct and inferred, is often not clear: in short, whether Catherine will turn out to be this or that kind of heroine is left in question. We do not yet have sufficient grounds for inference—or to put it another way, we have reason for reading on to discover how Jane Austen can possibly proceed after having so seriously undermined her heroine. In short, unlike Shakespeare, she has not said—not yet, and in a sense she never does—"My heroine is belied by these false compares —she is really more heroic than these false heroines." On the contrary, Catherine *is* unpromising as a heroine, the family *is* plain and dull and respectably unpromising—except for the purpose of burlesque.

All the more delight, then, in the hints that the word "heroine" will be redeemed. The short phrase—"for many years of her life"— tells us that she will *become* pretty (which is after all the essential virtue for a comic romance). We are thus prepared to learn, a moment later, that "at fifteen" "appearances were mending." It is not clear yet whether, like "my mistress' eyes," her qualities will finally come to seem more genuinely worthy than those of other authors' heroines; but that they will be worthily integrated into some kind of delightful anti-novel is by now highly probable. And the more we know about the sources of the mocked convention, the more we can enjoy the parody.[17]

17. With the last two examples, I have been relying on what amounts to a "historicism" that would, like my intentionalism, have shocked the "new critics" who, in the first half of this century, attempted to turn literary studies away from dry history to "the poem itself," the "autonomous work of art." Though all my interpretations are, I hope, based on a close reading of the text, and I thus profit from the revolutionary rejection of "mere history," they all rely on historical facts or inferences that could only be supported, finally, by going outside the text. That all literary interpretation is in this sense dependent on history should have been obvious to everyone, and it was obvious to the great originators of the rediscovery of close textual analysis: I. A. Richards, William Empson, the American New Critics, the "Chicago school of neo-Aristotelians." The first generation were historically trained, and they used their knowledge of history often quite explicitly (and, if I am right, *always* implicitly) whenever they read a poem. But in overstating their case for a return to the "text," they invited excessive rites of purification in their disciples: to rely on historical fact, "outside

Whatever the ups and downs of critical controversy, historical knowledge, including knowledge of genres, is thus often required when reconstructing stable ironies: a reconstructing of implied authors and implied readers relies on inferences about intentions, and these often depend on our knowing facts from outside the poem. Parody of previous historical models is thus just an extreme instance of a general process: we are often dependent on the assumption that in *that* time and in *that* place, this author most probably knew or believed or intended such-and-such, in contrast to what the surface says.

As we have seen, modern criticism has multiplied contradictions, and modern theory has been led to dwell upon the chaotic results almost to the point of speculative suicide. Disagreements multiplied beyond a given point cannot help suggesting that there is no real art of interpretation—only a game of competing improvisations. The critic with the most persuasive style wins, because there are after all no rules imposed by "the work itself," and there is no referee.

I think that we have grossly exaggerated the actual disagreement even about the hard cases: critical dispute is in fact made possible by agreement at a deeper level. When we say, "It's as if the two critics had read totally different works," we almost always find, looking closer, that it is not that way at all: they have clearly, in thousands of undisputed matters, read precisely the same work, but have chosen (quite naturally) to debate about what is debatable.

Even if this were not so, even if every current critical dispute about ironic readings represented totally antithetical responses, we ought surely to keep steadily before us the astonishing residue of unquestioned agreement: over the centuries every experienced reader has read these stable ironies of Swift, Shakespeare, and Jane Austen just as you and I do. We disagree about many "larger" issues: whether the Houyhnhnms are to be seen as totally admirable, whether the Duke in *Measure for Measure* behaves badly, whether Mary Crawford in *Mansfield Park* is not unfairly treated by Jane Austen's moralizing voice. But nobody has suggested, even in this age of critical fecundity, that "A

---

the poem," in resolving critical controversy was in some circles thought to be wicked.

Now we are, apparently, in the midst of another swing, back to history. The splendid journal *New Literary History,* for example, announces that its contributors "do not accept the dichotomy of literary historian and literary critic" (vol. 1 [October 1969]: 4). We may well wonder why there was ever a divorce in the first place.

Modest Proposal" is a tragedy, or a paean to the British landlords or to the Irish collaborators, or even a modest proposal for preventing the children of Ireland from being a burden to their parents or country. And nobody has suggested that "My Mistress' Eyes" or *Northanger Abbey* should be read either as non-ironic or as totally ironic, with no clear stop signs. Swift and Shakespeare and Jane Austen will not, after all, allow such freedoms; whether we like it or not, they determine, through the literary forms they created, both where we begin and where we stop.

Prince Hal: There is a devil haunts thee in the likeness of an old
fat man; a tun of man is thy companion. Why dost thou con-
verse with that trunk of humours, that bolding-hutch of beast-
liness, . . . that father ruffian, that vanity in years? Wherein is
he good, but to taste sack and drink it? . . . wherein worthy,
but in nothing?
Falstaff: I would your Grace would take me with you. Whom
means your Grace?

—*Henry IV, Part I*

And should I have the right to smile?
—T. S. Eliot, "Portrait of a Lady"

Was he free? Was he happy? The question is absurd:
Had anything been wrong, we should certainly have heard.
—W. H. Auden, "The Unknown Citizen"

I am this month one whole year older than I was this time
twelve-month; and having got, as you perceive, almost into the
middle of my fourth volume—and no farther than to my first
day's life—'tis demonstrative that I have three hundred and
sixty-four days more life to write just now, than when I first set
out; so that instead of advancing, as a common writer, in my
work with what I have been doing at it—on the contrary, I am
just thrown so many volumes back— . . . It must follow, an'
please your worships, that the more I write, the more I shall have
to write—and consequently, the more your worships will have to
read.

—*Tristram Shandy*

# FIVE | Ironic Portraits

In chapter 4 I deliberately limited myself, except in the section on parodies, to works in which the intended reconstruction could be described with only slight distortion as some kind of argument or message. Even in such direct works, ironic reconstruction never yields only a single, literal message, because the action of choosing irony and all of its consequences remains part of what is communicated. But in them the most evident purpose of the irony is achieved when unacceptable statements or arguments or judgments have been reconstructed into what the author believes and expects us to believe with him. In all of our reconstructions, it is true, we could be said to re-create not just ideas but speakers, dramatized or implied; but our attention was not primarily on the speaker and his deficiencies but on the false message and its true reconstruction. Even in "A Modest Proposal," which modern critics often read as if it were a work of pure literature, with conclusions about Swift's polemic far in the background, the reader has no doubt that the work's original center is its argument; Swift's art, like our art of reconstruction, was devoted to the attack on abuses, not to the portrayal of an interesting character or situation or story for its own sake.

In the works we turn to now, the order of importance is reversed: the reconstruction of messages or content seems to be for the sake of revising and completing a picture of the speaker or of an action in which he is involved. The act of reconstruction is not completed in a proposition or set of propositions but in a dramatic picture. It follows from the dramatic quality of such works that the speaker does not usually address the reader directly, as in most of our previous examples, but is shown addressing other characters or speaking or thinking to himself.

This description of the differences is one way, rather roundabout and cumbersome, of distinguishing what we sometimes call "rhetorical" or "discursive" or "didactic" works from "literary" or "poetic" or "imaginative" or "creative" works: novels and epics, plays and poems written because "the experience of writing and reading them is self-justifying," or because "all appetites aroused in the works are fulfilled within them," or because "they make no assertions about the real world." The distinction is often used pejoratively, as if we were now turning from non-art to Art. It is sometimes said, by people who see things this way, that "A Modest Proposal" survives in spite of its message, not because of it; the passage of time has rendered irrelevant its rhetorical impurities (who cares any more about political abuses of two hundred years ago?) leaving it to be enjoyed now as pure art. Other critics (e.g., Kenneth Burke) ignore or deny the distinction, because no art exists divorced from its practical consequences, or because all art, even the most abstract, is rich in ideological and even rhetorical content for the critic clever enough to discern it.

This is not the place to rehearse in detail the many positions that have been taken about the ends of art, the role of ideological or didactic purposes in art, or the resulting manifold views of how practical messages and purposes are opposed to or harmonizable with or even necessary for all "genuine art." But it is important to see that stable irony is in a peculiar way caught in the center of all such disputes.

At one extreme stable irony can be viewed as a device useful for enforcing or strengthening an argument that in itself could be formulated in perfectly straightforward non-ironic terms. In oratory, and in theories of oratory, the momentary touch of irony can be simply one of many verbal tropes, as in the example cited by Quintilian: "Rejected by him, you migrated to your boon-companion, that excellent gentleman Metellus" (9.2.46). Though I think that Quintilian erred in seeing such ornamental ironies as *merely* "verbal," it is clear that many such *are* inessential, expendable; they work at the periphery and not the center of the rhetorical art in which they appear. They can be expunged without changing the essential effect, which means that they can be translated into literal meanings without *great* loss: ". . . that vile monster Metellus" or whatever. Though their use and interpretation will always affect the speaker's *ethos,* it can still be said that at the extreme limit, where purposes are practical and clear-cut, the insertion of one or two such momentary ironies into an argument comes close to being a merely ornamental gesture.

But such ironies cannot come as close to the fungible as other, less intricately involving kinds of ornament. From the earliest discussions of irony it has been seen as something that, like metaphor, will not stay graciously in an assigned position, something that in fact can easily and quickly expand its own peculiar appeals, move toward dominance, and become some kind of end in itself. From the beginning, apparently,[1] the word tended to get itself attached to a type of char-

1. See Norman Knox, *The Word "Irony" and Its Context: 1500–1755,* pp. 3–7, summarizing G. G. Sedgewick's account in his unpublished dissertation, "Dramatic Irony" (1913) and *Of Irony* (Toronto, 1935). As every schoolboy knows, the standard work on the concept of the *eiron* in Greek literature is Otto

acter—Aristophanes' foxy *eirons,* Plato's disconcerting Socrates—
rather than to any one device. The ironist did not simply say something
about his subject, he said something about himself and the world.
Theophrastus' "Character" of the ironist (neatly balanced by his portrait of the *alazonist,* what we would call the ironic boaster) shows him
not as someone accomplishing clear rhetorical purposes in the world
by the controlled use of stable irony but as a man whose irony is his
character and for whom the establishing of his character is inseparable
from his rhetorical purposes. "The ironic man is like this: He is ready
to walk up to his enemies and make small-talk without hostility. He
praises present company, whom he secretly attacks, and then condoles
with his victims. . . . If it's a rumor he pretends he never heard it; if
he's a witness he says he didn't see a thing; if he admits he was there
he says he doesn't remember. . . . The tags of his speech are as follows:
'unbelievable,' 'I just can't understand it,' 'I'm amazed,' and 'you might
be describing another man; he's never behaved so to me,' and 'Oh, go
on.' "[2]

Some of the rhetoricians recognize, though almost as if in passing,
that irony was much more than an ordinary rhetorical figure. Quintilian
says that "in the *figurative* form of irony the speaker disguises his entire
meaning, the disguise being apparent rather than confessed. . . . The
meaning, and sometimes the whole aspect of our case, conflicts with the
language and the tone of voice adopted; nay, a man's whole life may be
coloured with *irony,* as was the case with Socrates, who was called an
*ironist* because he assumed the role of an ignorant man lost in wonder
at the wisdom of others. Thus, as continued *metaphor* develops into
*allegory,* so a sustained series of *tropes* develops into this *figure"* (9.2.
46–47).

But having touched on this borderline where irony ceases to be
instrumental and is sought as an end in itself, Quintilian draws back,
quite properly for his purposes, to his functional view, and in effect
carries nearly two millennia worth of rhetoricians along with him. It
was not until well along into the eighteenth century that theorists were
forced, by explosive developments in the use of irony itself, to begin
thinking about ironic effects as somehow self-sufficient literary ends.
And then of course irony burst its bonds so effectively that men finally

---

Ribbeck's "Über den Begriff des εἴρωτ" (1876), a work my detailed study of
which is reflected in at least two passages in this book.

2. Character Number 1. I owe the translation to James Redfield.

dismissed merely functional ironies as not even ironic, or as self-evidently less artistic.[3]

This imperialistic expansion is often discussed as resulting from the ironist's temptation to display his own ironic cleverness,[4] but it can equally well be seen as a natural and legitimate development of a literary quality into a supreme artistic end justified by the nature of things, or the nature of literature, or the nature of the modern world.[5]

It would be as pointless to debate whether irony *should* be a means to an end or an end in itself as to debate those related questions of whether there is a real and final distinction between didactic works and true literature, or between didactic art and mimetic art, or between impure and pure literature. To distinguish rhetorical and aesthetic appeals is useful for some purposes, useless and even destructive for others. It happens to be helpful in dealing with stable irony, because in deciding whether a given irony is a means to some didactic purpose, a means to some non-ironic aesthetic purpose, or somehow an end in itself, we obtain practical assistance in deciding where to stop in our reconstructions.

In reading ironic satire, probably the most widespread genre using stable ironies, we stopped ironic reconstruction only when we had found a convincing pattern of messages or satirical thrusts against

3. See for example Andrew H. Wright, "Irony and Fiction," *Journal of Aesthetics and Art Criticism* 12 (1953): 111–18. *"Jonathan Wild the Great . . . is not an ironic work, despite the author's free use of rhetorical irony. . . . For there is contrast merely, not contradiction"* (p. 116). Mr. Wright takes this back in his excellent review of Muecke's *Compass of Irony, College English* 31 (December 1969): 322–26.

Northrop Frye often suggests that the clearer the functionality of a given stroke, the less irony there is in it: "The chief distinction between irony and satire is that satire is militant irony: its moral norms are relatively clear, and it assumes standards against which the grotesque and absurd are measured. Sheer invective or name-calling ('flyting') is satire in which there is relatively little irony: on the other hand, whenever a reader is not sure what the author's attitude is or what his own is supposed to be, we have irony with relatively little satire" (*Anatomy*, p. 223). This is almost the direct opposite of the traditional view. See also Cleanth Brooks, "Irony as a Principle of Structure," in Morton Dauwen Zabel, ed., *Literary Opinion in America* (New York, 1951), pp. 729–41.

4. See Maximillian E. Novak, "Defoe's Use of Irony," in *The Uses of Irony: Papers on Defoe and Swift,* for an argument that Defoe's irony often proceeded from pleasure in his own genius (esp. p. 38). Kierkegaard discusses this "temptation" at great length.

5. See for example Kenneth Burke, "Thomas Mann and André Gide," *Counter-Statement* (Los Altos, Calif., 1931; paperback, 1968). The bibliography on the relation of irony to realities of various kinds is itself immense. See Muecke, *Compass of Irony,* for a selective list.

some belief or person or thing in the so-called real world—when the genre "covert attack" was seen to account for the whole. But in reading the works we turn to now, we stop not with a pattern of reconstituted messages which replace the overt message but with some kind of human character, situation, or story that we have been led to see as superior in interest, emotional quality, or poetic truth to the ostensible offering of the ironic words. Such ironies still fall short of the kind of pervasive domination of their worlds that we will find when we come to chapter 8; since they remain stable they invite reconstruction into stable views. They can thus be said to be either functional, in the service of those final stable views, or ends in themselves, depending on one's critical presuppositions; the point is that the ironic pursuit of the reader still comes to a decisive end.

"I could 'a' stayed if I wanted to, but I didn't want to," says Huck Finn when Colonel Sherburn aims his double-barreled shotgun at the lynching mob. Throughout *Huckleberry Finn* Huck's version of his motives and feelings differs considerably from the one we reconstruct; the story that Mark Twain tells us is consequently quite different from the story that Huck thinks he is telling, and of course the distance between the two is in itself our most interesting (and amusing) information about the events and about Huck's own character. The distance is greatest, and the resulting double-drama most intense, in the famous scene when Huck, rejecting the voice of his "conscience," decides not to turn Nigger Jim back into slavery: "All right, then, I'll *go* to hell." Few readers if any have ever learned from this scene that slavery is bad; we do not praise it because it teaches us a truth we did not know before, or because it is an effective attack on slavery. Any "messages" that are involved are in fact brought by most readers to the passage, not derived from it; it is upon the convictions shared by Samuel L. Clemens, Mark Twain, and every successful reader that the wonderfully warm moral comedy of Huck's "mistake" is built; it is thus Huck, with his verbal misjudgments and his essential moral integrity, that we read for.

### DRAMATIC MONOLOGUE

Such ironic portraits are perhaps more frequently slanted the other way around, with a character giving away more weaknesses or vices than he intends. There is a great difference in emotional effect between the self-condemned-revealed-as-secret-saint and the self-satisfied-re-vealed-as-fool-or-knave. But the contribution of the irony is the same so long as the reader's confidence in drawing to a halt springs from completed characters or actions or pictures and not completed argu-mentation or satirical thrusts outward into the real world. In reading

141

"A Modest Proposal" I would not feel comfortable saying, "This or this passage must be ironic because an ironic reading makes the proposer's character or actions more interesting or coherent." But in many novels, plays, or poems we do depend for our confidence precisely on some such assertion about the context.

In Browning's dramatic monologues, for example, the irony is clearly in the service of what in a misleading shorthand we call literary rather than practical effects.

Soliloquy of the Spanish
Cloister

### I

Gr-r-r—there go, my heart's abhorrence!
    Water your damned flower-pots, do!
If hate killed men, Brother Lawrence,
    God's blood, would not mine kill you!
What? your myrtle-bush wants trimming?
    Oh, that rose has prior claims—
Needs its leaden vase filled brimming?
    Hell dry you up with its flames!

### II

At the meal we sit together:
    *Salve tibi!* I must hear
Wise talk of the kind of weather,
    Sort of season, time of year:
*Not a plenteous cork-crop: scarcely*
    *Dare we hope oak-galls, I doubt:*
*What's the Latin name for "parsley"?*
    What's the Greek name for Swine's Snout?

### III

Whew! We'll have our platter burnished,
    Laid with care on our own shelf!
With a fire-new spoon we're furnished,
    And a goblet for ourself,
Rinsed like something sacrificial
    Ere 't is fit to touch our chaps—
Marked with L. for our initial!
    (He-he! There his lily snaps!)

### IV

*Saint,* forsooth! While brown Dolores
    Squats outside the Convent bank

With Sanchicha, telling stories,
    Steeping tresses in the tank,
Blue-black, lustrous, thick like horsehairs,
    —Can't I see his dead eye glow,
Bright as 't were a Barbary corsair's?
    (That is, if he'd let it show!)

### V

When he finishes refection,
    Knife and fork he never lays
Cross-wise, to my recollection,
    As do I, in Jesu's praise.
I the Trinity illustrate,
    Drinking watered orange-pulp—
In three sips the Arian frustrate;
    While he drains his at one gulp.

### VI

Oh, those melons? If he's able
    We're to have a feast! so nice!
One goes to the Abbot's table,
    All of us get each a slice.
How go on your flowers? None double?
    Not one fruit-sort can you spy?
Strange!—And I, too, at such trouble,
    Keep them close-nipped on the sly!

### VII

There's a great text in Galatians,
    Once you trip on it, entails
Twenty-nine distinct damnations,
    One sure, if another fails:
If I trip him just a-dying,
    Sure of heaven as sure can be,
Spin him round and send him flying
    Off to hell, a Manichee?

### VIII

Or, my scrofulous French novel
    On grey paper with blunt type!
Simply glance at it, you grovel
    Hand and foot in Belial's gripe:
If I double down its pages
    At the woeful sixteenth print,
When he gathers his greengages,
    Ope a sieve and slip it in 't?

## IX

Or, there's Satan!—one might venture
    Pledge one's soul to him, yet leave
Such a flaw in the indenture
    As he'd miss till, past retrieve,
Blasted lay that rose-acacia
    We're so proud of! *Hy, Zy, Hine* . . .
'St there's Vespers! *Plena gratiâ*
    *Ave, Virgo!* Gr-r-r—you swine!

One might at first think that there are no real differences between
the invitations this poem offers the reader and what he was asked to
do by "A Modest Proposal." In both works he must infer the qualities
of a speaker from evidence supplied entirely by that speaker, with no
direct assistance from any voice speaking reliably for the author. In
both the speaker stands in radical contrast to the author whom we infer
behind the scenes. In both most of the beliefs of the speaker must be
repudiated, and we reconstruct a picture of the speaker that undermines him. And in both there are other characters—Brother Lawrence
in the poem and a whole cast of villains in the satire—whose true
qualities must be discerned through the distorting glass of the speaker's
words.

But the differences are even more striking. The speaker in the
poem is in no sense conscious of making an argument to a reader or
audience; he is not making an argument at all. Even if we took his
words as spoken aloud, which they surely are not, they would not
remotely resemble a systematic argument. Somehow the coherent picture of the speaker's character and emotion as he gives himself away
is the center of our interest here. Browning is not saying something *by
means of* the poem; the poem *is* what he is saying. To discover a message in this poem—something about the corruption, say, of the Catholic
clergy, or "Down with the monasteries!"—gets us nowhere. Our job,
to put it crudely, is to re-create the qualities of the two men and the
drama between them as precisely and vividly as possible.[6]

6. We may then of course choose to talk about what the poem says about
Browning, or about Renaissance monasteries, or about Victorian views of pornography—or indeed about any of its unlimited relations to the world. The
poem's significance is limited only by our interests and ingenuity; it can even
include the fact—and it is a fact, though an "incredible" one—that some readers in the century after its composition cannot perform the acrobatics that it
requires. The critical issues involved in distinguishing major kinds of literary
interest are much more complex than I have suggested. The best argument for
using a radical distinction of ends is to me Sheldon Sacks's *Fiction and the Shape
of Belief* (Berkeley, 1964), especially the opening and closing chapters.

Experienced readers can do the job of re-creating the speaker in opposition to his own views without having to make every step conscious. But it is useful to pretend once more that we are not experienced readers and that we must move consciously and analytically. Only in this way can we be sure that our intuitive leaps have not been across imaginary gaps between nonexistent platforms.

We can begin by asking what we in fact learn about Brother Lawrence. Do we, for example, know whether to believe the speaker when he tells us that Brother Lawrence is sexually aroused by brown Dolores? "Can't I see his dead eye glow . . . ? (That is, if he'd let it show)"—which is to say that Brother Lawrence does *not* let it show, and we must ask, then, how the speaker knows it is there. What is not in doubt is something he does not—and possibly could not—say: that he is himself guilty of the sin he ascribes to Brother Lawrence. "Steeping tresses in the tank"—suddenly his mind is caught by the sensuous picture ("Blue-black, lustrous, thick like horsehairs,/—Can't I . . ."), and the dash tells us that he has wrenched himself back to Brother Lawrence.

The only facts we can be sure of about Brother Lawrence, when we have rejected those claims that the speaker fails to support, are that he gardens and loves to talk about gardening; that he surrounds himself with pleasant possessions (the platter, spoon, goblet); that he is called "Saint" by *someone* and that the narrator thinks the term ludicrously misapplied; that he *perhaps* gives a larger share of melons to the abbot than to the lesser monks; that he *perhaps* has some undue personal vanity (the initial L); and that he is not punctilious about the forms of religiosity.

These facts are not enough to build much of a portrait on; Brother Lawrence could be, for all we *know,* a saint with minor vanities, or a rival in corruption to the speaker himself. What is clear is that if Browning had wanted us to build a full portrait of Brother Lawrence, so that we would see *two* unmistakably vicious monks, he could easily have provided far more than he does. Instead, he deliberately undercuts what little absolute fact he does give, even casting doubt on the possibility of Brother Lawrence's interest in Dolores by adding the final line in stanza 4. The obvious inference is that Browning's attention is on the speaker's twisted soul. The details Browning has him provide are in every case chosen as a mode of self-betrayal. What they all "say" is that whatever Lawrence's virtues or faults, there is simply nothing in the poem to justify the extreme hatred displayed by the speaker. The contrast between the hatred and the slightness of the provocation is thus one of the points of the poem, since the greater the contrast—within limits—the more morally grotesque the narrator will seem, and hence the more interesting as a literary portrait.[7]

But just how twisted is this damned soul? It is interesting that we know very little more about his actions, taken alone, than we do about those of Brother Lawrence: he has watched Dolores, he eats "by the book," trying to make every gesture seem religious, he has "close-nipped" some of Lawrence's flowers, he owns and has read a pornographic French novel—a slim list to build on, if we had nothing more.

But of course we have much more: we have the inadvertent self-portrait provided by his thoughts. The silent curse that concludes stanza 1, the petty name-calling that concludes stanza 2, the childish glee that concludes stanza 3—all prepare us for the hypocrisy of stanzas 4 and 5 and the concentration on his ludicrous villainies in the final stanzas.

Perhaps the nicest irony of the whole poem is his unconscious confession as he talks of the pornographic French novel. How does *he* know that if you glance at the right page you will grovel hand and foot in Belial's grasp? Only by having had the experience, of course. The final revelation that he is willing to risk selling his soul to the devil for the sake of withering an acacia bush—though he thinks he is clever enough to escape—comes as no surprise; it is "in character"—meaning in harmony with the character we have constructed behind his back. Browning and we have been converting all the signs into a meaning that the speaker could never dream of, and when he turns to repeat the words appropriate to vespers, in the same breath hailing Mary and cursing Brother Lawrence, the contrast merely summarizes the hypocrisy that we have come to expect.

7. Critics who do not accept the universality of interest in the ironic process can mistake this interest for private obsession with a particular revealed vice. A. L. French, in an intelligent attack on ironic ambiguity as potentially a device for escaping the author's responsibility, underrates our general fascination with what is ironically difficult. "No one confuses Robert Browning with the Duke in 'My Last Duchess,' but Browning must have been attracted, and his art itself suggests that he was indeed attracted by the Duke's callous amorality. Perhaps the marked interest he shows in Renaissance Italian wickedness testifies to the power of instincts which, in nineteenth-century London or Italy, could find no natural outlet. And the drift of this argument is not towards amateur psychologising but towards talking about a writer's sensibility—the things that fascinate him, the things he finds significant" ("Purposive Imitation: A Skirmish with Literary Theory," *Essays in Criticism* 22 [1972]: 114). But it is precisely toward "psychoanalysing" that such speculation leads, if unchecked by our awareness that all of us find self-betraying hypocrisy fascinating to watch, and that almost all great writers, and particularly the dramatists who influenced Browning, had reveled in showing precisely his kinds of fools and knaves. I think it would be hard to show that the "hypocritical" Victorian period produced more literary portraits of hypocrisy than our own ostensibly uninhibited time.

The major irony in this poem, then, is the contrast between what the speaker (or "thinker") believes about himself and what we must infer about him. The steps we take in making this reconstruction are thus precisely those we have traced in chapter 1: a *required rejection* of the surface meaning; a consideration of *alternatives;* a *decision* about the author's position; and a *reconstruction* in harmony with what we infer about that position. The difference is that the reconstruction here is of a consistent character engaging in significant thought or action in a given scene, not finally of the revised convictions themselves.

The details of our reconstruction will depend, of course, on how our knowledge and experience relate to the implied author's intention. Browning knew that he could count on most of us to deplore the wanton destruction of gardens, or hypocrisy about pornographic novels. He could assume our instant recognition of a great disparity between the motives of the speaker and those that pious tradition would expect of the cloistered, yet he could also assume that most of the good Anglican readers in mid-Victorian England would expect precisely this kind of corruption in the clergy of the Renaissance. Most of us can be counted on to hold the same assumptions, but we may require a few added steps—e.g., looking up oak-galls or Manichee—depending on how much we know about gardening or theology. But such steps are by no means necessary in reconstructing the essential irony, as we can see if we ask ourselves what difference it makes that commentators cannot agree about the text in Galatians or that no one has found a convincing interpretation of *Hy, Zy, Hine*. Nothing would surprise us more than a cogent and genuinely novel reading of this poem, claiming that new information about Galatians and *Hy, Zy, Hine* or any other feature proves that Browning intended us to take the speaker and his opinions at face value.

The same point can be made, though less dramatically, with the word "Arian." Editions with footnotes invariably explain Arianism as the Unitarian heresy, opposed to the doctrine of the Trinity. This meaning can of course be inferred from the poem: to "frustrate the Arian" by drinking orange juice in three sips rather than one gulp can mean only one thing, in this context, and for those of us who have the essential knowledge that there has been controversy between Trinitarians and Unitarians. If we learned that Arius (256–336) was really a Tetrarian or (as Mark Twain once said in a similar context) a Septuagenarian, we would reject the new information as irrelevant, so strong is our security about what the implied author believes and expects us to believe.

Such shared clarities will not, of course, eliminate all controversy about other problems of interpretation and evaluation. Having seen the speaker for what he is, readers may encounter the same range of critical disagreement as surrounds straightforward lyrics like "Kubla Khan" or "Sailing to Byzantium." Differences of temperament will produce responses ranging from comic savoring to solemn condemnation of the portrait of corruption; differences of belief may yield readings all the way from amused tolerance to angry denunciation of Catholic corruption. The task of deciding precisely what emotional load Browning gave to his ironic portraiture, or what response a reader does or should give him, is not necessarily less difficult, once that portrait has been reconstructed, than in works that make no ironic demands. Since Browning's chosen form of irony allows him no direct interventions, the range of possibilities may seem initially much broader than when Coleridge's alter ego says, without an ounce of ironic discounting, that he "would build that dome in air,/ That sunny dome," and that he has fed on honey-dew and "drunk the milk of Paradise." But Browning's many unmistakable ironies narrow the choices sharply: no one will mistake the ironic portrait for a spiritual meditation, a bit of romantic longing for the past, or even a simple satire against the church.

We thus find ourselves with different levels of certainty about different acts of interpretation.

1. About the local ironies (does Browning intend, say, the contrast between the puritanical attack and the lecherous reality?) we are practically certain as soon as they are recognized, and experience of the whole poem bolts them firmly and permanently into place.

2. About the total character of this speaker we are only slightly less sure. We know him clearly for what he is, know him more surely (though less richly) than we ever know anyone in real life: he is permanently fixed as hypocrite, lecher, envious sadist.

3. We are not quite so sure about whether the author would share our precise tone in describing him. After all, Browning chose not to employ such melodramatic epithets, but to portray a lively mind in action. And legitimate critical debate will occur about the intended moral placement, if any: Browning was clearly "fascinated," as artist, by the problem, or the delight, of portraying such folk, and yet he clearly judges them as in some sense deplorable. It is here that so much talk of the ambiguity caused by irony comes about: Browning has chosen a genre that denies us the kind of larger context that to some degree fixes the moral judgments in nineteenth-century novels. Put into a novel, our priest could be made to threaten someone we love, say, and we would then be made to judge precisely. The poem is "looser"

than that novel would be, but it is a mistake to think this looseness the result of the irony: it is shared fully with every short portrayal of a non-ironized character. For fuller resolution of moral questions about such short works, one must be willing to construct the larger contexts that the author has, for the moment, denied us: his other works, including statements of intentions, the interpretations of readers in his own time, historical reconstruction of belief-probabilities and genre expectations, and so on.

4. About the exact emotional effect we are perhaps less sure still. Some readers of "Soliloquy" have seen it as a solemn satirical portrait of corrupt and vicious Catholic priests, and they have found the irony "biting"; others have found it essentially humorous, though admitting that the humor is "biting" or "grotesque." To me, the very nature of the speaker's sins undercuts any effort to read the poem with solemnity or even gravity. But to say that "solemnity is ironically undercut" by many details in the poem I must, once again, make certain inferences about the author. It is not simply his beliefs about cloisters and flowers, as implied in the poem, that are important to me. I also must either assume in advance or derive from the poem some picture of his artistic skill, including his concern for artistic coherence. Unless he cares about coherence in one sense or another, incongruity of details will tell us nothing. But of course I come to the poem with a strong conviction that Browning is a very good poet, famous for his "dramatic monologues," works which I already know present a great variety of self-betraying knaves, fools, sinners, and hypocrites. I also have an assumption, never held with great passion but strong enough to work with, that good poets make coherent poems, and they do what is necessary to realize the inherent intentions of a given poem in the most forceful way possible.

Now any good poet, if he were setting out to write a serious, grave, or bitter satire against the Catholic church would (my hidden assumption goes on) have done much better than this; he would certainly have been able easily to create a character more seriously threatening in his evil than this one. Instead of what Browning might have given in his picture of evil in the cloisters—a grave meditation on the nature of original sin, a savage indictment, a portrait of the horror at the heart of an absurd universe—this poem points invariably toward a kind of wry humor. Regardless of what Browning may have felt "in real life" about the various potential "subjects" here, in *this* poem the smile of wry amusement has, as it were, dominated his choices: he could so easily have done it other ways. Even I, a very feeble poet indeed, can think of ways to improve the poem if what he intended were these other things. But if I try to improve it under *this* conception, I can think of nothing.

My assumption is not, of course, that Browning always creates characters with precisely this tone. On the contrary, I know that his stage presents a great range of effects, from the solemn, even the tragic, to the farcical. In interpreting his ironies one cannot assume, from poem to poem—from "The Bishop Orders His Tomb at Saint Praxed's Church," to "Porphyria's Lover," "Johannes Agricola in Meditation," "My Last Duchess," "Fra Lippo Lippi," "Caliban upon Setebos," "Bishop Blougram's Apology," or "Mr. Sludge, The Medium"—that the speaker of any one poem will be essentially like the speaker of any other. But the process of reconstruction will in each case be similar, and our degree of final confidence will rest both on the internal coherence and force of our reconstruction and on our assumption that Browning knows what he is doing.

5. The ambiguities increase even more as we try to place the character and his milieu in a full world view. I doubt that anyone can be sure, from the poem itself, how Browning felt about monasteries or priests or the Catholic church or religion in general. It is conceivable that such a poem might have been written by a Catholic reformer, or by an atheist. It is thus at this level thoroughly ambiguous in itself, but no more so, one must insist, than any non-ironic lyrical expression taken from the historical context of its author and time.

In "telling us where to stop," then, the genre has only limited powers. Its rule is absolute against anyone who would try to make a new, interesting reading by reversing the local ironies once again: "Brother Lawrence is the *real* villain and the speaker is a man of God." But even in this domain the power of genre depends on probable inferences about the author and his intended readers, and as we move out from the autocratic center, we encounter more diversity, more controversy, and a growing need for explicit historical research in making our reconstructions. We need not know any more about Browning and his time (which is still, after all, very much *our* time in this respect) to read this poem with pleasure and some confidence; we would need to know more than anyone knows to be able to answer some of the broader questions that might be raised about it.

## FICTION AND DRAMA

Dramatic self-portraits by fools and knaves are relatively rare in short poetry, relatively frequent in drama and fiction and narrative poetry, where the greater length and variety make it easy for the author to provide corrective crosslights: contrasts of words with deeds, or words spoken early and words spoken later, or words spoken in soliloquy and words spoken to other characters, or points of view. Lacking such resources for correction, short poems are most often only incidentally ironic, in our sense, if ironic at all. The great lyric poems are for the most part written with little or no intended distance between the speaker and the implied author, and their ironies—if any—are likely to be so different from what we have seen so far as really to deserve a different name.

Fiction and drama are another matter. A very large number of short stories written since the mid-nineteenth century have been in effect extended dramatic monologues—extended "self-revelations" requiring of the reader a step-by-step reconstruction of the distances, sometimes large but often extremely subtle, between the presented view of things and the author's unspoken evaluation.

The first attempts in this curiously intense form presented relatively easy inferential tasks—I am thinking especially of the immensely influential stories of Poe told by madmen or fools like those we saw briefly in chapter 3. But the demands for subtlety of inference increased rapidly through the last half of the nineteenth and the early part of the twentieth century, for reasons perhaps too complicated for anyone to understand fully. Plausible explanations have been based on various social and moral and psychological and philosophical explorations and dissolutions; equally plausible accounts tell us that authors were extending the technical and formal possibilities opened by *Jacques le fataliste, Tristram Shandy,* and their imitators in the Romantic period.

For our present purposes, it is important only to recognize the absolute split between works designed to be reconstructible on firm norms shared by authors and readers, and those other "ironic" works that provide no platform for reconstruction. In the one kind, all or most of the ironies are resolved into relatively secure moral or philosophical perceptions or truths; in the other, all truths are dissolved in an ironic mist.

Even in the former kind there is a great difference between those works, like "A Cask of Amontillado," in which the norms of judgment are entirely public, conventionally shared by all or most readers (killing people in revenge for a petty insult is bad, or mad; gratuitous cruelty to children deserves extreme punishment), and those in which the author's norms, though intended to be shared, are to some degree private or idiosyncratic. It is often said that with the "breakdown of values" *all* values have come to be of the latter kind. Whether or not one shares this view, for the purposes of getting his work read a modern author can pretty well assume that he must create his world of values and thus his band of like-minded readers as he goes.

This is true even for writers working ostensibly within an established system of beliefs, but it is even more troublesome for those who see themselves as having to shape their own truths as well as their stories. Each of these kinds would justify a study in itself, but I can look briefly only at one example of each.

## "READY-MADE" VALUES

For sloganizing purposes, as Kenneth Burke would say, Flannery O'Connor is a Catholic. But whether such information, confirmed by all sorts of biographical evidence, will help us in reading the complex ironies in the following story, only a close encounter with the story itself can determine. To be a Catholic writer can mean many things, or it might even, in some kinds of writing, mean nothing. To see precisely in what sense it means something in her fiction—to see precisely how we use the author hidden in the work—it will be well to have the complete story before us.

## Everything That Rises Must Converge

[1]   Her doctor had told Julian's mother that she must lose twenty pounds on account of her blood pressure, so on Wednesday nights Julian had to take her downtown on the bus for a reducing class at the Y. The reducing class was designed for working girls over fifty, who weighed from 165 to 200 pounds. His mother was one of the slimmer ones, but she said ladies did not tell their age or weight. She would not ride the buses by herself at night since they had been integrated, and because the reducing class was one of her few pleasures, necessary for her health, and *free,* she said Julian could at least put himself out to take her, considering all she did for him. Julian did not like to consider all she did for him, but every Wednesday night he braced himself and took her.

[2]   She was almost ready to go, standing before the hall mirror, putting on her hat, while he, his hands behind him, appeared pinned to the door frame, waiting like Saint Sebastian for the arrows to begin piercing him. The hat was new and had cost her seven dollars and a half. She kept saying, "Maybe I shouldn't have paid that for it. No, I shouldn't have. I'll take it off and return it tomorrow. I shouldn't have bought it."

[3]   Julian raised his eyes to heaven. "Yes, you should have bought it," he said. "Put it on and let's go." It was a hideous hat. A purple velvet flap came down on one side of it and stood up on the other; the

rest of it was green and looked like a cushion with the stuffing out. He decided it was less comical than jaunty and pathetic. Everything that gave her pleasure was small and depressed him.

[4]    She lifted the hat one more time and set it down slowly on top of her head. Two wings of gray hair protruded on either side of her florid face, but her eyes, sky-blue, were as innocent and untouched by experience as they must have been when she was ten. Were it not that she was a widow who had struggled fiercely to feed and clothe and put him through school and who was supporting him still, "until he got on his feet," she might have been a little girl that he had to take to town.

[5]    "It's all right, it's all right," he said. "Let's go." He opened the door himself and started down the walk to get her going. The sky was a dying violet and the houses stood out darkly against it, bulbous liver-colored monstrosities of a uniform ugliness though no two were alike. Since this had been a fashionable neighborhood forty years ago, his mother persisted in thinking they did well to have an apartment in it. Each house had a narrow collar of dirt around it in which sat, usually, a grubby child. Julian walked with his hands in his pockets, his head down and thrust forward and his eyes glazed with the determination to make himself completely numb during the time he would be sacrificed to her pleasure.

[6]    The door closed and he turned to find the dumpy figure surmounted by the atrocious hat, coming toward him. "Well," she said, "you only live once and paying a little more for it, I at least won't meet myself coming and going."

[7]    "Some day I'll start making money," Julian said gloomily—he knew he never would—"and you can have one of those jokes whenever you take the fit." But first they would move. He visualized a place where the nearest neighbors would be three miles away on either side.

[8]    "I think you're doing fine," she said, drawing on her gloves. "You've only been out of school a year. Rome wasn't built in a day."

[9]    She was one of the few members of the Y reducing class who arrived in hat and gloves and who had a son who had been to college. "It takes time," she said, "and the world is in such a mess. This hat looked better on me than any of the others, though when she brought it out I said, 'Take that thing back. I wouldn't have it on my head,' and she said, 'Now wait till you see it on,' and when she put it on me, I said, 'We-ull,' and she said, 'If you ask me, that hat does something for you and you do something for the hat, and besides,' she said, 'with that hat, you won't meet yourself coming and going.'"

[10] Julian thought he could have stood his lot better if she had been selfish, if she had been an old hag who drank and screamed at him. He walked along, saturated in depression, as if in the midst of his martyr-dom he had lost his faith. Catching sight of his long, hopeless, irritated face, she stopped suddenly with a grief-stricken look, and pulled back on his arm. "Wait on me," she said. "I'm going back to the house and

take this thing off and tomorrow I'm going to return it. I was out of my head. I can pay the gas bill with that seven-fifty."

[11] He caught her arm in a vicious grip. "You are not going to take it back," he said. "I like it."

"Well," she said, "I don't think I ought . . ."

"Shut up and enjoy it," he muttered, more depressed than ever.

"With the world in the mess it's in," she said, "it's a wonder we can enjoy anything. I tell you, the bottom rail is on the top."

Julian sighed.

[12] "Of course," she said, "if you know who you are, you can go anywhere." She said this every time he took her to the reducing class. "Most of them in it are not our kind of people," she said, "but I can be gracious to anybody. I know who I am."

[13] "They don't give a damn for your graciousness," Julian said savagely. "Knowing who you are is good for one generation only. You haven't the foggiest idea where you stand now or who you are."

[14] She stopped and allowed her eyes to flash at him. "I most certainly do know who I am," she said, "and if you don't know who you are, I'm ashamed of you."

"Oh hell," Julian said.

[15] "Your great-grandfather was a former governor of this state," she said. "Your grandfather was a prosperous landowner. Your grandmother was a Godhigh."

"Will you look around you," he said tensely, "and see where you are now?" and he swept his arm jerkily out to indicate the neighborhood, which the growing darkness at least made less dingy.

[16] "You remain what you are," she said. "Your great-grandfather had a plantation and two hundred slaves."

"There are no more slaves," he said irritably.

[17] "They were better off when they were," she said. He groaned to see that she was off on that topic. She rolled onto it every few days like a train on an open track. He knew every stop, every junction, every swamp along the way, and knew the exact point at which her conclusion would roll majestically into the station: "It's ridiculous. It's simply not realistic. They should rise, yes, but on their own side of the fence."

"Let's skip it," Julian said.

"The ones I feel sorry for," she said, "are the ones that are half white. They're tragic."

"Will you skip it?"

"Suppose we were half white. We would certainly have mixed feelings."

"I have mixed feelings now," he groaned.

[18] "Well let's talk about something pleasant," she said. "I remember going to Grandpa's when I was a little girl. Then the house had double stairways that went up to what was really the second floor—all the cooking was done on the first. I used to like to stay down in the kitchen

154

on account of the way the walls smelled. I would sit with my nose pressed against the plaster and take deep breaths. Actually the place belonged to the Godhighs but your grandfather Chestny paid the mortgage and saved it for them. They were in reduced circumstances," she said, "but reduced or not, they never forgot who they were."

[19] "Doubtless that decayed mansion reminded them," Julian muttered. He never spoke of it without contempt or thought of it without longing. He had seen it once when he was a child before it had been sold. The double stairways had rotted and been torn down. Negroes were living in it. But it remained in his mind as his mother had known it. It appeared in his dreams regularly. He would stand on the wide porch, listening to the rustle of oak leaves, then wander through the high-ceilinged hall into the parlor that opened onto it and gaze at the worn rugs and faded draperies. It occurred to him that it was he, not she, who could have appreciated it. He preferred its threadbare elegance to anything he could name and it was because of it that all the neighborhoods they had lived in had been a torment to him—whereas she had hardly known the difference. She called her insensitivity "being adjustable."

[20] "And I remember the old darky who was my nurse, Caroline. There was no better person in the world. I've always had a great respect for my colored friends," she said. "I'd do anything in the world for them and they'd . . ."

[21] "Will you for God's sake get off that subject?" Julian said. When he got on a bus by himself, he made it a point to sit down beside a Negro, in reparation as it were for his mother's sins.

"You're mighty touchy tonight," she said. "Do you feel all right?"

"Yes I feel all right," he said. "Now lay off."

She pursed her lips. "Well, you certainly are in a vile humor," she observed. "I just won't speak to you at all."

[22] They had reached the bus stop. There was no bus in sight and Julian, his hands still jammed in his pockets and his head thrust forward, scowled down the empty street. The frustration of having to wait on the bus as well as ride on it began to creep up his neck like a hot hand. The presence of his mother was borne in upon him as she gave a pained sigh. He looked at her bleakly. She was holding herself very erect under the preposterous hat, wearing it like a banner of her imaginary dignity. There was in him an evil urge to break her spirit. He suddenly unloosened his tie and pulled it off and put it in his pocket.

She stiffened. "Why must you look like *that* when you take me to town?" she said. "Why must you deliberately embarrass me?"

"If you'll never learn where you are," he said, "you can at least learn where I am."

"You look like a—thug," she said.

"Then I must be one," he murmured.

155

"I'll just go home," she said. "I will not bother you. If you can't do a little thing like that for me . . ."

[23] Rolling his eyes upward, he put his tie back on. "Restored to my class," he muttered. He thrust his face toward her and hissed, "True culture is in the mind, the *mind*," he said, and tapped his head, "the mind."

"It's in the heart," she said, "and in how you do things and how you do things is because of who you *are*."

"Nobody in the damn bus cares who you are."

"I care who I am," she said icily.

[24] The lighted bus appeared on top of the next hill and as it approached, they moved out into the street to meet it. He put his hand under her elbow and hoisted her up on the creaking step. She entered with a little smile, as if she were going into a drawing room where everyone had been waiting for her. While he put in the tokens, she sat down on one of the broad front seats for three which faced the aisle. A thin woman with protruding teeth and long yellow hair was sitting on the end of it. His mother moved up beside her and left room for Julian beside herself. He sat down and looked at the floor across the aisle where a pair of thin feet in red and white canvas sandals were planted.

[25] His mother immediately began a general conversation meant to attract anyone who felt like talking. "Can it get any hotter?" she said and removed from her purse a folding fan, black with a Japanese scene on it, which she began to flutter before her.

"I reckon it might could," the woman with the protruding teeth said, "but I know for a fact my apartment couldn't get no hotter."

[26] "It must get the afternoon sun," his mother said. She sat forward and looked up and down the bus. It was half filled. Everybody was white. "I see we have the bus to ourselves," she said. Julian cringed.

"For a change," said the woman across the aisle, the owner of the red and white canvas sandals. "I come on one the other day and they were thick as fleas—up front and all through."

"The world is in a mess everywhere," his mother said. "I don't know how we've let it get in this fix."

[27] "What gets my goat is all those boys from good families stealing automobile tires," the woman with the protruding teeth said. "I told my boy, I said you may not be rich but you been raised right and if I ever catch you in any such mess, they can send you on to the reformatory. Be exactly where you belong."

"Training tells," his mother said. "Is your boy in high school?"

"Ninth grade," the woman said.

"My son just finished college last year. He wants to write but he's selling typewriters until he gets started," his mother said.

[28] The woman leaned forward and peered at Julian. He threw her such a malevolent look that she subsided against the seat. On the floor across the aisle there was an abandoned newspaper. He got up

156

and got it and opened it out in front of him. His mother discreetly continued the conversation in a lower tone but the woman across the aisle said in a loud voice, "Well that's nice. Selling typewriters is close to writing. He can go right from one to the other."

"I tell him," his mother said, "that Rome wasn't built in a day."

[29] Behind the newspaper Julian was withdrawing into the inner compartment of his mind where he spent most of his time. This was a kind of mental bubble in which he established himself when he could not bear to be a part of what was going on around him. From it he could see out and judge but in it he was safe from any kind of penetration from without. It was the only place where he felt free of the general idiocy of his fellows. His mother had never entered it but from it he could see her with absolute clarity.

[30] The old lady was clever enough and he thought that if she had started from any of the right premises, more might have been expected of her. She lived according to the laws of her own fantasy world, outside of which he had never seen her set foot. The law of it was to sacrifice herself for him after she had first created the necessity to do so by making a mess of things. If he had permitted her sacrifices, it was only because her lack of foresight had made them necessary. All of her life had been a struggle to act like a Chestny without the Chestny goods, and to give him everything she thought a Chestny ought to have; but since, said she, it was fun to struggle, why complain? And when you had won, as she had won, what fun to look back on the hard times! He could not forgive her that she had enjoyed the struggle and that she thought *she* had won.

[31] What she meant when she said she had won was that she had brought him up successfully and had sent him to college and that he had turned out so well—good looking (her teeth had gone unfilled so that his could be straightened), intelligent (he realized he was too intelligent to be a success), and with a future ahead of him (there was of course no future ahead of him). She excused his gloominess on the grounds that he was still growing up and his radical ideas on his lack of practical experience. She said he didn't yet know a thing about "life," that he hadn't even entered the real world—when already he was as disenchanted with it as a man of fifty.

[32] The further irony of all this was that in spite of her, he had turned out so well. In spite of going to only a third-rate college, he had, on his own initiative, come out with a first-rate education; in spite of growing up dominated by a small mind, he had ended up with a large one; in spite of all her foolish views, he was free of prejudice and unafraid to face facts. Most miraculous of all, instead of being blinded by love for her as she was for him, he had cut himself emotionally free of her and could see her with complete objectivity. He was not dominated by his mother.

[33] The bus stopped with a sudden jerk and shook him from his

meditation. A woman from the back lurched forward with little steps and barely escaped falling in his newspaper as she righted herself. She got off and a large Negro got on. Julian kept his paper lowered to watch. It gave him a certain satisfaction to see injustice in daily operation. It confirmed his view that with a few exceptions there was no one worth knowing within a radius of three hundred miles. The Negro was well dressed and carried a briefcase. He looked around and then sat down on the other end of the seat where the woman with the red and white canvas sandals was sitting. He immediately unfolded a newspaper and obscured himself behind it. Julian's mother's elbow at once prodded insistently into his ribs. "Now you see why I won't ride on these buses by myself," she whispered.

[34] The woman with the red and white canvas sandals had risen at the same time the Negro sat down and had gone further back in the bus and taken the seat of the woman who had got off. His mother leaned forward and cast her an approving look.

[35] Julian rose, crossed the aisle, and sat down in the place of the woman with the canvas sandals. From this position, he looked serenely across at his mother. Her face had turned an angry red. He stared at her, making his eyes the eyes of a stranger. He felt his tension suddenly lift as if he had openly declared war on her.

[36] He would have liked to get in conversation with the Negro and to talk with him about art or politics or any subject that would be above the comprehension of those around them, but the man remained entrenched behind his paper. He was either ignoring the change of seating or had never noticed it. There was no way for Julian to convey his sympathy.

[37] His mother kept her eyes fixed reproachfully on his face. The woman with the protruding teeth was looking at him avidly as if he were a type of monster new to her.

"Do you have a light?" he asked the Negro.

Without looking away from his paper, the man reached in his pocket and handed him a packet of matches.

[38] "Thanks," Julian said. For a moment he held the matches foolishly. A NO SMOKING sign looked down upon him from over the door. This alone would not have deterred him; he had no cigarettes. He had quit smoking some months before because he could not afford it. "Sorry," he muttered and handed back the matches. The Negro lowered the paper and gave him an annoyed look. He took the matches and raised the paper again.

[39] His mother continued to gaze at him but she did not take advantage of his momentary discomfort. Her eyes retained their battered look. Her face seemed to be unnaturally red, as if her blood pressure had risen. Julian allowed no glimmer of sympathy to show on his face. Having got the advantage, he wanted desperately to keep it and carry it through. He would have liked to teach her a lesson that would last

her a while, but there seemed no way to continue the point. The Negro refused to come out from behind his paper.

[40] Julian folded his arms and looked stolidly before him, facing her but as if he did not see her, as if he had ceased to recognize her existence. He visualized a scene in which, the bus having reached their stop, he would remain in his seat and when she said, "Aren't you going to get off?" he would look at her as at a stranger who had rashly addressed him. The corner they got off on was usually deserted, but it was well lighted and it would not hurt her to walk by herself the four blocks to the Y. He decided to wait until the time came and then decide whether or not he would let her get off by herself. He would have to be at the Y at ten to bring her back, but he could leave her wondering if he was going to show up. There was no reason for her to think she could always depend on him.

[41] He retired again into the high-ceilinged room sparsely settled with large pieces of antique furniture. His soul expanded momentarily but then he became aware of his mother across from him and the vision shriveled. He studied her coldly. Her feet in little pumps dangled like a child's and did not quite reach the floor. She was training on him an exaggerated look of reproach. He felt completely detached from her. At that moment he could with pleasure have slapped her as he would have slapped a particularly obnoxious child in his charge.

[42] He began to imagine various unlikely ways by which he could teach her a lesson. He might make friends with some distinguished Negro professor or lawyer and bring him home to spend the evening. He would be entirely justified but her blood pressure would rise to 300. He could not push her to the extent of making her have a stroke, and moreover, he had never been successful at making any Negro friends. He had tried to strike up an acquaintance on the bus with some of the better types, with ones that looked like professors or ministers or lawyers. One morning he had sat down next to a distinguished-looking dark brown man who had answered his questions with a sonorous solemnity but who had turned out to be an undertaker. Another day he had sat down beside a cigar-smoking Negro with a diamond ring on his finger, but after a few stilted pleasantries, the Negro had rung the buzzer and risen, slipping two lottery tickets into Julian's hand as he climbed over him to leave.

[43] He imagined his mother lying desperately ill and his being able to secure only a Negro doctor for her. He toyed with that idea for a few minutes and then dropped it for a momentary vision of himself participating as a sympathizer in a sit-in demonstration. This was possible but he did not linger with it. Instead, he approached the ultimate horror. He brought home a beautiful suspiciously Negroid woman. Prepare yourself, he said. There is nothing you can do about it. This is the woman I've chosen. She's intelligent, dignified, even good, and she's suffered and she hasn't thought it *fun*. Now persecute us, go ahead

and persecute us. Drive her out of here, but remember, you're driving me too. His eyes were narrowed and through the indignation he had generated, he saw his mother across the aisle, purple-faced, shrunken to the dwarf-like proportions of her moral nature, sitting like a mummy beneath the ridiculous banner of her hat.

[44] He was tilted out of his fantasy again as the bus stopped. The door opened with a sucking hiss and out of the dark a large, gaily dressed, sullen-looking colored woman got on with a little boy. The child, who might have been four, had on a short plaid suit and a Tyrolean hat with a blue feather in it. Julian hoped that he would sit down beside him and that the woman would push in beside his mother. He could think of no better arrangement.

[45] As she waited for her tokens, the woman was surveying the seating possibilities—he hoped with the idea of sitting where she was least wanted. There was something familiar-looking about her but Julian could not place what it was. She was a giant of a woman. Her face was set not only to meet opposition but to seek it out. The downward tilt of her large lower lip was like a warning sign: DON'T TAMPER WITH ME. Her bulging figure was encased in a green crepe dress and her feet overflowed in red shoes. She had on a hideous hat. A purple velvet flap came down on one side of it and stood up on the other; the rest of it was green and looked like a cushion with the stuffing out. She carried a mammoth red pocketbook that bulged throughout as if it were stuffed with rocks.

[46] To Julian's disappointment, the little boy climbed up on the empty seat beside his mother. His mother lumped all children, black and white, into the common category, "cute," and she thought little Negroes were on the whole cuter than little white children. She smiled at the little boy as he climbed on the seat.

[47] Meanwhile the woman was bearing down upon the empty seat beside Julian. To his annoyance, she squeezed herself into it. He saw his mother's face change as the woman settled herself next to him and he realized with satisfaction that this was more objectionable to her than it was to him. Her face seemed almost gray and there was a look of dull recognition in her eyes, as if suddenly she had sickened at some awful confrontation. Julian saw that it was because she and the woman had, in a sense, swapped sons. Though his mother would not realize the symbolic significance of this, she would feel it. His amusement showed plainly on his face.

[48] The woman next to him muttered something unintelligible to herself. He was conscious of a kind of bristling next to him, a muted growling like that of an angry cat. He could not see anything but the red pocketbook upright on the bulging green thighs. He visualized the woman as she had stood waiting for her tokens—the ponderous figure, rising from the red shoes upward over the solid hips, the mammoth bosom, the haughty face, to the green and purple hat.

160

His eyes widened.

[49] The vision of the two hats, identical, broke upon him with the radiance of a brilliant sunrise. His face was suddenly lit with joy. He could not believe that Fate had thrust upon his mother such a lesson. He gave a loud chuckle so that she would look at him and see that he saw. She turned her eyes on him slowly. The blue in them seemed to have turned a bruised purple. For a moment he had an uncomfortable sense of her innocence, but it lasted only a second before principle rescued him. Justice entitled him to laugh. His grin hardened until it said to her as plainly as if he were saying aloud: Your punishment exactly fits your pettiness. This should teach you a permanent lesson.

[50] Her eyes shifted to the woman. She seemed unable to bear looking at him and to find the woman preferable. He became conscious again of the bristling presence at his side. The woman was rumbling like a volcano about to become active. His mother's mouth began to twitch slightly at one corner. With a sinking heart, he saw incipient signs of recovery on her face and realized that this was going to strike her suddenly as funny and was going to be no lesson at all. She kept her eyes on the woman and an amused smile came over her face as if the woman were a monkey that had stolen her hat. The little Negro was looking up at her with large fascinated eyes. He had been trying to attract her attention for some time.

"Carver!" the woman said suddenly. "Come heah!"

[51] When he saw that the spotlight was on him at last, Carver drew his feet up and turned himself toward Julian's mother and giggled.

"Carver!" the woman said. "You heah me? Come heah!"

[52] Carver slid down from the seat but remained squatting with his back against the base of it, his head turned slyly around toward Julian's mother, who was smiling at him. The woman reached a hand across the aisle and snatched him to her. He righted himself and hung backwards on her knees, grinning at Julian's mother. "Isn't he cute?" Julian's mother said to the woman with the protruding teeth.

"I reckon he is," the woman said without conviction.

The Negress yanked him upright but he eased out of her grip and shot across the aisle and scrambled, giggling wildly, onto the seat beside his love.

[53] "I think he likes me," Julian's mother said, and smiled at the woman. It was the smile she used when she was being particularly gracious to an inferior. Julian saw everything lost. The lesson had rolled off her like rain on a roof.

The woman stood up and yanked the little boy off the seat as if she were snatching him from contagion. Julian could feel the rage in her at having no weapon like his mother's smile. She gave the child a sharp slap across his leg. He howled once and then thrust his head into her stomach and kicked his feet against her shins. "Be-have," she said vehemently.

[54] The bus stopped and the Negro who had been reading the news-paper got off. The woman moved over and set the little boy down with a thump between herself and Julian. She held him firmly by the knee. In a moment he put his hands in front of his face and peeped at Julian's mother through his fingers.

"I see yooooooooo!" she said and put her hand in front of her face and peeped at him.

[55] The woman slapped his hand down. "Quit yo' foolishness," she said, "before I knock the living Jesus out of you!"

Julian was thankful that the next stop was theirs. He reached up and pulled the cord. The woman reached up and pulled it at the same time. Oh my God, he thought. He had the terrible intuition that when they got off the bus together, his mother would open her purse and give the little boy a nickel. The gesture would be as natural to her as breath-ing. The bus stopped and the woman got up and lunged to the front, dragging the child, who wished to stay on, after her. Julian and his mother got up and followed. As they neared the door, Julian tried to relieve her of her pocketbook.

"No," she murmured, "I want to give the little boy a nickel."

"No!" Julian hissed. "No!"

[56] She smiled down at the child and opened her bag. The bus door opened and the woman picked him up by the arm and descended with him, hanging at her hip. Once in the street she set him down and shook him.

Julian's mother had to close her purse while she got down the bus step but as soon as her feet were on the ground, she opened it again and began to rummage inside. "I can't find but a penny," she whis-pered, "but it looks like a new one."

[57] "Don't do it!" Julian said fiercely between his teeth. There was a streetlight on the corner and she hurried to get under it so that she could better see into her pocketbook. The woman was heading off rapidly down the street with the child still hanging backward on her hand.

[58] "Oh little boy!" Julian's mother called and took a few quick steps and caught up with them just beyond the lamp-post. "Here's a bright new penny for you," and she held out the coin, which shone bronze in the dim light.

[59] The huge woman turned and for a moment stood, her shoulders lifted and her face frozen with frustrated rage, and stared at Julian's mother. Then all at once she seemed to explode like a piece of ma-chinery that had been given one ounce of pressure too much. Julian saw the black fist swing out with the red pocketbook. He shut his eyes and cringed as he heard the woman shout, "He don't take nobody's pennies!" When he opened his eyes, the woman was disappearing down the street with the little boy staring wide-eyed over her shoulder. Julian's mother was sitting on the sidewalk.

"I told you not to do that," Julian said angrily. "I told you not to do that!"

[60] He stood over her for a minute, gritting his teeth. Her legs were stretched out in front of her and her hat was on her lap. He squatted down and looked her in the face. It was totally expressionless. "You got exactly what you deserved," he said. "Now get up."

[61] He picked up her pocketbook and put what had fallen out back in it. He picked the hat up off her lap. The penny caught his eye on the sidewalk and he picked that up and let it drop before her eyes into the purse. Then he stood up and leaned over and held his hands out to pull her up. She remained immobile. He sighed. Rising above them on either side were black apartment buildings, marked with irregular rectangles of light. At the end of the block a man came out of a door and walked off in the opposite direction. "All right," he said, "suppose somebody happens by and wants to know why you're sitting on the sidewalk?"

[62] She took the hand and, breathing hard, pulled heavily up on it and then stood for a moment, swaying slightly as if the spots of light in the darkness were circling around her. Her eyes, shadowed and confused, finally settled on his face. He did not try to conceal his irritation. "I hope this teaches you a lesson," he said. She leaned forward and her eyes raked his face. She seemed trying to determine his identity. Then, as if she found nothing familiar about him, she started off with a headlong movement in the wrong direction.

"Aren't you going on to the Y?" he asked.

"Home," she muttered.

"Well, are we walking?"

[63] For answer she kept going. Julian followed along, his hands behind him. He saw no reason to let the lesson she had had go without backing it up with an explanation of its meaning. She might as well be made to understand what had happened to her. "Don't think that was just an uppity Negro woman," he said. "That was the whole colored race which will no longer take your condescending pennies. That was your black double. She can wear the same hat as you, and to be sure," he added gratuitously (because he thought it was funny), "it looked better on her than it did on you. What all this means," he said, "is that the old world is gone. The old manners are obsolete and your graciousness is not worth a damn." He thought bitterly of the house that had been lost for him. "You aren't who you think you are," he said.

[64] She continued to plow ahead, paying no attention to him. Her hair had come undone on one side. She dropped her pocketbook and took no notice. He stooped and picked it up and handed it to her but she did not take it.

[65] "You needn't act as if the world had come to an end," he said, "because it hasn't. From now on you've got to live in a new world and face a few realities for a change. Buck up," he said, "it won't kill you."

She was breathing fast.

"Let's wait on the bus," he said.

"Home," she said thickly.

[66] "I hate to see you behave like this," he said. "Just like a child. I should be able to expect more of you." He decided to stop where he was and make her stop and wait for a bus. "I'm not going any farther," he said, stopping. "We're going on the bus."

[67] She continued to go on as if she had not heard him. He took a few steps and caught her arm and stopped her. He looked into her face and caught his breath. He was looking into a face he had never seen before. "Tell Grandpa to come get me," she said.

He stared, stricken.

"Tell Caroline to come get me," she said.

[68] Stunned, he let her go and she lurched forward again, walking as if one leg were shorter than the other. A tide of darkness seemed to be sweeping her from him. "Mother!" he cried. "Darling, sweetheart, wait!" Crumpling, she fell to the pavement. He dashed forward and fell at her side, crying, "Mamma, Mamma!" He turned her over. Her face was fiercely distorted. One eye, large and staring, moved slightly to the left as if it had become unmoored. The other remained fixed on him, raked his face again, found nothing and closed.

[69] "Wait here, wait here!" he cried and jumped up and began to run for help toward a cluster of lights he saw in the distance ahead of him. "Help, help!" he shouted, but his voice was thin, scarcely a thread of sound. The lights drifted farther away the faster he ran and his feet moved numbly as if they carried him nowhere. The tide of darkness seemed to sweep him back to her, postponing from moment to moment his entry into the world of guilt and sorrow.

This is an extremely complex story, not only in its ironic under-cuttings but in its affirmations. No reading of it can be considered adequate unless it somehow relates the curious title to the various attempts to "rise" and to the failures to "converge." In the web of inference that we must create to see the story whole, our running translation of Julian's judgments into alternative judgments is only one strand. But once we have discerned that strand clearly, the rest of the story gives few difficulties.

Since Julian's is the only mind offering us opinions (except for a few observations and metaphors from the narrator, most notably the final sentence), we must sooner or later decide how far we can trust him. It is not hard to see that he is unreliable about many things. "He never spoke of it without contempt or thought of it without longing" (par. 19)—what kind of man is it, we ask, who always belies his true feelings? His life is full of such contradictions, showing that in his own

164

way he is as far out of touch with reality as he takes his mother to be. His radical self-deception is perhaps clearest in the long fantasy that begins when he "withdraws into the inner compartment of his mind where he spent most of his time" (29). No one could misread his own character more thoroughly than Julian does in thinking that he has "turned out so well" (32), that he has a "first rate education," that he has a "large" mind, that he is "free of prejudice and unafraid to face facts" (32)—remember, this is the boy who "did not like to consider all she did for him" (1) and who can take pride in having "cut himself emotionally free of her" (32). The closer we look at the disharmonies among his various opinions and actions, the more vigorously we must work in reconstructing the terrible lost young man we see behind his self-defensive rhetoric. His childish efforts to hurt his mother begin in a comic light, as he poses like a martyr (2) and does everything he possibly can to spoil her one pleasant time of the week (e.g., 21–22). But the comedy slowly gives place to pathos and horror as he runs over in his mind the possible tortures he might subject her to (42, 43), then enjoys her humiliation about the duplicate hat (49), and finally—so wrapped up in his own petty bitterness and futility that he cannot see what is in front of his eyes—shouts petty insults at the stricken woman. "You aren't who you think you are" (63), he says, summarizing himself as much as his mother. "You've got to live in a new world and face a few realities for a change. Buck up, it won't kill you" (65). It *is* killing her, and *he* is the one who must now begin to "face a few realities for a change."

These disharmonies are simple and clear. But the reconstruction of what "the realities" are—of what Julian must face—is not so easy. It is obviously not to be found in the "unreal," absurdly "innocent" world of the class-bound mother, nor in the equally unreal and absurd but vicious world of Julian. One kind of unmistakable reality is found in the irreducible, often harsh details of the life that Julian and his mother encounter but cannot see because of the abstractions that blur their vision. The mother does not see real "Negroes," for example, only the stereotypes that her childhood has provided her with (e.g., 17). But Julian does not see real people either; instead he sees only the stereotypes that his liberal opinions dictate (e.g., 36). Similarly, neither of them can see the other: Julian cannot see his mother for what she is; she cannot see what a miserable failure she has helped to create in him.

Our question then becomes: is there some ordering of values that for this story constitutes an alternative reality, one that in a sense judges everything the characters do? Our knowledge that Flannery O'Connor was known as a devout Catholic, or even that she herself talked about her stories in religious terms can only alert us to one possible direction of interpretation. She might, after all, write one story that was entirely different from the others; for all I know, independently of my reading, she could have written this one before being converted, or after losing her faith. Even the most detailed knowledge about the author's life and statements of purpose can only alert me to certain possibilities; I must finally ask what kinds of clues the story itself provides to aid in the task of reconstructing a world of values that contrast with Julian's inanities.

The curious title is itself a kind of warning that seems to be spoken, as it were, in a special tone of voice. It simply does not harmonize easily with most of the surface, and indeed at first hardly makes sense at all. Does everything that "rises" in the story "converge"? Hardly. The black characters are "rising" (17), but in spite of the liberal platitudes of Julian, there is no sign in the story that in their rising they will converge with the whites or with each other; one must thus ask whether or in what limited sense they are rising at all. Julian's liberal abstractions lead him to expect all Negroes to want his sympathy and interest, and to conform to his stereotyped demand that they "rise" to "talk on subjects that would be *above* the comprehension of those around him" (36). But they insist on dwelling in a totally inaccessible world.

Julian has been "rising," too, as he obtains what he likes to think was a "first-class education." But his sense of elevation has, obviously, separated him not only from his mother but from all of his roots, without providing him with any other allegiances that could possibly support the claim of the title. What, then, can the title mean? It does not help us much to learn that it comes from the works of Teilhard de Chardin, the Catholic priest whose scientific and theological speculations earned him the accusation of heresy.

Is there any genuine change in the story that could be considered a "rising"? There is one, indeed, if we take seriously the change in Julian produced by the catastrophe. Julian is not just nasty and petty throughout the story; he is totally absorbed in his own ego. In contrast to his mother, who is "innocent," he is corrupt. Her desire is not to do ill in the world, but good, and only the limitations of what Julian calls her "fantasy world" betray her. But Julian, as we discover him behind his rationalizations, is actually malevolent, totally incapable of "converging" with the interests of any other person. His thoughts run constantly on his hatred of the world and his desire to "justify" himself (42, 49) in ways that he knows will hurt his mother deeply. "He would be entirely justified [in bringing home a Negro wife] but her blood

166

Ironic Portraits

pressure would rise to 300. He could not push her to the extent of making her have a stroke, and moreover, he had never been successful at making any Negro friends."

Throughout his absurd but vicious fantasies there thus run clues that prepare us for his discovery at the end. "For a moment he had an uncomfortable sense of her *innocence,* but it lasted only a second before *principle* rescued him. *Justice* entitled him to laugh" (49) Dimly aware of her "innocence," passionately devoted to proving his own "principles" and obtaining "justice," he can be touched only by the greatest of disasters. Having never once been genuinely touched by any trouble, having in fact used his mother and her innocence as a shield against knowledge of himself, he is at last "stricken," "stunned." The change in him is as startling as the physical change produced in her by the stroke which he has helped to induce: "Darling, sweetheart, wait!" He is "crumpled," crushed into letting his defenses down and trying, too late, to call to his mother in love.

It would probably be a mistake to see anything strongly affirmative in this final dropping of all his egotistical defenses and crying "Mamma, mamma." He has not risen very far, but as he watches her destruction, falls at her side, and then runs for help, there has been, at last, a "convergence," a meeting of two human wills, that *might* presage his genuine "entry into the world of guilt and sorrow." For the Julian we have known throughout the story to experience either genuine guilt or sorrow would be a "rise" indeed, a rise based on the final convergence. The honest nightmare of his nothingness moving into "nowhere" in the final paragraph is thus a great improvement—in the light of this view of reality we now share with the implied author—over the "mental bubble" in which he established himself, where "he was safe from any kind of penetration from without" (29). In his bubble he had been able to "see her with absolute clarity," or so he thought. Now, at the end, his bubble has been penetrated; he is swept by a "tide of darkness," and we are led to feel that he is for the first time in a position from which some sort of genuine human life is conceivable.

Whether this interpretation is sound or not, it certainly is never stated. Except for the ending, most of the words report Julian's misguided thoughts without open correction, and they must consequently be reconstructed. But they are not translated into a message.

There is perhaps no absolute need to go further than this. Readers of many different faiths and anti-faiths can presumably participate in this story of punishment and discovery, without pushing toward any special meaning for words like sin (21), innocence (4, 49, etc.), faith (10), realities (65), guilt and sorrow (69). But those of us who have read many of Flannery O'Connor's stories and studied her life will be unable to resist seeing Julian's final problematic redemption as presented in a religious light, even a specifically Roman Catholic light. Once the story is reread from this point of view, many additional ironies accumulate, ranging from Julian's name and his saintly posings at the beginning to the gratuitousness of grace at the end. But Flannery O'-Connor was eager to write stories that were not mere allegories; as she intended, this story can be experienced by anyone who catches the essential contrast among the three systems of norms, Julian's, his mother's, and the cluster of traditional, conventional values we share with the author. Though it may seem thinner to those for whom Julian's self-absorption and cruelty are judged in secular terms than for a Catholic who sees him as in mortal sin, the structure of experience will be the same for both: everyone will be forced to reject all or most of what the words seem to say.[8] At every point we must decide on one out of many possible reconstructions, on the basis of a set of unshakable but silent beliefs that we are expected to share (however fleetingly) with the author. No one who fails to discern and feel some sympathy for these

---

8. When the story was published in the collection by the same name (New York, 1965), Irving Howe reviewed it (*New York Review of Books,* 30 September 1965, pp. 16–17) in terms that to me showed a failure to perceive the depths of irony the story offers. "Reading the title story, one quickly begins to see the end toward which it moves and indeed must move. The climax is then realized effectively enough—except for the serious flaw that it is a climax which has already been anticipated a number of pages earlier, where it seems already present, visible and complete, in the preparatory action. One doesn't, to be sure, know that the Negro woman will strike the white woman; but more important, one does know that some kind of ironic reversal will occur in the relationship between mother and son. There is pleasure to be had in watching Miss O'Connor work it all out, but no surprise, for there has been no significant turning upon the premises from which the action has emerged." Howe then compares the story unfavorably with some of his favorites, mainly by other authors, which, in contrast, build to a "moment of revelation" "when the unexpected happens, a perception, an insight, a confrontation which may not be in accord with the writer's original intention and may not be strictly required by the logic of the action, but which nevertheless caps the entire story." This seems to me to describe precisely—except perhaps for the note about the author's lack of control—the way grace operates at the end of "Everything That Rises Must Converge." It has *not,* in naturalistic terms, been fully prepared for by the story, and it would thus be objected to by many critics sharing Howe's naturalistic biases. But if I am right he has not even been able to see how the irony works. It goes, as he says of the story "Revelation," which he admires, "beyond the schemes of irony"—beyond, that is, his notion of the limited ironies of generational conflict, and moves to the religious ironies that violate Howe's basic beliefs (see, for further evidence, his curious reduction of "Revelation," in his final paragraph, to "a vision of God's ingratitude").

beliefs—only a few of them specifically Roman Catholic—is likely to make very much of the story.

For the reader who does see behind Julian's absurd and egotistical words, the energy devoted to the act of seeing will of course increase the emotional effect and thus his estimate of the story's worth. This will not necessarily lead him to agree with me that it is a first-class story. But if he likes it at all, the force of his liking will have been strengthened by the active engagement with the ironies.

## CUSTOM-BUILT WORLDS

By comparison with many characters in modern literature Flannery O'Connor's sinners stand in a relatively bright light. Many modern authors have, for a variety of reasons, created clashes of character and secret value that are immeasurably more difficult to reconstruct. Some authors whom we shall come to shortly would of course repudiate the very notion of trying to separate out the points on which they stand *with* their characters and the points on which they stand above them. But other authors write from equally firm though highly personal or idiosyncratic standpoints; their characters thus present more elusive mixtures of praise and blame, of sympathy and irony, and of stable ironies and indecipherables. In doing so their works contribute, for good or ill, to the fantastic explosion of controversies about readings that has occurred in the last few decades. I have written at length in *The Rhetoric of Fiction* about what this explosion has meant for readers of fiction, and I shall therefore be very brief about it here, simply pausing long enough to make clear that the two obvious pitfalls in reading irony—not going far enough and going too far—are especially threatening when the mixtures of praise and blame are intricate, when the "distances" are small, when the clues are subtle, and especially when the unexpressed norms are, in contrast to Flannery O'Connor's, exploratory or private. I should also make clear, since there has been so much misunderstanding of my "moralizing" about such matters, that I do not see any necessary connection between moral clarity or conventionality and literary quality. Obscurity can contribute to the badness of some works, just as clarity can betray the inanities of others.

Wright Morris's *Love Among the Cannibals* (1957) begins like this:

> This chick, with her sun-tan oil, her beach towel, her rubber volleyball, and her radio, came along the beach at the edge of the water where the sand was firm. Soft sand shortens the legs and reduces their charms, as you may know. This one pitched her camp where the sand was dry, slipped on one of these caps with

169

the simulated hair, smoked her cigarette, then went in for a dip. Nothing particular, just a run-of-the-mill sort of chick. She was out beyond the surf when I noticed that the tide was dampening her towel. I got up and dragged it back alongside our own. When she came out of the water I explained what had happened and she thanked me without being coy. She dried her hair and accepted one of our cigarettes. We got to talking, the way you do, and since everyone in California is from somewhere else it gives you something, at the start, to talk about. She was from Dubuque. The one in Iowa. Married a boy from Port Chester during the war. That didn't pan out, so she had come to California on a scholarship good for fifty bucks. All she had to do was earn her own living and raise the other three hundred twenty-five. She lived with two other chicks at the school and they all worked as waitresses at the same Wilshire drive-in. They all liked California, but they thought the people were cold. Her childhood had not been too happy and her mother often complained that her father was too small for a satisfactory sexual partner. Her mother didn't use those words, of course, but that was what she meant. If her father had not been so *conventional* it might have worked out. Why were men so perverse they always had to be on *top*?

That's what she said. She said why are men so perverse. Then she asked me if I had any ideas, and I had a few ideas but what I said was that the *conventional* sort of thing, with maybe a million years behind it, had a lot to recommend it. How do you know what's conventional *now,* she said, was conventional *then*? Her shift at the drive-in began before I had an answer to that.

I'd never seen her before. I'll probably never see her again. She was twenty-two or -three, I suppose, and I'll be forty-one the ninth of September, having lived and loved more or less conventionally. Things can change in twenty years. More, I mean, than I have changed myself. When I was her age I didn't know beans. She knows too much.

It is not surprising that many readers have had trouble recognizing that this narrator does not speak unequivocally for the author. Surely he does so when he says, "She knows too much." We are with him in *his* ironies about the girl's unconscious inversion of the word "perverse," and we are with him in his ironic observations on the California scene. But where are we when he goes on to say, "I don't mean to be ironic. California is that way naturally. It's hard to do malice to California. . . ." His flippant "corny" wit and cynical vision, later undermined when he gets involved with a rootless, conventionless blond, would be intolerable if the book did not impose at almost every point an ironic knowledge that this is not Wright Morris's own true voice at all—this is his presentation of the least objectionable member of a contemptible world; he is one of the "Cannibals," less ignorant, more self-aware than the others, but still so different from Wright Morris that our ironic judgment must operate upon him at almost every stroke. I know this partly by knowing Wright Morris's other works, partly by inferring it in this work, but my inferences are rarely as secure as they often are in reading O'Connor. In fact, I can be certain that I sometimes judge when judgment is not intended, sometimes fail to judge when Morris expects me to, and sometimes judge on the wrong axis: Morris may intend undercuttings that many readers will overlook, yet many a reader may make moral and aesthetic judgments against Morris that he in fact intends to be made against the narrator.

In short, such works call for a reconstruction more difficult, if not more delicate, than any I have before described. And they are of course not confined to fiction. In viewing drama we have long since reveled in invitations to flounder, while knowing that simply to flounder will be to misinterpret: from Pirandello and Brecht, those old-fashioned affirmers of undermining, through Albee and Ionesco and even Beckett, the verdict "ambiguous" can account for only a fraction of our successful reconstructions of the plays. In poetry, extensions of the dramatic monologue into further reaches of subtle ironic distance have left sophisticated readers assuming that whatever speaker they encounter is not simply the author; but they all know that he will not be *not* simply the author either. From T. S. Eliot's *The Waste Land*—the interpretation of which is still wildly controversial, though I would have you believe that *I* know how to read it—through, say, Robert Lowell's "To Speak of the Woe That Is in Marriage"—a poem that A. L. French and I both find opaque,[9]—readers have been asked to decipher mixtures of distance and sympathy that resist even those who specialize in the life and work of any one author. Stable irony always depends on the sharing of norms with an implied but covert author, and yet many modern authors, themselves not at all confused about at least some values underlying their ironies, have encouraged the notion that sharing values doesn't matter.

The least important damage done by the resulting "obscurity" is the most often lamented: the particular misunderstandings that result. Misunderstanding in itself does not matter very much, in doses small enough and local enough to allow for antidotes. We have all misunderstood each other from the beginning of time, and then used our misunderstanding as roads to occasional understanding and then further

9. "Purposive Imitation," pp. 128–30.

misunderstanding. I am especially unconcerned about what some critics seem to think is the only problem of obscurity—the impossibility of making out the meaning in some poems that are *deliberately* ambiguous or obscure. Let them be. Enjoy their obscurity. The serious loss comes when readers, barraged with critical talk hailing the discovery of ambiguities as a major achievement, learn to live with blurred senses and dulled attention, and deprive themselves of the delights of precise and subtle communication that skillful stable ironists provide. As Kierkegaard says, talking of the boredom that results not only in literature but in the whole of life when everything—history, literature, metaphysics—is ironized: "Irony [pushed to its ultimate power] is free, to be sure, free from all the cares of actuality, but free from its joys as well, free from its blessings. For if it has nothing higher than itself, it may receive no blessing, for it is ever the lesser that is blessed of a greater. This is the freedom for which irony longs."[10]

10. *The Concept of Irony,* p. 296.

I believe the danger which I am indicating to be a perfectly real one, however fantastic it may sound—the danger, I mean, that we have lost, or are losing, the power to take ridicule seriously. That our habituation to humorous reading has inoculated our systems against the beneficent poison of satire. Unhappy the Juvenal whom Rome greets with amusement; unhappier still the Rome, that can be amused by a Juvenal!

—Ronald Knox

After Trout became famous, of course, one of the biggest mysteries about him was whether he was kidding or not. He told one persistent questioner that he always crossed his fingers when he was kidding.

"And please note," he went on, "that when I gave you that priceless piece of information, my fingers were crossed."

And so on.

He was a pain in the neck in a lot of ways.

—Kurt Vonnegut, Jr., Breakfast of Champions

Happy who in his verse can gently steer,
From grave to light; from pleasant to severe.

—Dryden

# SIX | The Ironist's Voice

In the preceding two chapters I have been probing a variety of ways in which ironic authors make it possible for us to know when to stop reconstructing and settle comfortably, as it were, into our new location. In every case we rely both on an intuition of a genre and on a picture of the author, sometimes as he is implied in the work, sometimes as we know or think we know about his likely intentions from our other experience. In reading a satire like "A Modest Proposal," what enabled us to make our way confidently through potentially baffling shifts of tone and argument was an emerging picture, an intended form, implying a Swift whose values could make sense out of what otherwise was incoherent. In reading poems and stories we reconstructed portraits or events from unreliable voices, and we could do so only because clear artistic intentions emerged that were backed up by the affidavits provided silently by a coherent view of the implied author: the O'Connor whose secret views could make imaginative sense out of Julian's actions and words, the Browning whose amusement we confidently shared behind his monk's back.

In every case, we stopped when we had arrived at what we took as the true end of the discourse. But everyone who has read much modern literature knows that clear patternings of ends and means are often not to be found. Even in the works I have selected to illustrate a functional, stable irony, I have often felt as if I were holding back a very frisky pony, that in fact the heady, threatening pleasures of irony were already trying to drag me ahead of my story—just as they ran away with literary history from the Romantic period on. Like the sublime, which Longinus and others admired regardless of specific formal demands of differing literary kinds, irony has seemed to many to have a life of its own; whenever critics with an idealist bent have dealt with it they have turned it into a very aggressive Idea indeed. Stable ironies, savored, demand more stable ironies; the stabilities soon crumble, and we find ourselves talking about "the ironic man," "the ironic universe," "the ironic mode," "the mythos of irony," and "irony, the master trope."

The remarkable story of how "irony" took over so much of the modern literary world would be out of place here.[1] Nor can I attempt

1. It is told well by Muecke in the final chapters of *The Compass of Irony,* building on Knox's detailed reconstruction of the first stages in *The Word "Irony" and Its Context: 1500–1755.*

175

justice to the psychological and moral issues that are raised when irony becomes a way of life and a norm for literature, though I shall touch on them through the remaining chapters. But even someone attempting only a rhetoric of irony—not a psychology or sociology or metaphysics or ethics of irony—cannot refuse to move onto the treacherous terrain that stretches before us. The more difficult ironies we are moving toward manage in curious ways to get themselves understood, or at least enjoyed, somehow, sometimes, and insofar as they do, they become a part of our subject.

But there are, as we have begun to see, many stages between the clear and simple stabilities of chapters 1 to 3 and the uncharted domains of Samuel Beckett and Ionesco. Perhaps the last outpost this side of the open frontier is provided by what might be called "The Ironist's Voice as Context."

As soon as an ironic voice has been used to any extent in any work of any kind, readers inevitably begin to take interest and pleasure in that voice—in the tasks it assigns and the qualities it provides; it thus becomes part of whatever is seen as the controlling context. I am not thinking here of the mocked voices that the ironist may take up for a time—the various unreliable narrators that may be given a single poem or a part of a novel or play to tell. Rather I am thinking of the reliable but ironic authors who convince us that they are pretty much the real man or woman speaking to us: the Henry Fielding, the Laurence Sterne, the Jane Austen, the George Eliot, the Max Beerbohm, the Mark Twain, the E. M. Forster, the Henry James, the Emily Dickinson, the W. H. Auden who stand behind each ironic stroke as warrantors of the continuing validity of what we are about. Once we have read a few pages by any of these authors we have experienced so many stable ironies that the appetite for more of them becomes essential to whatever effects the works intend. And the appeal is of course not confined to individual works; it can lead us on to work after work by the same author, even when we know that we have already exhausted his best and must plow through inferior stuff of other kinds just to get more of that *voice*.

## OTHER TIMBRES: METAPHOR ONCE AGAIN

This kind of supra-formal appetite—the passion for a style or tone—is by no means confined to ironists. But in a time when most good artists have been ironists, other sustained timbres have been harder to hear.

The main rival is of course rich-flowing metaphor, the sort of miraculous gift we find in Proust and Faulkner and Dylan Thomas, and of course in most traditional lyric poets. The history of metaphor would in fact make an interesting parallel with that of irony, since metaphor also has ranged from a minute oratorical device, one among many, to an imperialistic world conqueror. Traditionally, the capacity to make original metaphors was generally given much higher status than the ability to use irony; in Aristotle, for example, it is the most important single gift of the poet. But like irony, the device was not content until it had become a concept, an Idea. And with romanticism, it began to expand its domain, until it finally became for some the whole of the poetic art. As Wallace Stevens wrote, echoing Mallarmé, who in turn was simply extending romantic commonplaces, "Reality is a cliché from which we escape by metaphor. It is only *au pays de la métaphore qu'on est poète*" (from *Adagia*). Stevens and others have often talked as if the whole poem were a metaphor (sometimes a "symbol") and as if its *raison d'être* were to *be* metaphoric.

We thus have two curiously parallel projects of expansion in modern times. Two devices of indirection that once kept their place in a classically defined order, performing metaphoric or ironic functions in genres with larger or at least different demands, have expanded themselves—in Symbolism and what might be called Ironism—to fill the whole world of the maker. "The Metaphor" and "the Irony" have thus been proclaimed as genres in their own right.

Saving for later our discussion of whether there is in fact any such literary genre as "the irony," it is important to note a crucial difference between the two imperialisms. As we saw in chapter 1, metaphor is essentially "additive"; nothing of importance in "the words themselves" need be discarded en route to understanding. The consequence is that when metaphor is made into the central poetic category, no paradox results. The essential metaphoric act is a putting together, a synthesis of what had not been unified before; when larger and larger elements are thus unified, when finally the universe itself is seen as one grand Metaphor for Itself, there is no problem in claiming, like Coleridge, that it is all held together by the Great Imaginer himself.

But when irony refuses to keep in place, when it becomes increasingly like an end in itself, paradox is inescapable. And the paradox is not just of that happy rich kind which the ironist originally seeks—the perception of wheels within wheels, the vertiginous but finally delightful discovery of depths below depths; it is a paradox that can weaken and finally destroy all artistic effect, including the perception of paradox itself. Since irony is essentially "subtractive," it always discounts something, and once it is turned into a spirit or concept and released upon the world, it becomes a total irony that must discount itself, leaving . . . Nothing.

We cannot entirely dodge the metaphysical implications of these two uncaged devourers, but our main interest is still in how they contrast rhetorically. They somehow have become representative of two grand fundamental human passions (or perhaps one should use the current jargon and call them structures): the conviction that "there is more here than meets the eye" and the suspicion that there is less. Unbridled metaphor clearly feeds one of these, and when it reaches its highest successes it can produce an expansiveness of soul that Longinus knew as the sublime. But irony in a curious way feeds both while in a sense pretending to feed only the second. The shrewd skeptic that we all learn to become as we meet life's con-men is delighted to find, behind the presented words, a fellow skeptic, demolishing illusions; and *then*—marvel of marvels—that skeptic turns out to be a great dreamer, a man of passion who can multiply implications and proclaim mysteries: here is a soul-mate indeed. It is not hard to forgive the ultimate paradox in the position of such a companion—are we not all caught in the same lugubrious undertow that has led him to his infinite negations?

It is not surprising, then, that the ironic voice has come to rival and for some to surpass the metaphoric. Even when the ironist finally ends in Nothingness, he has been doing more for us along the way than the relatively uncomplex Symbolist. Or so it has seemed to many. To me the metaphoric gift must be said to be supreme, if we persist in talking in such global terms. But there can be no denying that in modern times more authors have established themselves in our consciousness through ironic voices than through metaphoric richness. Even our masters of metaphor—Yeats, Auden, Eliot, Stevens, Roethke—tend to qualify their strongest affirmations with a wry twist of irony.[2]

But for now I must draw back from such speculations and look once again at that opposite kind of qualifying—the steady clarities that some ironists still provide as substrata to their teasings.

It will be useful now to look at two of the great, relatively secure voices, as a summary of what we have done so far and as an illustration of how pervasive stable irony provides a further kind of context telling us when to stop.

2. For a fine brief study of how Auden makes his ironies contribute to his special kind of modern "sublimity," see Robert Roth, "The Sophistication of W. H. Auden: A Sketch in Longinian Method," *Modern Philology* 48 (1950–51): 193–204.

## FIELDING

Let us trace first the lightning changes of tone through a passage from the beginning of *Tom Jones,* one of the greatest and most persistently ironic of all novels.[3]

### A short description of Squire Allworthy, and a fuller account of Miss Bridget Allworthy, his sister

[1]  In that part of the western division of this kingdom which is commonly called Somersetshire, there lately lived and perhaps lives still, a gentleman whose name was Allworthy, and who might well be called the favourite of both Nature and Fortune; for both of these seem to have contended which should bless and enrich him most. In this contention Nature may seem to some to have come off victorious, as she bestowed on him many gifts, while Fortune had only one gift in her power; but in pouring forth this, she was so very profuse, that others perhaps may think this single endowment to have been more than equivalent to all the various blessings which he enjoyed from Nature. From the former of these he derived an agreeable person, a sound constitution, a sane understanding, and a benevolent heart; by the latter, he was decreed to the inheritance of one of the largest estates in the county.

[2]  This gentleman had in his youth married a very worthy and beautiful woman, of whom he had been extremely fond: by her he had three children, all of whom died in their infancy. [a] He had likewise had the misfortune of burying this beloved wife herself, about five years before the time in which this history chooses to set out. [b] This loss, however great, he bore like a man of sense and constancy, though it must be confessed he would often talk a little whimsically on this head; for he sometimes said he looked on himself as still married, and considered his wife as only gone a little before him, a journey which he should most certainly, sooner or later, take after her; and that he had not the least doubt of meeting her again in a place where he should

---

3. One persistent fashion denies that works like Fielding's are ironic, because they are morally clear. See Andrew H. Wright, *Jane Austen's Novels* (London, 1961 reprint), pp. 29–30. But see chap. 5, n. 3, above. Clearly this notion, often put as a distinction between irony, which must be ambiguous, and satire, which is making a clear point, depends entirely on one's definition. If "the ironist has nothing to prove," if he must play "with those very epistemological possibilities that eat away proof" (as Claudette Kemper puts the same case), then of course Fielding is not an ironist ("Irony Anew, with Occasional Reference to Byron and Browning," *Studies in English Literature* 7 [1967]: 708). There is no point in quarreling about definitions, so long as we remember that in almost all discussions of "irony" and "the ironist" we must figure out what silent modifiers, like stable or satiric or ambiguous or metaphysical, are implied.

never part with her more—sentiments for which his sense was arraigned by one part of his neighbours, his religion by a second, and his sincerity by a third [c].

[3]   He now lived, for the most part, retired in the country, with one sister, for whom he had a very tender affection. [a] This lady was now somewhat past the age of thirty, an era at which, in the opinion of the malicious, the title of old maid may with no impropriety be assumed. She was of that species of women whom you commend rather for good qualities than beauty, and who are generally called, by their own sex, very good sort of women—as good a sort of woman, madam, as you wish to know. Indeed, she was so far from regretting want of beauty, that she never mentioned that perfection, if it can be called one, without contempt; and would often thank God she was not as handsome as Miss Such-a-one, whom perhaps beauty had led into errors, which she might have otherwise avoided. [b] Miss Bridget Allworthy (for that was the name of this lady) very rightly conceived the charms of person in a woman to be no better than snares for herself, as well as for others; and yet so discreet was she in her conduct, that her prudence was as much on the guard as if she had all the snares to apprehend which were ever laid for her whole sex. Indeed, I have observed, though it may seem unaccountable to the reader, that this guard of prudence, like the Trained Bands, is always readiest to go on duty where there is the least danger. [c] It often basely and cowardly deserts those paragons for whom the men are all wishing, sighing, dying, and spreading every net in their power; and constantly attends at the heels of that higher order of women for whom the other sex have a more distant and awful respect, and whom (from despair, I suppose, of success) they never venture to attack.

[4]   Reader, I think proper, before we proceed any farther together, to acquaint thee that I intend to digress, through this whole history, as often as I see occasion, of which I am myself a better judge than any pitiful critic whatever; and here I must desire all those critics to mind their own business, and not to intermeddle with affairs or works which no ways concern them; for till they produce the authority by which they are constituted judges, I shall not plead to their jurisdiction.

This famous opening is straightforward and trustworthy, though packed with irony. It is clear to all that the narrator is not being ironic when he says that Allworthy was blessed by both Nature and Fortune; we learn later, if we are not already sure, that in calling him All*worthy,* the narrator is not really jesting, though Allworthy does have a few intellectual faults. But what does the last part of the first paragraph say? Most obviously it continues to give us the plain facts; we do not question for a moment that Allworthy is handsome, healthy, sensible, good, and rich. But it also manages to incorporate an ironic slap at the "others" who think that the last of Allworthy's gifts, wealth, is "more than equivalent to all the others." The reader who gets nothing more from the paragraph than the literal introduction of Allworthy's gifts of Nature and Fortune will never discover his mistake, as he might if the praise for Allworthy were also ironic; he can read on with the essential facts in hand. But he will have missed most of the richness of the paragraph, depending as it does on Fielding's ability to be ironic and straightforward almost at the same instant. The narrator does not think money more important than goodness. "Others perhaps may," but we soon learn that to read this novel properly we must agree with Fielding —that is, with the version of himself he offers here, the implied author —and not with the "others."[4]

Fielding immediately returns (par. 2) to literal praise of the "very worthy and beautiful woman," the "beloved wife" who died five years before the story begins. We accept these words of praise without question. But if so, how do we then recognize that the last half of the paragraph is again ironic? The narrator himself "says" that Allworthy's religious belief in the hereafter is "whimsical." Yet we are expected to recognize that this is a momentary pretense, and that the three kinds of neighbors (*c*), who accuse Allworthy of credulity, superstition, and hypocrisy, are the true butts of the irony. How is it that we can make such shifts with confidence?

Before trying to answer, it will be useful to move on through the passage, describing other shifts of tone. We come next to a paragraph (3) that, except for the first sentence, is entirely ironic. "Somewhat past the age of thirty"? We must suspect that she is *far* past it; an old maid not just "in the opinion of the malicious" but in the narrator's opinion

4. It is sometimes useful to consider even the "Fielding" whom we trust as to some degree a mask, in contrast with the "real Fielding"—whatever he may have been like: he is a created character who may not be very much like the living man. For our purposes it is perhaps better to reserve the popular term "persona" for such an invented version of the author, because it is not in itself ironic in our sense. The author clearly intends us to trust him, even as we learn *not* to trust the various ironic poses he puts on. Similarly Mark Twain, the humorist, was to some degree a persona invented by Samuel L. Clemens, and we know from Clemens's biography that there were often great differences between what the real man was thinking and feeling and what he chose to show under the guise of "Mark Twain." A mask is ironic only if the literary effect of the work depends on our seeing behind the mask; in this sense, Mark Twain is ironic when he pretends to be a moron: "He spelt it Vinci, but he pronounced it Vinchy; foreigners always spell better than they pronounce." But Clemens is not ironic when he assumes, in work after work, the basic persona of the shrewd, kindly humorist. (See *The Rhetoric of Fiction*, chaps. 3 and 7–12 for much fuller discussion of these points.)

and in the opinion of the author who stands behind him. What does he think of her personal appearance? He says that she "very rightly" thinks of beauty as merely a threat to chastity (3*b*). Does the narrator agree with his own "very rightly"? Obviously not; irony is being used to make fun of Bridget's self-advertised concern for her virtue.

But Fielding is surely not saying that personal beauty is *never* a snare for virtue. We cannot, in fact, discover from this passage alone what the narrator's true attitude toward personal beauty will prove to be; all we know is that Bridget is ugly and yet is ridiculous not so much for being ugly as for pretending that beauty is only a snare.

With this known, we have no trouble making the reconstructions required by the rest of the paragraph (e.g., "higher," "distant and awful"), though there is perhaps a slightly different tone introduced with "I suppose" (in the final sentence).

Note how easily Fielding next (4) adopts a different tone entirely, with the address to the reader and the critics. Is he serious? Partly, partly not, and I think it would be impossible, on the basis of the paragraph alone, to decide exactly where to draw the line. Readers of the entire book know that most of its seeming digressions are strictly to the point. The narrator *does* digress, occasionally, but on the whole the book has seemed to most critics extraordinarily tight in construction. The narrator is, then, exaggerating the digressive nature of the book, and the verdict must be: irony! But on the other hand, Fielding *is* a better judge of his book than the critics he mocks; as we read along, we become convinced that he has established a new authority in a new type of fiction, and this statement is thus discovered to have been sound: no irony! And this complex mixture, which some would call ironic just because it is a mixture, is rendered more complex as soon as we think of how the attack on imaginary critics works rhetorically on us. "Am I potentially one of these critics? Well, yes, and now I must decide whether to take this quarrelsome tone seriously."

So far I have given you my decisions about the details of this passage, and not my reasons. If your decisions are the same as mine, then you may not care about my reasons. But what would we both say to a reader who protests that he simply does not see, even now, on what grounds we have decided to take "agreeable person," and "benevolent heart" (1) and "beloved wife" (2*a*) without question and then to reject, though spoken by the same narrator, such judgments as "whimsically" (2*b*), "in the opinion of the malicious" (3*a*), and "higher order" (3*c*)?

Let me once again artificially isolate a series of reasons, any one of which might be most important—though perhaps not brought into conscious play—for this or that reader.

1. The most useful test here is the presence of incredible disparities. How can I reconcile praise for Allworthy's "sane understanding" and "benevolent heart" with the dismissal of his talk about the resurrection as "whimsical" in paragraph 2? Either Fielding is carelessly inconsistent, or deliberately inconsistent; if the latter, he must be joking with either his praise or his blame. But it is extremely improbable that any author—especially one who has been praised by so many critics for his subtlety—could be so dense as to fall inadvertently into such obvious inconsistencies. Indeed, there is a pattern of inconsistency throughout the passage that can hardly be accidental: one of the two Fieldings must be rejected.

2. Admitting this, it might still be that the praise for benevolence and good sense is ironic, and the praise of Bridget's hypocrisy and the attack on Allworthy's "whimsical" religious convictions serious. In deciding which voice is false, I can appeal first to the three classes of clues discussed in chapter 3. Since there are no out-and-out conflicts with knowledge that I possessed when I came to the work (only the kind of internal conflicts that I described in no. 1 above), and since the style in itself is not obviously repudiated by the author, I must appeal to the third class of clues: how do the conflicting beliefs jibe or clash with my own, and with my assumptions about what Fielding would believe?

For many modern readers, this test will be misleading, because they will think that for a man to believe in the resurrection, as the narrator says Allworthy does, is in fact a whimsical sign that he does *not* enjoy a "sane understanding." But what about the other beliefs? "No one," I am convinced (not even that rare reader who resembles Bridget herself), would ever accept as stated the beliefs of paragraph 3. They are so "obviously absurd" that they could never be intended seriously. Of course if our hypothetical reader does not see them as absurd, if he or she is in fact a prude who believes that lack of "charms of person in a woman" is a blessing, because it protects her from pursuit by men, and that even an ugly woman should be constantly on guard "as if" she were under attack, then we are back where we started.

If I were dealing with the whole novel instead of this fragment, the problem would evaporate, no doubt, because Bridget's prudishness is later revealed to be entirely hypocritical and her virtue entirely imaginary. But for now I am left depending on the "self-evident" illogicality of Bridget's behavior: If beauty *is* a snare, ugliness should be a protection. Such a violation of everyday logic is absurd, so absurd that Fielding must have intended it.

3. No one has yet written a defense of Bridget as a moral center of *Tom Jones,* but her time may come. What would be our last line of defense, if someone pushed current ironizing trends and argued either that Fielding wrought better than he knew, or—which may be the same thing—that he fell accidentally into these absurd contradictions but really did not mean the irony to work so strongly against Bridget?

We must turn, I think, to another line of argument entirely, one that I have often touched on but not yet developed.

What is the effect on the quality of the passage—or, to a rhetorician almost the same thing, what happens to my pleasure in it—if I assume that Fielding is ironic in praising Allworthy's benevolence and entirely serious in praising Bridget's virtue and discretion? Such an interpretation simply destroys most of the fun and convinces me—if I hold to it—that I am in the hands of a bumbler. The marvelous ironist simply disappears. If it were correct, what would the point be, for example, of the lines about the neighbors who doubt his sense, his religion, and his sincerity? If the three groups described are not victims of Fielding's wit but are rather to be seen as right in their condemnation of Allworthy, why did Fielding bother to mention them? What is the literary value of their being here? The answer is important: there is no value, and the sentence describing them has become lifeless. The groups become deadwood, unless Fielding's ironic voice is on All-worthy's side against them. Similarly, what happens to the description of Bridget if we assume that Fielding is seriously praising her? Its wit evaporates into long-windedness. Only if he is at each step puncturing her pretensions—to youth, to indifference about good looks, to prudence—does every point count for our pleasure. Only if read as irony does the passage yield a new delight with every phrase.

The principle underlying this test might read as follows: other things being equal, one should always accept the reading that contributes most to the quality of the work. Of all the tests we have used so far, this one is the most troublesome. Readers show even less agreement about literary value than about descriptions of style or moral beliefs. What is worse, books that are in fact flat and dull will merely confuse us if we try to liven them up by reading them ironically. But difficult as it is, the test of whether a given interpretation—however plausible in itself—destroys or enhances a work is sometimes the only final arbiter of disputes about irony. The test will work most clearly when we are reasonably sure of the generic grooves in which we travel, and of how irony or its absence will incise them further. But sometimes the only part of the work that will be seriously destroyed or enhanced will be the quality of the ironist's voice, and then we inevitably have more difficulties.

Without some such test, overly ingenious readers sometimes go astray in their search for ironies. Once they have learned to suspect a given speaker, they are tempted to suspect every statement he makes. To them, there seem to be no clear signposts telling them where to stop, and soon the master of subtle shifts is reduced to a monotonous sneering drawl. The main—and sometimes the only—objection to such imaginative re-creations is that they diminish the works they are intended to illuminate. On the ground cleared by his demolition the reader erects monuments to his own ingenuity.

Fielding combats such excesses by "training" the reader to draw up short, to move back and forth from ironic to straight readings. Having caught the irony against Bridget, why not go on ironizing and doubt the words praising Allworthy, and later on the words praising Tom? Why not decide that Blifil, the man everyone else has taken as villain, is really a misunderstood victim of the vicious Allworthy? In doing so we could take great pleasure, no doubt, in thinking of all the fools who had misread this book for two hundred years, but at the same time we would be forced to throw away most of what is in the actual book, so dull it would have become. *Tom Jones* would no longer make sense as a whole, and we would be left with a few isolated fragments, delightfully ironic but nonetheless fragments. In effect we would have imagined another book entirely, a possible book but not the book Fielding wrote. There is no law against this, of course, but anyone who decides to make a practice of it should be quite sure, first, that he can really write a better book than the one the author offers. If the new, more ironic version is in fact immeasurably inferior as a work of art, the sense of my own cleverness in having penetrated to it beneath Fielding's deceptive surface is meager compensation for my loss.

## E. M. FORSTER AS ESSAYIST

Like Fielding, many of the great personal essayists provide experience in the art of deciding when to stop; that is, they provide subtle mixtures that require us to shift gears constantly and skillfully. They do not invent a radically distinct mask and offer every word in his tone of voice; rather they develop a tone which becomes known as their true style and which includes frequent stable ironies.

E. M. Forster, for example, has invented (or so we might put it) an "E. M. Forster" who seems to be the real man addressing us, a man who wears something like the same ironic smile from essay to essay.

185

We know, as we approach any new essay, that it will have manifold ironies. But we also come to know that he will never allow us to take refuge in a generalized verdict, "It's ironic." What is he "really saying," for example, in the following famous essay?

## Me, Them and You

[1]  I have a suit of clothes. It does not fit, but is of stylish cut. I can go anywhere in it and I have been to see the Sargent pictures at the Royal Academy. Underneath the suit was a shirt, beneath the shirt was a vest, and beneath the vest was Me. Me was not exposed much to the public gaze; two hands and a face showed that here was a human being; the rest was swathed in cotton or wool.

[2]  Yet Me was what mattered, for it was Me that was going to see Them. Them what? Them persons what governs us, them dukes and duchesses and archbishops and generals and captains of industry. They have had their likenesses done by this famous painter (artists are useful sometimes), and, for the sum of one and six, they were willing to be inspected. I had one and six, otherwise I should have remained in the snow outside. The coins changed hands. I entered the exhibition, and found myself almost immediately in the presence of a respectable family servant.

[3]  "Wretched weather," I remarked civilly. There was no reply, the forehead swelled, the lips contracted haughtily. I had begun my tour with a very serious mistake, and had addressed a portrait of Lord Curzon. His face had misled me into thinking him a family servant. I ought to have looked only at the clothes, which were blue and blazing, and which he clutched with a blue-veined hand. They cost a hundred pounds perhaps. How cheap did my own costume seem now, and how impossible it was to imagine that Lord Curzon continues beneath his clothes, that he, too (if I may venture on the parallel), was a Me.

[4]  Murmuring in confusion, I left the radiant effigy and went into the next room. Here my attention was drawn by a young Oriental, subtle and charming and not quite sure of his ground. I complimented him in flowery words. He winced, he disclaimed all knowledge of the East. I had been speaking to Sir Philip Sassoon. Here again I ought to have looked first at the clothes. They were slightly horsey and wholly English, and they put mine to shame. Why had he come from Tabriz, or wherever it was, and put them on? Why take the long journey from Samarcand for the purpose of denouncing our Socialists? Why not remain where he felt himself Me? But he resented analysis and I left him.

[5]  The third figure—to do her justice—felt that she was Me and no one else could be, and looked exactly what she was: namely, the wife of our Ambassador at Berlin. Erect she stood, with a small balustrade and a diplomatic landscape behind her. She was superbly beautiful and

incredibly arrogant, and her pearls would have clothed not mere hundreds of human beings but many of her fellow-portraits on the walls. What beat in the heart—if there was a heart—I could nòt know, but I heard pretty distinctly the voice that proceeded from the bright red lips. It is not a voice that would promote calm in high places, not a voice to promote amity between two nations at a difficult moment in their intercourse. Her theme was precedence, and perhaps it is wiser to allow her to develop it in solitude.

[6]   And I drifted from Them to Them, fascinated by the hands and faces which peeped out of the costumes. Lord Roberts upheld with difficulty the rows of trinkets pinned on his uniform; Sir Thomas Sutherland was fat above a fat black tie; a riding costume supported the chinless cranium of a Duke; a Mr. John Fife "who showed conspicuous ability in the development of the granite industry" came from Aberdeen in black; and a Marquess actually did something: he was carrying the Sword of State on the occasion of King Edward's Coronation; while a page carried his train. Sometimes the painter saw through his sitters and was pleasantly mischievous at their expense; sometimes he seemed taken in by them—which happens naturally enough to a man who spends much time dangling after the rich. In spite of the charm of his work, and the lovely colours, and the gracious pictures of Venice, a pall of upholstery hung over the exhibition. The portraits dominated. Gazing at each other over our heads, they said, "What would the country do without us? We have got the decorations and the pearls, we make fashions and wars, we have the largest houses and eat the best food, and control the most important industries, and breed the most valuable children, and ours is the Kingdom and the Power and the Glory." And, listening to their chorus, I felt this was so, and my clothes fitted worse and worse, and there seemed in all the universe no gulf wider than the gulf between Them and Me—no wider gulf, until I encountered You.

[7]   You had been plentiful enough in the snow outside (your proper place), but I had not expected to find You here in the place of honour, too. Yours was by far the largest picture in the show. You were hung between Lady Cowdray and the Hon. Mrs. Langman, and You were entitled "Gassed." You were of godlike beauty—for the upper classes only allow the lower classes to appear in art on condition that they wash themselves and have classical features. These conditions you fulfilled. A line of golden-haired Apollos moved along a duck-board from left to right with bandages over their eyes. They had been blinded by mustard gas. Others sat peacefully in the foreground, others approached through the middle distance. The battlefield was sad but tidy. No one complained, no one looked lousy or overtired, and the aeroplanes overhead struck the necessary note of the majesty of England. It was all that a great war picture should be, and it was modern because it managed to tell a new sort of lie. Many ladies and gentlemen fear

that Romance is passing out of war with the sabres and the chargers. Sargent's masterpiece reassures them. He shows that it is possible to suffer with a quiet grace under the new conditions, and Lady Cowdray and the Hon. Mrs. Langman, as they looked over the twenty feet of canvas that divided them, were still able to say, "How touching," instead of "How obscene."

[8]  Still, there You were, though in modified form, and in mockery of your real misery, and though the gulf between Them and Me was wide, still wider yawned the gulf between us and You. For what could we do without you? What would become of our incomes and activities if you declined to exist? You are the slush and dirt on which our civilization rests, which it treads under foot daily, which it sentimentalizes over now and then, in hours of danger. But you are not only a few selected youths in khaki, you are old men and women and dirty babies also, and dimly and obscurely you used to move through the mind of Carlyle. "Thou wert our conscript, on Thee the lot fell. . . ." That is as true for the twentieth century as for the nineteenth, though the twentieth century—more cynical—feels that it is merely a true remark, not a useful one, and that economic conditions cannot be bettered by booming on about the brotherhood of man. "For in Thee also a godlike frame lay hidden, but it was not to be unfolded," not while the hard self-satisfied faces stare at each other from the walls and say, "But at all events we founded the Charity Organization Society—and look what we pay in wages, and look what our clothes cost, and clothes mean work."

[9]  The misery goes on, the feeble impulses of good return to the sender, and far away, in some other category, far away from the snobbery and glitter in which our souls and bodies have been entangled, is forged the instrument of the new dawn.

Let me test our agreements one more time by recording in detail my impressions of the opening lines:

*I have a suit of clothes.*
A strange way to begin. It sounds like a grade school pupil. But this is "E. M. Forster," so something tricky is going on—the flat obviousness in the style must be deliberate—a subdued but inescapable joke of *some* kind.

*It does not fit, but is of stylish cut. I can go anywhere in it.*
Making fun of himself a bit, no doubt, but even more of conventions of style? If the suit were not stylish, could he *not* go anywhere? Right! So he's attacking superficial standards of judging who can go where?

*Underneath . . . wool.*
This settles it: he is satirizing dress.

*Yet Me was what mattered . . .*
True, true. Forster and I agree—the real person is of course
what matters. No irony here, only the fun of the grammar.

*Them persons what governs us . . .*
Working class "accent" here. Why? "Us" puts Forster on "our"
side against Them? Possibly.

*(artists are useful sometimes)*
Quotation marks implied. Spoken by *Them* as sign of Their absolute indifference to real, as distinct from merely "useful,"
values of art.

*I had one-and-six . . .*
Like "I have a suit of clothes." Money lets Me (Forster) in, as
an outsider, but he is clearly siding with those who have not
one-and-six.

The satire against the ruling classes is by now fairly obvious,
and we can see that the ironies almost all operate in one direction. So
there is little difficulty, perhaps, until the shift to "You" (7). Now
slowly the levity declines, the tone becomes more and more direct,
until at the end we no longer are translating distorted statements; we
are listening to E. M. Forster, direct social critic, as he warns the upper
classes, quite directly, of revolutionary change to come.

Thus if the last sentence is ironic, it is only so in a very special
sense: though like most of the essay it seems to be spoken in E. M.
Forster's own voice, that voice is not the direct voice of a revolutionary
shouting "Workers of the world unite; you have nothing to lose but
your chains." Forster is addressing the ruling classes, not the workers,
but even so his message is deflected from direct exhortation to a kind
of wry, almost mystifying allusion to "some other category" where
others whom we cannot hope to know—the "You" of the essay—are
forging the instrument of the new dawn. It is almost as if he were refusing to be involved in any implicit message his essay contains: "You
comfortable readers may infer from this that you ought to disentangle
your souls and bodies from the 'snobbery and glitter,' but don't expect
me to help you. Or even to become deeply involved in your inevitable
doom."

And yet we know that he is not finally ironic when he speaks of
"the misery," "the feeble impulses," and "the instrument of the new
dawn." If anyone tried to argue that the final phrase satirizes the work-
ing-class hopes for socialism, we could easily show that such a reading
would be entirely inconsistent with the rest of the essay, that indeed it
would make hash of the essay by destroying the ending: it would carry

only a feeble thrust, and an inconsistent one, if it were really directed against its own overt meaning. Taken entirely straight it is a forceful final stroke against those whose petty kindnesses and apologies will have no effect on whatever new dawn is to come.

Where then do we stop in our search for ironic pleasures? Where the work "tells" us to, wherever it offers us other riches that might be destroyed by irony. It takes a clever reader to detect all the ironies in a Fielding or a Forster. But it takes something beyond cleverness to resist going too far: the measured tempo of the experienced reader, eager for quick reversals and exhilarating turns, but always aware of the demands both of the partner and of the disciplined forms of the dance.

In our day an ironic provincialism, which looks everywhere in literature for complete objectivity, suspension of moral judgments, concentration on pure verbal craftsmanship, and similar virtues, is in the ascendant.

—Northrop Frye

Tho I have endeavour'd to defend the Use of *Ridicule* and *Irony,* yet it is such *Irony* and *Ridicule* only as is fit for polite persons to use. As to the gross *Irony* and *Ridicule,* I disapprove of it, as I do other Faults in Writing; only I would not have Men punish'd, or any other way disturb'd about it, than by a Return of *Ridicule* and *Irony.*

—Anthony Collins

. . . These are questions of fact, not of sentiment. Whether any particular person be endowed with good sense and a delicate imagination, free from prejudice, may often be the subject of dispute, and be liable to great discussion and inquiry; but that such a character is valuable and estimable will be agreed in by all mankind.

—Hume, "Of the Standard of Taste"

# SEVEN | Is There a Standard of Taste in Irony?

## I

The search for knowledge about interpreting irony has led us now to a curious kind of assertion. I began by trying to discover firm tests for the presence of stable irony and found that there was no escaping the question of when to stop. In looking for what the work *means* I was forced, by irony, to look for what it *meant*: the historical fact of what the author intended. Either he did or he did not intend stable irony. Yet that search—already based on assumptions which many critics would reject—led finally to the test of the work's relative excellence: if we carry ironic reading too far, we diminish Fielding's and Forster's work.

Now here is a curiosity indeed—a claim to settle matters of historical fact by reference to assertions of value. I have not been simply saying that value judgments are a legitimate part of literary criticism, though that in itself would be bad enough for some. Mr. Northrop Frye, for example, has said repeatedly, though with some slight wavering, that we cannot pursue the study of literature "with the object of arriving at value judgments, because the only possible goal of study is knowledge. The sense of value is an individual, unpredictable, variable, incommunicable, indemonstrable, and mainly intuitive reaction to knowledge."[1] But I am forced, by my close look at how we actually make our decisions about irony, to the outlandish assertion that our knowledge, in Mr. Frye's sense—our shared, predictable, not-entirely-variable, communicable, demonstrable (though of course in some sense intuitive) conviction about what a work means—is dependent on knowledge of a kind that he rules out: knowledge of value.

I am thus dragged by the inquiry itself into the thickets of theories about evaluation. A rhetoric of irony cannot avoid any of the actions

1. "On Value Judgments," *Contemporary Literature* 9 (Summer 1968): 311–18. See also his "Polemical Introduction" to the *Anatomy of Criticism*. The issue of *CL* contains three other essays on evaluation, by Murray Krieger, E. D. Hirsch, Jr., and Wayne Shumaker. Together they give a good introduction to the grounds of current controversy. See also *Problems of Literary Evaluation,* ed. Joseph Strelka (University Park, Pa., 1969). Most of the contributors would agree that some kinds of evaluation have some sort of general validity, but most would pull up short of the claim that Mr. Hirsch and I share—that some kinds of literary evaluation constitute knowledge. See his "Literary Evaluation as Knowledge," *CL* 9: 319–31.

authors and readers perform reliably together. Some ironic works claim for themselves that they have, as it were, stopped at the right point, while others would seem to demand that we "go all the way" with them, and that to make such a demand is inherently superior to the stodginess of stability. To accept either claim is to assume that there is a standard of taste in irony.

But this is only to make explicit what has been implied at every point: every ironist has asked us, as we saw in describing the four judgments of chapter 2, to assume that his form of rhetorical display is a worthy one. The ironist makes more claims for himself, and thus risks more, than does the literal speaker. He insists on inviting us to join him in constructing his hierarchies, and it is scarcely surprising that he thus invites more aggressive praise and denunciation than all but the most extreme addicts of other figures. The ironic stroke that for one critic is brilliant and subtle will for another be cheap trickery, yet each critic is likely to feel that a great deal is at stake in the disagreement. Irony thus once again heightens a problem shared to some degree by all verbal art: it forces us to judge, and yet it produces disagreements that seem to render all judgment capricious. How can there be a standard of taste in irony, when it is so clearly true that each critic is his own arbiter, and when we see that critics for the most part offer only a statement of preferences, with no effort to give ultimate reasons?

Why?—I want to ask F. R. Leavis when he asserts that Gibbon's irony, which "habituates and reassures, ministering to a kind of judicial certainty and complacency," is superior to Swift's, which is "essentially a matter of surprise and negation." Why is it bad for Swift to attempt "to defeat habit, to intimidate and demoralize"—assuming for the moment that Leavis's summary is accurate? Where would he be forced to look for his answer?

But again I want to ask Why? when William Frost, rightly offended by Leavis's distortion of Swift, replies that Swift's achievement is greater *because* he reorients the reader's patterns of sensibility "in unexpected ways," while Gibbon merely confirms, habituates, reassures.[2] I do not assume that either Leavis or Frost would be unable to

---

2. Leavis's essay appeared in *Scrutiny,* March 1934, pp. 364–78; Frost's reply, "The Irony of Swift and Gibbon," in *Essays in Criticism* 17 (1967): 41–47. John Preston argues that Gay's irony in *The Beggar's Opera* is superior to Fielding's in *Jonathan Wild,* because Fielding's irony is only "a verbal trick," less "complex," more "conservative": "It consolidates prepared positions and draws its effectiveness from our relief that we have not lost our bearings." Gay's irony, on the contrary, "does not resolve into a 'moral,'" and it "threatens our faith in the qualities we most admire: honesty, honour, friendship, loyalty, and

develop a reply; I only report that they saw no reason, in these published evaluations, to develop the moral or metaphysical or religious or political reasons for asserting that affirmative or destructive irony is superior.

Such disputes fill our books and journals, and it is hardly surprising that they have seemed to support relativism. And in exchange, a thoroughgoing relativism frees us to conduct such disputes with happy irresponsibility: if genuine knowledge of value judgments is impossible, we can with a clear conscience use whatever devices of persuasion are available to enforce our private views.

On the one hand, we have then critics like Mr. Frye ruling out evaluation from the provinces of criticism, because they seek a subject matter that can be known, not merely asserted;[3] and on the other a host of critics like Mr. Herbert Lindenberger who repudiate even the limited hope for knowledge expressed by Mr. Frye; not just all evaluation, but all interpretation is "subjective": ". . . I do not believe that we can or should seek 'objective knowledge' about literary works. . . . Instead of seeing ourselves in the pursuit of objective knowledge, desperately trying to impress the scientists with our 'lace-curtain' respectability, let us substitute the image of a dialogue in which one party is using *the most forceful means of persuasion* he can muster to convince another of his point of view. One of the advantages of this dialogue image is, I think, the fact that it releases us from the need to measure our endeavors against a prescriptive outer standard such as Hirsch's notion of objectivity, and instead makes the quality and nature of criticism a function of *the critic's relationship with his audience"* (my italics).[4] It does indeed, and at the same time condemns us perpetually to a sense of ultimate futility in what we do. Though the pursuit of knowledge on the model of science has indeed been constricting, the opposing Pyrrhonism, which revels in an illusory sense of freedom while binding us to whichever suitor woos most winningly, is far more destructive.

---

love" ("The Ironic Mode: A Comparison of *Jonathan Wild* and *The Beggar's Opera," Essays in Criticism* 16 [1966]: 268–80, esp. pp. 274–79).

3. A rather different attack on evaluation is contained in C. S. Lewis's *An Experiment in Criticism* (Cambridge, 1961); Lewis is not so much concerned about the impossibility of evaluating as the inadvisability—the critic should not, he says, treat the great classics like so many lamp posts for a dog. A popular polemic asserting the total capriciousness of all literary judgment is contained in *Precious Rubbish,* by Theodore L. Shaw (Boston, 1956).

4. "Keats' 'To Autumn' and Our Knowledge of a Poem," *College English* 32 (November 1970): 132–33.

Our troubles seem to stem in part from the habit of insisting on all or nothing. Either "value judgments," en masse, are defensible, or they are nothing; if they are not "scientific knowledge," they are not subject to meaningful inquiry at all. Either they are "objective" or they are "subjective"—and if they are subjective, as they quite obviously are, they cannot be objects of knowledge. If we are to cast some skeptical light on the romantic dogma that the ironic view is always right, while at the same time building a modest confidence in the validity of critical judgment, we must abandon such large labels and begin with some discriminations.

## FOUR LEVELS OF EVALUATION

Literary evaluation is not a single act. Critics engage in at least four radically different processes; the structure of justification in each process differs from all the others, and our decision about whether asserted judgments can be defended will depend on knowing which of the four structures we are implying. Are we (A) judging parts as they contribute to whole works, or (B) judging parts according to universally desirable qualities, critical constants, or (C) judging completed works according to their own implicit standards, their intentions (and thus in comparison with other works, real or implicit, of the same kind or intention), or (D) judging kinds compared with other kinds, like Frost or Leavis in their controversy?

Though we may easily think of borderline cases and subspecies, I think that these four types cover the range of possible evaluations of literary works (though not, of course, of authors, periods, nations— and so on). In the first and third, the criteria are found "in" the particular work: only its inferred intentions can tell us whether a given part is suited to the whole, and whether its own inherent powers or possibilities have been achieved to the full. On the other hand, the second and fourth lead us away from the individual work to other works, other kinds, and hence other sources of criteria. There seems to be no definable limit to the number of larger contexts that particular literary works can be fitted into and judged by: the author's other work, or his personal development; other works of the same kind; other works of the time or of a particular political or sexual or psychological temper; man's nature or needs; God's will; and so on.

As I turn to a closer look at the four kinds of evaluation, working under the pitiless (though perhaps a bit strabismic) gaze of Irony, I should warn that it will not lead to a simple list of useful rules for judging. But at least it should free us from the surprisingly widespread and hopelessly inhibiting view that our judgments can be based on those two flat true-false tests: "Is irony present?" And "Is the irony honest (i.e., negative)?"

## A. Judging Parts According to Function

Nobody has ever successfully argued against the possibility of saying, "This device is better for this task in this work than that device would be." Few have even tried, so obvious is it that critical agreement is possible about some relations of parts and wholes. If you would heighten the tragedy, then you must heighten the sympathy. If you would make men laugh, you cannot make your characters entirely noble. Given certain desired effects, certain means are more likely to succeed.

This hypothetical reasoning, always dependent on the unproved givens, can often yield clear, unequivocal choices among possible parts. Given the aim of writing a neatly satiric couplet, one ironic word will (sometimes) be demonstrably better than another at a particular spot.

Describing Belinda's toilet table, Pope says

> Here files of pins extend their shining rows,
> Puffs, Powders, Patches, Bibles, Billet-doux.

He might have written "novels" instead of "Bibles," but he did not, and the irony (to say nothing of the alliteration) is clearly superior as it stands, because the contrast is greater. Similarly, given the aims of Butler's *Erewhon,* to have the narrator exclaim, of a danger escaped, ". . . As luck would have it, providence was on my side," is a very good ironic stroke indeed. We can test such judgments simply, by trying out other readings: "As luck would have it, God was on my side," or "Fortunately, God chose to save me." Butler's choice of *providence* rather than *God* heightens the contrast with the secular luck, while his choice of *luck* rather than *fortune* heightens the contrast with the pious notion of providence.

In both of these examples, then, one word is clearly better than another, given the ironic intention of the sentence. And in both, we could easily show that larger sections surrounding the sentences are strengthened by the sharpest possible contrasts at precisely these points; and thus on to the whole work.

There is a kind of obviousness about many such judgments: a given work silently demonstrates for us, without any need for theory or analysis, that a given ironic effect is appropriate or necessary at a given spot. No reader without a critical axe to grind has ever looked for a justification of the innumerable ironic strokes in, say, *Pride and Prej-*

*udice*. We enjoy them, hope for more, and only in artificial analysis find ourselves offering justifications (e.g., Elizabeth must be shown surrounded by absolutely impossible fates—stupid or unfeeling parents and sisters, gruesome suitors, threatening models for marriage—if her hopeless isolation and our consequent 'longing' for Darcy is to be savored). We do not ask, when we read the wonderfully self-betraying speech of proposal by Mr. Collins, what the general requirements of irony are in novels, or in novels of this or that kind; we know without taking thought that this precise self-portrait of a grasping foolish clergyman is just right, at *this* spot in *this* novel. And we know that other ironic delights will not do: a confusing monologue by Samuel Beckett's Watt or a self-revealing soliloquy by Joyce's Molly Bloom will not be good here though they are good where they belong. Mr. Collins's outpourings are, however, very good indeed, and the criterion of our judgment is known to every reader: the worse his words are as an actual proposal the better:

> Believe me, my dear Miss Elizabeth, that your modesty, so far from doing you any disservice, rather adds to your other perfections. You would have been less amiable in my eyes had there *not* been this little unwillingness; but allow me to assure you that I have your respected mother's permission for this address. You can hardly doubt the purport of my discourse, however your natural delicacy may lead you to dissemble; my attentions have been too marked to be mistaken. Almost as soon as I entered the house I singled you out as the companion of my future life. But before I am run away with by my feelings on this subject, perhaps it will be advisable for me to state my reasons for marrying—and moreover for coming into Hertfordshire with the design of selecting a wife, as I certainly did. . . .
>
> My reasons for marrying are, first, that I think it is a right thing for every clergyman in easy circumstances (like myself) to set the example of matrimony in his parish. Secondly, that I am convinced it will add very greatly to my happiness; and thirdly— which perhaps I ought to have mentioned earlier, that it is the particular advice and recommendation of the very noble lady whom I have the honour of calling patroness. Twice has she condescended to give me her opinion (unasked too!) on this subject; and it was but the very Saturday night before I left Hunsford— between our pools at quadrille, while Mrs. Jenkinson was arranging Miss de Bourgh's foot-stool, that she said, "Mr. Collins, you must marry. A clergyman like you must marry.—Chuse properly, chuse a gentlewoman for *my* sake; and for your *own,* let her be an active, useful sort of person, not brought up high, but able to make a small income go a good way. This is my advice.

Find such a woman as soon as you can, bring her to Hunsford, and I will visit her." Allow me, by the way, to observe, my fair cousin, that I do not reckon the notice and kindness of Lady Catherine de Bourgh as among the least of the advantages in my power to offer. You will find her manners beyond any thing I can describe; and your wit and vivacity I think must be acceptable to her, especially when tempered with the silence and respect which her rank will inevitably excite. Thus much for my general intention in favour of matrimony; it remains to be told why my views were directed to Longbourn instead of my own neighbour- hood, where I assure you there are many amiable young women. But the fact is, that being, as I am, to inherit this estate after the death of your honoured father, (who, however, may live many years longer,) I could not satisfy myself without resolving to chuse a wife from among his daughters, that the loss to them might be as little as possible, when the melancholy event takes place—which, however, as I have already said, may not be for several years. This has been my motive, my fair cousin, and I flatter myself it will not sink me in your esteem. And now nothing remains for me but to assure you in the most animated language of the violence of my affection. To fortune I am perfectly indif- ferent, and shall make no demand of that nature on your father, since I am well aware that it could not be complied with; and that one thousand pounds in the 4 per cents. which will not be yours till after your mother's decease, is all that you may ever be en- titled to. On that head, therefore, I shall be uniformly silent; and you may assure yourself that no ungenerous reproach shall ever pass my lips when we are married.

Not only can we say with confidence that the worse Collins is the better he is; we can discover here standards even about such elusive matters as proper length. A much shorter speech is conceivable, and if Jane Austen had written it we probably would not suspect what we had missed; what is more, according to any abstract notion of proper proportion this one is much too long: Collins is simply not *that* impor- tant, even as a threat. But to do its full comic job, the speech must be as long as possible. Since our delight stems in part from Collins's tediousness, the firstlys, secondlys and thirdlys must move forward at a pace that in real life would be as intolerable to us as it is to Elizabeth: the magnificence of the anticlimax, when he finally gets around to her value and then loses it immediately in talk of money and himself, de- pends on stretching the speech to the uttermost limits. These are loosely but decisively determined by the demands that the novel makes as it goes about its business. Just how firmly all of these constraints operate can be seen if one tries either to lengthen the speech or to capture its

199

essence in selections. Though the quotation above is, for example, "much too long," according to my notions of how citation should be handled in a work like this one of mine, I find simply nothing that can be scuttled without weakening my point about proper length.

By the same criterion we can see that this kind of irony would destroy other parts of the same novel. Most obviously, to make Darcy's letter to Elizabeth similarly absurd—an easy task, for Jane Austen—would destroy important romantic effects without which the novel would be maimed. In short, only *Pride and Prejudice,* looked at in very close detail, can tell us where and how irony of a given kind can be effective in *Pride and Prejudice.*

To see this clearly is already to see limitations on the kind of judgment Mr. Reuben Brower makes against the abandonment of irony in the last third of *Pride and Prejudice.*[5] It is clearly not a functional judgment, since to increase the irony at the end, or to shorten the last parts because they cannot be kept ironic, would require a complete rewriting of the novel. It can only be seen as a judgment against the novel as a whole for failing to allow for continuation of a quality that is universally desirable, our second kind of judgment. It does not say that the non-ironic parts are failures in what they have to do—they do it as well as they can—or that the novel fails "in its own terms," but that its "terms" are deficient from the beginning: insufficient provision for irony through to the end. Two pages of irony are good and four pages are twice as good.

Flushed out into the open like this, the criterion might or might not be acceptable to Mr. Brower. It may be that he would make a case for irony as a universally desirable quality, as Mr. Brooks does in *The Well Wrought Urn.* At least we would then know what we are discussing—not a question of what Jane Austen could or should do with this or that part of her novel, but what kinds of literary effects the world would contain if it were run properly—the fourth kind of judgment.

Many absurdities about too much or too little of this or that character or scene or stylistic quality could thus be avoided simply by noticing that the work as a whole requires things to be as they are, if

5. "Occasionally, we feel a recovery of the richer texture of amusement and of the more complex awareness of character revealed in the central sequence. . . . It is perhaps not 'rational,' as Elizabeth would say, to expect the same complexity when a drama of irony has once arrived at its resolution. But it is probably wise for the novelist to finish up his story as soon as possible after that point has been reached" (*The Fields of Light: An Experiment in Critical Reading* [New York, 1951; paperback, 1962], pp. 180–81).

it is to come into existence at all. But to say this raises two very serious difficulties. If we all decided to become functional critics and place every line in its context before judging it, would we not be reduced finally to critical particularism, unable to judge any literary touch except instrumentally? Can I say only that a type of irony suited to *Gulliver's Travels* may destroy *Pride and Prejudice* or Kafka's *The Castle,* and that Kafka's ironies would destroy *Erewhon, Finnegans Wake,* or *Pilgrim's Progress*? Is the only possible generalization about the quality of irony that a piece of it is good when it works in its context, that is, that it's good when it's good? If so, the critic can only limp from work to work, description to description, led by his assumptions to a helpless relativism of judgment, except when judging parts in wholes.

And there is a second objection: with functionalism, cannot one justify almost anything, however shoddy, if it is seen to fulfill the intentions of its context? Reading a detective story, I come across this scintillating passage:

> The young woman's smile revealed a streak of cruelty.
> "I think your guesses are ridiculous," she said.
> "Is that so?" ("Vraiment!") [said the detective].
> Hillen had put as much irony as possible into this phrase.

It is not hard to think of ironies handled more cleverly or subtly than this. Surely it is the author's job to make the words carry the irony, not simply tell the reader that a word is packed with irony. Here, then, is a critical constant, applied as general standard, and it tells us that this irony is poor. But what about the reader who manages to get to page 213 in this shabby detective story, *Panique à Fleur de Peau,* by one André Lay. Is this undemanding reader not part of the context we must take into account? If we say only that an author succeeds when he manages to lead his reader to join him, surely the author has chosen best here—providing an obvious irony for dull readers. Whether by nature or temporary torpor, the reader of *Panique . . .* cannot be very quick or demanding—any alert reader, eager for clever invitations to reconstruction, would have quit on the first page.[6] So then, we say, this is just right for this context and therefore good irony? The conclusion seems absurd, but if there are no valid general standards, we seem to be forced to it.

## B. Qualities as Critical Constants

The quality of "being ironic" has perhaps more than any other in modern times been taken as the distinguishing mark of all good litera-

6. Yes, yes, clever one. I have thought of what this says about me as I arrived at p. 213. But I do not choose to explain.

ture.[7] The abstract, deductive method of criticism that the belief leads to is so often destructive that one is tempted to go to the opposite extreme of claiming that there are no critical constants whatever. The case against them might run like this:

> There is no evidence that any one quality marks "all literature" or "all good literature." There is no single common element in all good literature, and, more obviously, there is no single common element in all good ironic literature—not even irony in any one definition: to say that all ironic literature must be ironic gets us nowhere, so long as one man's irony is another man's literal statement. Anyone who thinks the claim too sweeping can be asked to name his quality. We then lead him, through the most obvious and easy questioning (why? why?), back to his general aesthetic principles (which he will find are not exemplified in all literature that he and other men consider good), and from those to his basic philosophy of value (which again will not be accepted by all critics).
>
> If he tells, us, for example, that all good literature is ironic he can be asked *why*, and if he says, "Because literature ought to reflect life and life is ironic," he can be asked to prove that literature ought to reflect life and to prove that life is always in all respects ironic. If, in answer to the second challenge, he says it is always in all respects ironic because the universe is essentially absurd, casting an ironic light on all human endeavors, he can be asked how he knows *that*. If he can show to our satisfaction that each of his steps is convincing (we do not ask for scientific proof, simply for evidence that he has taken the obvious objections into account), then we will follow him back to his general prescription about "all ironic literature." If he cannot give any reasons for thinking that the whole universe is absurd or hollow to the core or essentially against affirmation, reasons other than that it is fashionable to say so, then we can say to him that we know such-and-such a work (say *Middlemarch* or *War and Peace* or *Four Quartets*) that, while admitting a great richness of ironies, finally affirms certain values without the slightest ironic discounting, and both to him and to us they are great works; his general principles do no more than get in our way in trying to understand their greatness. Note that we do not say to him that they are great

7. The treatment of irony as universally desirable had clear beginnings in earlier centuries (see, for example, chapter 4 in Knox's *The Word Irony*, "Criticism of the Art of Irony"). But it really came into its own with the development by some New Critics of romantic theories of irony, especially as derived from Coleridge. It continues with surprising vigor, and in many different versions. See, for example, Charles I. Glicksberg, *The Ironic Vision in Modern Literature* (The Hague, 1969), esp. chaps. 1, 13, and 14.

*because* they affirm—that would be to assert a counter universal constant, equally indefensible outside a full philosophical system —but that we find them great and know that he does too. Since they do in fact affirm, there must be something wrong with the notion that *all* great works are essentially ironic—or essentially negative, which is the more usual way of putting this dogmatic demand.

One way of viewing the inadequacy of critical constants is to ask what we do when we find our pleasure in a character or scene or technique conflicting with somebody's claim that it violates some critical standard. We immediately proceed to work out some ingenious interpretation that will show how the suspected part really does belong in its context, or we search about until we find a rival constant to throw back at the critic. The truth is that we care more, or should care more, about the works that excite our admiration than we do about any possible constant they might follow or violate.

In short, the challenge to the defender of constants is to find a single bad quality that cannot be shown to be useful at some point in at least one work of recognized importance, or a single good quality that cannot be shown to be inappropriate or destructive in some contexts. Now if he can show us one, or two, or ten exceptions, we shall of course have to retreat a bit: but only a bit, because the more general case is that the search for qualities as constants in judging parts of works is critically useless even if we find them. Whatever constants we found would necessarily still be so general that any work, however wild, would exhibit them.

We must conclude, then, that though there are many qualities that are *sort-of-constant,* since they are suitable or useful in *many* works, there are none that can be universally applied to the parts or elements of works. When we say, "I like this work for its ironic language," or "This work fails because there is no ironic vision," the most we can mean, if we are pressed to defend ourselves, is, "This work as a whole succeeds with me and I find that the ironic language contributes to its success," or "This work as a whole is *of the kind* that cannot succeed without an ironic vision."

Though I would like to place this sweeping rejection above the desks of all those who rely on constants, to keep them honest, it is unfortunately subject to what Kenneth Burke would call ironic discounting in at least two points. First, taken absolutely it would, like the radical functionalism described in section A above, leave us in a forest of particulars, moving without accumulated profit from unique work to unique work, unable in each new experience to make use of our past experience, forced finally to admit that except in relating means to ends, the rankest beginner's preference is worth as much as the experienced reader's; if one reader likes the quality of blunt pornographic excitement and the other likes ironic complexity, who is to judge between them? The effort to develop a loophole with some "sort-of-constants" is surely unsatisfactory.

But secondly, a close look shows that the argument was itself dependent on a critical constant, one that I must admit to holding throughout this book, even when I have not been thinking about it: my refutation of constants holds good only *if* it is always a good thing for literary parts to contribute appropriately or necessarily to the works in which they occur; otherwise the form cannot be apprehended. If I surrender *that* constant for one moment, then a defender of irony as a constant can say that irony is always a good thing (when done well), even if and when it destroys other effects in the works containing it. Just as a true aficionado of the sublime will sacrifice everything for a sublime moment, just as Aristotle seems to be willing to sacrifice any other principle in the name of increased tragic effect, so can a defender of *any* effect reject my argument, if I surrender *my* constant, artistic coherence that is in some degree sharable.

But of course I am not willing to surrender it. Though there are some works that fail as wholes but that are in some sense saved by brilliant parts, it is still true that all good literature must hold together, somehow, to be good. Even the "parts" that I admire out of context hold together in themselves; there can be, for me, no literary achievement without some sort of form or coherence, yielding the pleasure, more or less conscious, that apprehending "multeity in unity" gives.[8]

I could perhaps claim that this is not really a constant of the kind the argument rejects, because it is merely a restatement of the first kind of judgment: pleasure in any coherent whole is made up of a recognition that the parts do their job in the best possible way. But I have relied on a second constant, implicit in the first, one that surely cannot be dismissed in this way: the rhetorical standard of "the meeting of minds." It is always good, I have assumed, for two minds to meet in symbolic exchange; it is always good for an irony to be grasped when intended, always good for readers and authors to achieve understanding (though the understanding need not lead to mutual approval

8. Almost every critical position offers some kind of equivalent for Coleridge's phrase. It is itself "ironic," we should remind ourselves, according to those who broaden the term to include any sharp contrast or seeming contrast: How can there be unity of what is multiple?

—that is another question entirely). This is a critical constant which I cannot in any degree explain away, and it is thus as vulnerable to my initial objections as any other; if another reader decides that maximizing private ironic pleasure is more important than the meeting of minds, then he and I are formally on the same ground—to my great discomfort. Though we could, I believe, engage in profitable discussion about the consequences of choosing our constants, I cannot claim, as I at one time thought, that my position is somehow logically purer than his.

For the moment all I can say is that our constants ought to be put in hypothetical form, so that we know where we stand: *If* you agree that *one* valuable thing that literature can do is to mold readers into shapes previously created by authors—if you agree that it is good for readers to experience effects created for them by skillful authors—then a further range of relative prescriptions can be stated. All of them will be non-universal at least in the sense that nobody can prove that they should be everywhere in all works.

If, for example, a work calls for intense active involvement in making any kind of judgment, then stable irony will be valuable—provided, of course, that circumstances allow for it, a large proviso indeed. The question then becomes, in this small corner where three vast subjects, irony, rhetoric, and value theory, intersect: what makes the difference between strong and weak in an effect held to be desirable? The answers are disappointingly general, leaving all particulars to be settled by the detailed demands of each work in its special kind.

1. Each ironic stroke should be neither too difficult nor too easy. If it is too difficult it will of course be overlooked or, if detected, blurred in effect. If it is too easy we cannot resist blaming the author for pretending to be a clever ironist. In practice, of course, we have experience with the first extreme only when other readers have pointed out our oversights, or perhaps when we reread. This may be why there are far more complaints about the blatant than the subtle.

2. The second golden mean is no more helpful than the first, though we cannot in practice avoid it: the judgment required must be neither too harsh nor too generous. Note that this mean, to some degree operating in all communication of judgments, comes into much more powerful play as soon as irony is used. An ironic stroke simply will not work unless the judgment it both relies on and reinforces is somehow "reasonable." At the extremes the irony will again be simply overlooked; short of that, it cannot be judged as clever unless the judgment it asks for is at least plausible. Yet it asks to be judged as clever. Once again we see why it is so risky.

3. Closely related to clarity is economy. Since the essence of

success in this kind of irony is swift communion of meanings that make the reader himself feel clever for seeing so much in so little, the less the better. A *Candide* twice as long would be half as good. Not: "I have always been a lucky sort of person, and in this case luck was again mine: indeed I can say that providence was on my side." Rather: "As luck would have it, providence was on my side." Not: "In my considered opinion, Bolingbroke is—if you take my meaning—a holy man." Rather: "Bolingbroke is a holy man."

In short, even when the ironist in this mode must nudge—and he frequently must—he must not be *thought* to nudge. Recognizable nudging, anything that might be seen as increased bustle on the author's part, decreases the active role of the reader. In the language of J. L. Austin, the speech act moves from being a performative—*"do* something for or with me"—to descriptive, from dance to assertion. Since irony "claims" to be performative, nudging contradicts its claims.[9]

But—to move to a second hypothetical general standard—if instead of strong judgment a work calls for the greatest possible intensity of what might be called "deciphering energy," then all these rules are modified. It must, as in *Finnegans Wake,* mix into its stable ironies a generous sprinkling of instabilities. It will make every proper reader feel, at no matter what stage in his reconstruction:

> that many of his reconstructions must again be reconstructed, perhaps *ad infinitum;*

> that he has missed many clues and must now try harder;

> that there is thus never any chance that he can fully reconstruct the author's intentions, so clever was the author in foreseeing and forestalling every possible final closure; and

> that enough stabilities have still been found so that he knows himself to be on the right path, in contrast to all the possible dullards who would be totally, not just partially, baffled.

All of this means that the work of *this* kind should be maximally prodigal rather than economical. A sense of richness is all; even when simple clear judgments are employed, they should be underplayed or disguised.[10]

Such rules will scarcely simplify the lot of the practicing critic.

---

9. See chap. 3, n. 11. We now make explicit why Alcanter de Brahm's plea for a punctuation mark was misguided. If he had ever developed his system he would surely have wanted a set of evaluative sub-symbols: * = average; † = superior; ‡ = not so good; § = marvelous; || = perhaps expunge.

10. See the discussion of Beckett in chap. 9.

They are far less general than those implied in what most critics say, yet they are not sufficiently particular to help us when we are doubtful about any actual bit of irony. At best they might explain, after the event, why a critic has found himself praising a passage. But since they all depend on the initial "if," they all force us, for their validation, to the close consideration of larger contexts that can call into play this or that hypothetical judgment.

## C. Success of Particular Works

How do we know a good work when we see one, and how do we share our knowledge? Every critic must face this question in his own way, as the cliché goes, but there really are not that many ways to go around. In deciding whether a work *does* something well that is worth doing, or *is* something good that is worth being, the critic has only four or five general directions to look. We can admire a work because it is constructed unusually well (objective or formal criticism); because it expresses its author or his situation effectively (expressive); or because it does something to us with unusual force (rhetorical); or because it contains or conveys a true or desirable doctrine (didactic, or ideological); or because it culminates or illustrates a tradition or initiates a fashion (historical).

Since every work *is* all of these—a construction, an expression, an action on its audience, an embodiment of beliefs, and a moment in history—a critic stressing any one interest will find all works amenable to his judgments. And there is no reason to expect in advance that judgments generated by any one of these five interests will agree or disagree with judgments coming from the others. While it often happens, for example, that a work everyone sees as "well constructed" also produces powerful effects on readers or expresses its author's deepest dreams, we often find that the historically important work, or the truest poetry, or the hard hitter may seem, to expressionist or objectivist critics, seriously deficient. The point is that we should expect different evaluations, each quite possibly valid in its own terms, when critics are dealing with radically different questions.

In a rhetorical inquiry our direction is clearly marked: we look at kinds and degrees of effectiveness. And we find ourselves in a curious circularity: what is good is what we really admire, and what we really admire is good. It is not a circularity peculiar to the rhetorical direction; in fact I think all the other paths can be easily shown to end in similar circularities, and to be none the weaker for that. But the rhetorical mode dramatizes the inescapably social nature of literary standards. We do not obtain our criteria through some private intuition or

207

divine revelation or strictly logical deduction from known first principles: we experience something together, sense its value as we experience, and then confirm that value in discourse with other valuers. Instead of some final cogent argument demonstrating to the world that
*since* S is an absolute standard and *since* work X realizes it, *therefore*
X is good, we really say, in effect, "I experienced X and found it
teaching me the value of that kind of work, which I therefore now
value. It also taught me that it realizes that value in high degree—better
than others of the kind I know of or can imagine—and *therefore* I
know it to be a good member of a 'good kind.' " In short, we judge
the work by the values which we have learned to employ by reading
the work.

What saves the scandal of this circularity from being also a scandal of radical and arbitrary particularism is that we experience every
work under the aspect of its implied general kind, or genre. We may or
may not know of other works in the same kind; I think that for most
of the works we admire, we do not know rivals in the genre. It is the
misleading experience of "epic" and "tragedy" and "comedy," some
classic versions of which spawned progeny, that has confused us here:
because certain major works like *Oedipus* produced close descendants,
criticism has always tended to make do with an impoverished list of
kinds. It has thus too often imposed constants derived from a few
genres, when it should have sought multiple values discerned in innumerable genres.

Just what makes a literary genre is a vexing topic that now fills
many a book and journal.[11] It will always be a vexing topic, because
what we take to be a kind will always depend on our reasons for classifying, and these will legitimately vary from critic to critic. Fortunately,
we do not need here an elaborate theory, since my purpose is mainly
to cast a skeptical light on all criteria that assume identical intentions in
works that are radically different. For such a purpose, we need only a
rough-and-ready reminder that works are not usefully grouped unless
they are similar in quite precise ways: in general pattern or sequence,
in technique, in medium, and in effect. A genre, in this approach, will
consist only of works sufficiently alike on all four counts[12] to allow

11. See, for example, the much discussed argument in Hirsch, *Validity in
Interpretation,* and the journals *New Literary History, Genre,* and *Novel,* all
relatively new and all containing genre theory in almost every issue.

12. One might want, for some purposes, to use instead Burke's five "drama-
tistic" terms, or his more recent list of seven. Aristotle's four are especially
useful whenever one looks closely at the intentional product of a human
action. For the simple purposes of the list below, I reduce the four to three:

me to say: these two authors were, almost certainly, trying for similar achievements, and they could presumably have learned from each other how to do it; consequently I may, by learning from each, discover standards for judging the achievement of either. Needless to say, this way yields no rounded number of four or ten or thirty-six or any other determinate number of literary forms or genres but rather hundreds of forms known to me, to say nothing of the presumed thousands unknown or of those that will be invented tomorrow.

To describe very many of these would be pointless, and to describe any one of them in adequate detail—distinguishing techniques, subjects, structures, and effects—would require a chapter in itself. But I must hint, in shorthand, at the enriched repertory of genres, the sheer variety of effects and shapes that must be recognized by anyone who seeks to judge the success of "ironic works." If I am right, my list errs in giving too few differences, not too many, but even these few ought to make the point that a predominantly "lumping" style in criticism of ironies has obscured much that we in fact care about. Each class is intended to hint at effects, at overall form, and at the structure of what is ironized and what left firm.

1. The Tragedy of Emptiness: In Malcolm Lowry's *Under the Volcano,* to me a deeply moving tragic novel, what limits the ironies is the inescapable human importance of the characters, particularly the Consul. Though he denigrates himself in every imaginable way, the book does not and cannot deny his human significance. The effect is compounded of terror at the "emptiness of life," regret that things cannot be otherwise, lament over the loss of such a creature (or rather, such creatures—the others are wasted too), and wry intellectual communion with Lowry about the way the ironies of life are here realized. In contrast with The Snotty Sublime (no. 5 below), the *caring* is never discounted.

2. The Discovery of the Abyss: This is closely related to no. 1 but quite distinct. Here the central character(s) must learn through the course of the work what the Consul in *Under the Volcano* knows from the beginning, as Marlow in Conrad's *Heart of Darkness* learns that the heart of man, like the heart of the universe, is dark. The horror

---

predominant literary effect, overall shape, and the beliefs that serve as a kind of matter formed. Genre terms that leave out the first of these (e.g., "sonnet," "novel," "lyric") give us no help with irony at all; terms that suggest nothing about shape (e.g., "epic," "elegy") are similarly useless. What we need are terms that imply effect and shape and belief, as *tragedy* still does, at least in some critical contexts.

lies in wait to be discovered by anyone who is spiritually adventure-some. The *Erziehungsroman,* invented by Goethe and others on the assumption that beneath ironic undercuttings there were some solid truths that a hero could be educated to, turned into this even more ironic form when authors became convinced that the only final education for a mature man was to recognize the emptiness, the abyss. But there are still limits here; nothing undercuts the sense of *importance* of the quest, of *honesty* in unmasking error and facing the truth, of *courage* in facing the horror. Though everything else may be ironized, the nobility of the quest is not.

3. The Defiance: Often called ironic, works in this genre are different from 1 and 2 in dramatizing defiant response to the emptiness. Though the universe itself and every *other* response to it are subject to ironic undercutting, courageous, even fist-shaking choice of resistance is not. Perhaps the paradigmatic work here is Camus's *The Plague,* in which Dr. Rieux, who knows the plague on all its levels, literal and metaphorical, and who chooses to fight it, is never ironically discounted.

4. The Whimpering: Facing the same facts as the hero of The Defiance, the author, his characters, and his readers here see everything as ironic except their own self-pity; everything is unsure except that their hollow fate is pitiable. Naturally I can think of no fully admirable examples of a genre I have named so contemptuously, expressing an attitude that Eliot satirizes. No long work will merely whimper throughout, and it is not surprising that most works that come to mind here are lyric poems: e.g., Hardy's "Hap," once a favorite of mine, seems to me now to whimper. (It still seems to me a very good poem, in the class of whimperers; that I have demoted the class does not mean that I can no longer admire one of the best poems in it. What's more, I may tomorrow feel like whimpering again and find that the poem has regained all of its original power.) Many who object to *Jude the Obscure* claim that it is too close to a prolonged bleat of Hardy's self-pity. Much of Sylvia Plath's *The Bell Jar,* unlike her best poetry, seems to me unintentionally painful as an appeal for sympathy from those rare spirits who know the Truth of Things, as against the slobs and knaves. Mark Twain's last works, when he began to speak seriously about the universe, often whimper. Even Joyce's "Araby," despite its attempts to show that Joyce is himself ironically superior to the whimpering, seems to me now to whimper a bit. But the point is not the aptness of my examples or the justness of my damning but the limits found in the writing self and his sensitive readers: *they* still matter, and the universe is blamed for not recognizing their worth.

5. The Nauseating Wallowing: Perhaps Burrough's *The Naked*

*Lunch,* or Hubert Selby, Jr.'s *Last Exit to Brooklyn.* Here "everything is undermined," "there is no meaning"—except that disgust is still intended: the irony is limited still by a genuine revulsion, which means a genuine regret that life is so awful. If nothing really mattered, nothing portrayed in words could nauseate me, and what is more, I would not try to nauseate others with a picture of how things are.

6. The Snotty Sublime: Here the special limiting delight is that of the sophisticated, *méchant* puncturing: what fun we can have if we recognize that all values except our superior ironic insight can be ridiculed. The value system is the same as in no. 5, but the pleasure is entirely different. Author and reader relate as do the two characters in Richard B. Wright's *The Weekend Man*:

> Our conversation now gathers in upon itself and becomes a full-scale put-down of Harold's party. Everything from Hank Bell-amy's dirty jokes to Duncan MacCauley's gabardine trousers are [*sic*] raked with a mild pleasing scorn. Near the lighted Christmas tree we talk in whispers, like two bored teen-agers at a movie. Our remarks are unfair and ungracious and not terribly funny but they bring us together and we are soon hitting it off, feeling comfortable with one another in our isolation.[13]

These two (5 and 6) come perhaps closest of any so far to being an "ironic genre plain." Nothing limits the piling up of ironies but the reader's patience and—in some—the blessed need to keep things fun. Many short "put-ons" in *The New Yorker* of recent years have seemed to me redeemed only by Cleverness: Donald Barthelmé, though he often rises above this objection, to me often falls beneath it.

7. The Revolution: Everything is undermined with irony—everything, that is, connected with the bourgeoisie, or the establishment. As in the plays of Brecht, one unfailing limit to the irony is the implication that to overthrow All This, with words or with actions, will be a Good Thing.

8. The Comic Freeing: Another kind of revolution, the over-throwing of forms and conventions. Past restraints are undermined, comically, in the service of a joyful sense of release from inhibition. Life's invitations to fun are celebrated, including the delights of irony and its capacity to free. But, fellow romantics, do not push the irony too far, or you will pass from the joyful laughter of *Tristram Shandy* into Teutonic gloom. Read Schlegel.

9. The Aesthetic Manifesto: The Freeing moves imperceptibly into the Program for Art as Savior. Art views everything ironically

13. 1970. Signet ed. (New York, 1972), p. 101.

except art itself, whose ironic light imitates either the vision of God or the mockery of Satan. Not "Ah, love, let us be true to one another," but "Ah, reader, let us make beautiful things, or true things, together; naught else is worth the having." Carried out with Gallic logic, the program leads to works purged of every interest except their Art, as in the attempts of Robbe-Grillet. And once the value of art itself is put under radical questioning, you get infinite instability, as in no. 10.

10. The Serio-Comic Groping: Samuel Beckett here. Meaning where? Knowing nothing, least of all why I write, call that writing, why my characters speak, call that speaking. Lonely down here (where?) where it is known (by whom?) that even to express loneliness is absurd . . .

It is clear by now, surely, how futile would be any effort to make systematic such varieties of "ironic works," though I must attempt a different kind of system in the next chapter. Without half trying one could extend the list to any required good round number—nineteen, say—of *the* ironic genres:

11. The Comic Apotheosis of the Coping Self (Max Beerbohm)

12. The Comic Apotheosis of the Escaping Self (*Catch-22*)

13. The Comic Consolation (Thurber's helpless and wonderful disaster-mongering)

14. The Ironic Warning (*Brave New World, 1984*)

15. The Game (*Ada*; perhaps *V*; perhaps *Tiny Alice*)

16. The Ironic though Serious Elegy (Auden's "In Memory of W. B. Yeats")

17. The *Perhaps* Triumphant Meditation, against "Impossible" Odds (*The Waste Land*)

18. The Encyclopedia of All Ironic Wisdom (*Finnegans Wake*)

19. The Celebration of Infinitely Ironic Existence. A kind of extension of the Comic Freeing, this becomes in "post-modernist" times a portrayal of existence freed from the intellectual worries of Modernism. *Herzog,* for example, takes us through and beyond the abyss, "proves" that talk about the void can be funny, not tragic, and discovers for us that life can be lived here and now, in spite of anything Nietzsche or Kafka can say.

And so on, through a circle of increasingly firm undergirdings, back to confirmations like "The Ironic Prayer of Thanksgiving or Wonder," as offered by Flannery O'Connor or François Mauriac or W. H. Auden.

The point is that one could go on indefinitely, discovering more and more ironic kinds, each of which will determine its own unique standards of too much and too little, of too gross and too subtle, of too sweeping and too narrow, of stability and instability. If we worked at it—and it would be better to do so than to work at many critical tasks that are more common—we would find "ironic works" intending almost every general human attitude toward the mysteries of existence: purifying, pardoning, indicting, condoling, exorcising, dispassionately contemplating, mocking, uniting, inciting, terrifying ("The Lottery"), preaching (*Lord of the Flies*), and offering sacrificial victims (*Light in August*). And we would similarly find formal structures of almost every known shape. Whatever anatomy of shapes you use—Frye's, Burke's, your own—you will find that somebody has called every item ironic, and that irony under any particular definition will be prescribed by some shapes, proscribed by others. In short, few if any of these works can be said to belong to a genre, "*the* ironic," to be "an irony," not at least in the sense that a tragedy like *Oedipus Rex* has been thought to belong wholeheartedly to the genre "tragedy."

Regardless of the accuracy of my generic descriptions, then, I hope that my general point stands: no rule for creating or judging irony suitable to any one of these will precisely suit any other.

We come to rest then on a third form of hypothetical standard, closely related to the first: *if* you conclude that this ironic work is striving to become a Tragedy of Emptiness or Discovery of the Abyss, or Nauseating Wallowing, *then* such-and-such norms may be relevant. But by now we have escaped from the particularism which threatened earlier. We do not limp from work to work; rather we discover kinds and relate works to their generic possibilities.

But are there no good works in a more general sense? Are there only works good for the generic ends I have postulated? Have we no way of judging among different kinds, different essential forms, different genres? If so, can we never say that this work is excellent of its kind but its kind is bad, or at least inferior to others?

## D. Comparison of Kinds

Although I was making some effort to keep my catalog of ironic genres neutral, every reader will have noticed just how much bias crept into both the names and the descriptions. I was willy-nilly judging the "Tragedy of Emptiness" as inherently superior to, say, "The Whimpering"—though of course this or that whimpering might be judged on other grounds as superior to this or that tragedy of emptiness. In doing so, I was turning into a genre distinction what critics who employ larger groupings would consider differences of excellence between works within a single genre.

By the use of commodious genres, we might thus dodge for a while the question of whether cross-genre judgments are in any way defensible. But it would be only a dodge; the sharper distinctions of genre that I have used make explicit a universal practice.

A great deal has been written, from Aristotle on, about the superiority of tragedy to epic, or of comedy to farce, or of dramatic narrative forms to discursive, or of Ibsenian tragedy to Millerian, or of tragedy-with-ironic-denouement to tragedy-with-resounding-resolution. So much of such evaluation has been so crudely assertive, with so little effort to give reasons, that one can understand the recent impulse to damn the whole effort to compare and simply appreciate or interpret. But everyone does in fact judge among kinds, concluding that Elizabethan tragedy, say, is (or even that it is not) superior as a kind to science fiction or hard-core pornography, or that a long satiric poem like *The Dunciad* is greater than the best couplet Pope ever wrote.

Have such choices any aesthetic standing whatever? Can they be defended with critical reasoning? The reasons against attempting to do so are obvious: as soon as we decide to treat such questions, we can no longer answer them by a simple structural reference to the work in hand and its implied genre, at levels A and C; our arguments will become less and less firmly based on textual evidence, the more we try to show that even the best work of one kind will be inferior to the best of another kind. As soon as we try to deal with such questions we inevitably infringe on the patents of other disciplines.

We can see this easily if we ask where we are to turn for arguments to decide whether the comprehensiveness and depth and tragic force of *King Lear*, say, are more important artistically (or any other way) than the perfect concision and clarity and ironic force of the couplet by Pope:

> I am his Highness' Dog at *Kew*;
> Pray tell me Sir, whose Dog are you?

In defending a choice which everyone who knows both works will make, we have only four *general* directions left open to us, once we assume that each is a superlative construction in its kind.

Those who like to talk about the artist's powers will naturally turn to what the two works imply of their makers. I cannot, for example, avoid thinking that the imaginative and constructive powers required to write *Lear* were greater than those required to write the couplet. The author implied by the play seems to be a magnanimous, profound, sensitive, imaginative human being, while the author implied by the couplet is at most a clever sardonic man. If I am inclined to be envious,

214

I will envy Shakespeare his work much more than I will envy Pope (and of course I will envy the implied author of *The Dunciad* far more than the author of this couplet). But how do I argue for such value judgments about human beings, imagined ones at that? What must I do if someone disputes my evaluation? Where can I turn? Only, I think, to the kind of debate that would conventionally go on—or that ought to go on—in a department of philosophy or theology or psychology or anthropology or sociology.

The same will happen, secondly, to critics who deal with the "reality" or "truth" that the works reflect. I simply cannot, try as I will, claim that the total picture of man and his universe implied by Pope's couplet is as interesting, as comprehensive, as true, as important, as the picture I get from *Lear*. But again, if you disagree with me, where are we to turn for genuine grounds of debate? Obviously we can turn only to other disciplines, many of which we will find plagued by the dogma that value judgments are essentially indefensible.

Thirdly, those who prefer to talk about the audience or reader will find themselves treating the relative importance of the effect of either work. But how does one *prove* that it is better to be moved to tragic depths than to be momentarily amused?

Finally, historical critics may want to show that *Lear* has meant more in all historical perspectives than the couplet—all, that is, but one, the history of the couplet. But again, to prove their claims, they will not be able to use "specifically literary" standards, whatever they might be.

Wherever we turn, then, we open up problems of value theory that some would say cannot be reasonably argued, and that all would agree are not specific to "literary criticism."

If we choose, as I think we must, to defy such doubts and limitations, we encounter more dangers than when we remain within the protective boundaries of individual works or carefully defined specific forms. The most obvious is that once we have admitted a general criterion for judging the importance of a literary kind, we are sorely tempted to apply it to works that don't really fit our kind, or (which may amount to the same thing) we are tempted to collect as many instances of our admired kind as possible. For example, supposing our subsuming criterion comes from some notion of man's ironic plight, or of man's nature as exemplified in the "ironic" American experience. We discover a wide variety of significant works that reflect more or less fully what we think of as the truth of man's situation, or the American experience, and we write our book on The American Adam or Radical Innocence or Love and Death or The Landscape of Nightmare or The

Dungeon and the Heart or The Eternal Adam and the New World Garden in the American novel—and we are naturally tempted to find more and more instances, to find instances at all costs. And when we have found works that *almost* fit the pattern, it is hard to know whether the work's failure to fit our pattern is an artistic failure or simply the fulfillment of another, equally valid pattern.[14]

This danger can be guarded against, but the second one can only be endured. Once we move to the level of trying to defend our general values, it will always be harder to decide what makes a persuasive, or even a relevant, argument in support of a given evaluation. How do we convince ourselves that a work is, say, true to the higher reaches of the human spirit, in contrast to an equally well constructed work that finally must be said to lie? Immediately we are landed in controversies that most of us have not been "trained" to deal with, controversies requiring the kind of encounter that we find in the major philosophers but that some modern philosophers would repudiate as meaningless. It is clear, for example, that much of the steam behind our zealous explications of ironies in recent decades comes from religious or metaphysical convictions that many have not thought through: general beliefs about the universe and about how man is totally alone or at home or astray in it; about how authors and readers should behave—beliefs about the value of comprehensiveness, of adequacy to the complexities of reality, of honesty in the face of absurdity, of humility in the face of mystery, of good humor or anger or *angst* in the face of inevitable disaster.

One such belief is especially important in all work on this fourth level. Once modern man had developed the notion that facts and values are sharply distinct, that one can never derive an "ought" from an "is," and that knowledge is obtainable only about the world of fact, the world of values was left to fend for itself. Values can be believed in, asserted, preached, and died for, but they cannot be defended with rational argument. In such a world—inescapably "ironic" because no one can resist valuing—it would be futile for a critic to seek to provide solid argument either for his critical constants (level B) or for his ultimate concerns—they are clearly value terms, implicating a sharp "ought," and knowledge about them is thus clearly impossible. Where in the name of reason could a critic go for his proof about the belief, say, that all good literature must be ironic in this or that sense, or must be coherent, or must somehow communicate its effects to a proper reader, or must express its author's deepest feelings sincerely? The two

14. For examples see *The Rhetoric of Fiction,* pp. 29–37.

kinds of proof that are, we have all been taught, the only proper kinds are flatly denied him. He cannot provide deductive or hypothetico-deductive proof, of the sort that we are able to use in functional criticism at levels A and C—by definition these values are ultimate, universal, and therefore not deduced from something else. But on the other hand, they clearly are not inductive, based on factual observation, because no values can be inferred from mere facts. Even if we could conduct a laboratory experiment, which we cannot do, or if we could devise the best questionnaire of all time, the results could not demonstrate that this or that quality is universally desirable.

Recently, as I have reported in *Modern Dogma and the Rhetoric of Assent,* men in a variety of fields have been rebelling against this impossible restriction. Fact and value are being reunited in many different ways. I cannot repeat any of the arguments here, but anyone who looks even briefly at what has been written on the subject of facts and values in the last five or ten years (instead of what was commonplace in the middle third of this century) will discover a crumpling of the dogma that values and commitments are inherently non-rational, non-cognitive, and hence indefensible in the courts of reason.[15]

For a rhetorician none of this recent shift is terribly surprising, because rhetoric has always provided a way of establishing values in the world of fact. Consider once again a value that has run implicitly throughout this book, not as a constant demand of *all* literature but as a constant value if and whenever achieved: from page 1 I have assumed that to achieve ironic communication is a worthwhile thing in itself. The assumption, unprovable in the courts of science or logic in the modern view of things, is thoroughly testable in the courts of rhetoric: the fact is that you and I without exception know from experience that we value this sort of thing. We seek it out; we practice it, and we know that others do the same, whether scholars or ditch-diggers. We deplore the impoverishment of those who cannot manage it. When we add to our agreement the agreement of generations in the Western tradition, and of all the other cultures that also have valued ironic communication,[16] we have an astonishing consensus of "experts" that gives us all we need to conclude that here is a genuine value. Our confidence is made all the stronger when we realize that there are no real experts on

15. See the *Journal of Value Inquiry* (1967—) for one source among hundreds. See also chap. 3, n. 9, above.

16. See pp. 30–31, n. 24, p. 40, n. 4. In our tradition the value starts with the Bible and Homer (when C. M. Bowra says, in *Tradition and Design in the Iliad,* that "Homer knows nothing of either irony or fustian" [Oxford, 1930, p. 240], he is clearly using a very special definition).

the other side—there simply are no great authors and no readers we could consider qualified who have acted or argued as if irony of all kinds should be eschewed. (Even the older Tolstoy, after he had attacked the ironies of Western literature because they divided man from man, went on writing ironic tales like "How Much Land Does a Man Need." And in his attack he affirmed, in fact, the very value I am affirming: successful communication.) With such consensus, the burden of disproof is surely placed upon the critic who would attack all irony.

But now consider the difference when we turn to any such proposition as that *all* good literature—or that the best literature—is ironic. Immediately our consensus is destroyed and we are landed in the bogs of controversy. Many a man or woman who has created or savored ironies in great number, and who therefore could qualify in some sense as an expert, would get off the boat at once, and our confidence in this constant should be reduced accordingly.

Does this mean that we cannot then resolve controversy about values except when we have clear consensus? Not in the least. For one thing, most constants are not in fact ultimates; they can be related to other larger or deeper generalizations about life and art where more consensus may be found. In fact every argument I have seen for irony as a universal criterion has been related to some kind of claim about "the nature of things" which is to be reflected in literature. "The metaphysical principle of irony . . . resides in the contradictions within our nature and also in the contradictions within the universe or God," says George Palante. "The ironic attitude implies that there is in things a basic contradiction, that is to say, from the point of view of our reason, a fundamental and irremediable absurdity."[17] The discussion is by this move thrust back into metaphysics, which does not make things any easier, but it does make for a different stage of the argument: "Literature must . . . *because* the universe is. . . ." This lends plausibility to the demand for universal irony that was not there before: since everyone who has thought about metaphysics would agree that the universe at least *"feels* like that" part of the time, since even the most religious persons will agree that "from the point of view of our reason" the universe often seems full of contradictions, the burden of proof is now placed back upon anyone who, like me, wants to question the universal standard.

In reply I can move in one of two directions, either arguing that the universe is not quite like that after all (which would require philo-

17. "L'ironie: étude psychologique," *Revue philosophique de la France et de l'étranger,* February 1906, p. 153; quoted in Muecke, *Compass of Irony,* p. 120, his translation.

sophical inquiry among those willing to stick with the subject for many hours and many days) or pointing back to the empirical data about what kinds of literature we in fact enjoy and admire. And here I think is where the argument for irony as a universal value finally must be abandoned, except in the self-proving form advanced by Cleanth Brooks. We in fact have hailed and do hail many works which assert unequivocal values without ironic undercutting. Would Wordsworth's "I Wandered Lonely as a Cloud" be improved if he had known enough to change the point to something more like that of Keats's "Ode to Melancholy," with the bliss explicitly undermined by the traditional melancholy truth that those daffodils are all dead by now, as the poet writes his poem, and he himself will die tomorrow? Would Burns's "Green Grow the Rashes O" be improved by giving it a new ending?—a rapid wrenching shift from the affirmation of

> Auld Nature swears, the lovely dears
> Her noblest work she classes, O;
> Her prentice han' she try'd on man,
> An' then she made the lasses, O.

to

> And yet I know as well as ye,
> That false are all the lasses, O.

or

> That love's a joy that passes, O.

Hardly, though I'll warrant that if two poems, identical except for such endings, were given to a random sampling of critics for judgment, the ironic poem would be chosen by many.[18]

It is true that one cannot think of works of any length and quality that do not encompass, as the formula has it, some realization of whatever forces run counter to the major affirmations. If the only claim were that every *Paradise Lost* must portray the devil fairly, every *Divine Comedy* include its *Inferno*, every *Herzog* do justice to the modernist problems its hero somehow surmounts, then we would have no trouble: a simple principle of reading interest requires that there must be conflict in any work running more than a few lines. If that is what a critic means by irony—and it is all that some critics do mean—then there is no argument. But sometimes what is meant is that every really great

18. I have tried it out on fifty graduate students, and though I did not find as many ironists as I had predicted (a majority), I did find that one-third chose the ironic version and gave the irony as their reason.

work must portray the way in which every potential affirmation is finally vulnerable to irony; and when that is the claim, all we can say is that few readers if any have found this to be uniformly so; we all reconstruct and share a wide range of solid affirmations. A determined irony hunter can of course make Satan the hero of *Paradise Lost,* turn Dante into an ironist in the *Paradiso,* show Dickens as a satirist when he portrays Esther Summerson in her final happiness, prove that George Eliot's Dorothea is ridiculous to worry so much about doing her duty by Casaubon. It is not hard to "demonstrate" that Dostoevsky and Kierkegaard and any other Christians who happen along could not have been serious.[19] In this way—but in this way only—is the argument for universal irony made self-proving. A good source of such improvising is Charles I. Glicksberg. The ironic vision requires us to recognize, he says, that we live in a meaningless void: such recognition produces a fusion of the tragic and the comic that is peculiarly "modern," a laughter that "has a ghastly ring," "the universal language of irony."[20] Yet he can, in his "meaningless world," cheerfully embrace standards dependent on meanings that contradict his general views: "Hardy voices an irony that is never shrilly derisive or condemnatory but instinct with pathos and compassion" (p. 99).

Thus Mr. Glicksberg imports the value of pathos and compassion back into his valueless universe. And his very effort to write a book that will actually say something contradicts his own denials.

None of this is more than a beginning to what might be said about evaluation across generic lines. But I hope it is enough to cast real doubt on those twin dogmas—that such evaluation is always meaningless and that the ironic genres are always superior. There are, I believe, many valid ways of pursuing further the conviction that one can speak about what Wittgenstein once told us we could not speak about.[21] The rhetorical way is to inquire carefully into what one means by words like "one" and "we." If "we" are to speak about values, who

---

19. For a typical argument that Dostoevsky simply *cannot* have been as serious in his Christian assertions as he was in his modernist ironies, especially in the Grand Inquisitor episode, see Vasily Rozanov, *Dostoevsky and the Legend of the Grand Inquisitor,* trans. Spencer E. Roberts (Baltimore, 1971). Jean Malaquais explores the thesis that Kierkegaard's conversion was unreal; the only genuine part of his thought, in spite of his own assertions to the contrary, was what negated Christian traditions and rebelled against the traditional God (*Søren Kierkegaard: Foi et paradoxe* [Paris, 1971]).

20. Glicksberg, *Ironic Vision,* p. 35. See Norman Knox, "On the Classification of Ironies," *Modern Philology* 70 (August 1972): esp. pp. 59–62.

21. "What we cannot speak about we must pass over in silence"—the concluding proposition of *Tractatus logico-philosophicus.*

are we? Rhetorical validation finally becomes validation of rhetoricians.

## II

### THE RHETORICAL MEETING AS A SOURCE OF NORMS

The notion that values are found and established *in valuers* entails the notion that some valuers are better at the task than others—not a popular notion these days but one we cannot avoid. Again and again I have had to say something like, "In *fact*, we *do* such-and-such, or *think and feel* such-and-such, when we read so-and-so. We—the readers who qualify each other as 'experts' by sharing our results—we value these actions and thoughts and emotions and this valuing establishes this value, for us." As one way of cutting traditional metaphysical knots, the theory of such circular dances is certainly controversial. It can be helpful, however, taken up not as a dogmatic solution to fixed problems but simply as a way of discovering "confidence enough" about questions of value.

We follow Hume's lead, then, given in the famous essay on the standard of taste, and ask: Who is the paragon who determines critical norms? Though I may often have sounded as if I offered myself for the job, everyone who has grappled with much irony knows his own fallibility. The rhetorical path questions in the sharpest possible way the notion that each man is for himself the best judge of what is. It questions that popular view, "If it seems good to me, it *is* good." It requires me to see "my personal view" as limited. But it also allows me to see in myself and others a natural capacity to respond with pleasure and admiration to qualities that a given work possesses, *unless* I am hampered by some momentary or permanent disability. We all have known in ourselves both the condition of fallibility and the condition of growing expertise, and we thus have shared thoroughly reasonable grounds for the conviction both that some readings are better than others and that each of us is capable of falling away from the standard of full alertness and sensitivity.

As Hume might say here, some stable ironies, because of the peculiar nature of the human mind, are capable of pleasing persons qualified to reconstruct them. Others will displease, and "amidst all the variety and caprice of taste [in irony], there are certain general principles of approbation or blame."[22] The problem then becomes that of detecting those deficiencies that will obscure our representative re-

22. Quoted and paraphrased from "Of the Standard of Taste," (1756), par. 10.

sponse to something designed to have a "natural" relationship to the properly attuned mind. As Hume implies, no one of us can hope to *be* "the expert" on all occasions; accidents of time and place and personal limitations will prevent our representing the "common sentiments of human nature." "Those finer emotions of the mind are of a very tender and delicate nature, and require the concurrence of many favourable circumstances to make them play with facility and exactness, according to their general and established principles. The least exterior hindrance . . . or the least internal disorder, disturbs their motion" (par. 8).

## FIVE CRIPPLING HANDICAPS

It should be useful to draw up a short list, like Hume's, of the "external hindrances" and "internal disorders" that are implicit in what has been said so far.[23] Such a list can remind us that though the judgments we are talking about are all in one sense "subjective," they are, as Hume says, "questions of fact, not of sentiment. Whether any particular person be endowed" with sound taste for ironies "may often be the subject of dispute . . . ; but that such a character is valuable and estimable will be agreed in by all mankind" (par. 12 to end).

I find in myself and others five major kinds of crippling handicap, with many sub-varieties of each: Ignorance, Inability to Pay Attention, Prejudice, Lack of Practice, and Emotional Inadequacy.

## Ignorance

Nobody knows very much compared with what might, being known, prove useful in reading ironies. As every true ironist knows, nobody knows very much about *anything,* compared with what we would need to know to walk securely or wisely through the world.

Since crippling ignorance can be about anything, there is no point in starting on a classification that could only end with a revision of *Roget's Thesaurus.* Nobody can work on removing ignorance in all directions at once; and therefore no particular exhortation or art can emerge from this greatest and most troubling of deficiencies.

Fortunately, there are often clues about special kinds of ignorance that may hamper us. Most of the "incredible" misreadings I know of have occurred when intelligent readers have ventured with too much confidence onto unfamiliar ground. There is in fact a neat and absolute law here, in a field that I have said presents no absolutes: the more remote a work is from my home province (my century, my country, my

23. See also I. A. Richards's *Practical Criticism* (London, 1929), pp. 13–18: "The Ten Difficulties of Criticism."

family, my profession, my church, my club, my generation) the more mistakes I will make in a given reading period.

This can all be put scientifically. My graduate student Gertrude Impersney has studied 273 famous cases of failure in comprehension, plotting degrees of error (E) and the period of duration of incomprehension (DI) against the distance (D) of the cultural milieu of the ironist from the victim's cultural milieu (CMV). We were both gratified when her results yielded the "straight line curves" illustrated in figure 4.

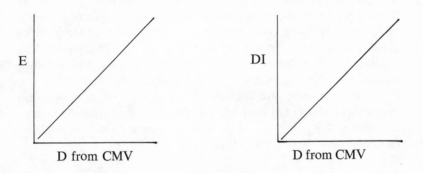

Fig. 4

The obvious lesson to be learned from this law is that confidence in my inferences should vary inversely with my distance from "home," and that if I must make inferences when away from home (and I frequently must), my special efforts to obtain essential knowledge must be directly proportional to the distance. Members of boards of trustees should send land-mine experts ahead of them when they travel into the underground press, or even into the official student newspaper; specialists in Swift will do well to withhold comment on Confucius' sayings until they have done some homework.

### Inability to Pay Attention

Lack of full attention to the words that sweep over us daily may not matter very much; indeed a certain amount of inattentiveness may be necessary to survive them. One can read most pages of the daily newspaper at a great rate, while watching a baseball game on TV. But then one comes to Art Buchwald's daily ironies, or—more dangerous still— to Russell Baker's column, one day ironic, the next day literal, the third day a mixture, and one sits down, morally alert and mentally torpid, to write an indignant letter to the editor, attacking the ironist for a position that he was himself attacking. It is the virtue of irony—perhaps its supreme moral justification—that it wakes men by punishing them for sleep.

I know of no law quite so generally applicable under "attention" as the one concerning ignorance and distance from home, though Ms. Impersney is now conducting studies to see whether her results will not also obtain here. No one can be perpetually alert, yet perpetual alertness is in a sense what is required. About all we can say, beyond shouting "Wake up," is that we should modulate our confidence in our results to the degree of alertness we know ourselves to have shown. As Hume says, "A man in a fever would not insist on his palate as able to decide concerning flavours; nor would one affected with the jaundice pretend to give a verdict with regard to colours. In each creature there is a sound and a defective state; and the former alone can be supposed to afford us a true standard of taste and sentiment" (par. 12). This means that we must also cultivate the chancy art of assessing other readers' alertness (as of their other qualities): I must simply pay more attention to the judgments of those who seem to have attended most carefully.

## Prejudice

But this suggestion, useful and indeed inescapable if one is to survive without nervous apprehension at all moments, cannot preserve one from difficulty with ironies that do not fit one's own precise beliefs. What I. A. Richards called "doctrinal adhesions" can keep me from understanding and enjoying a non-ironic poem that violates my norms, but so can they prevent my inferring ironies when the implied author's norms seem to me less plausible than the surface statement that violates them. The readers who were trapped by Samuel Butler's pseudonymous work *The Fair Haven for the Just*,[24] were victimized by their prejudices in favor of Christian miracles and against the "higher criticism": they presumably could not believe that a defense of Christianity against the unbelievers could be in fact an attack on Christian miracles by an unbeliever.

In 1970 a faculty member published in a college paper an ironic plea for revolution, attributed to a freshman; he filled it with a great list of follies and irrationalities and sentimentalities—a list sufficiently absurd for "anyone" to infer his satiric point when he said in his own name that "this paper expresses some of my own views better than I

24. London, 1873.

can myself"—that is, the "paper" attacks itself by its own absurdity. But it was taken literally by many readers who attacked the professor for what he was attacking. Presumably their picture of what a professor would probably say was confirmed by the silly and internally inconsistent gabble the paper displayed. And no doubt the seeming offense against their passionately held beliefs blinded them to the intent of a conclusion like this:

> ... only when we realize that after a person has been corrupted by the System, he can't be uncorrupted. When people have become repressive . . . (up-tight, rule-making, and Pig-minded), they *become* the System, which we are out to destroy. It's an objective fact, I feel, that they are not true free individuals any more but only a kind of inferior scum that doesn't deserve to live, and there is only one way to deal with them: KILL THE PIGS!
> In conclusion, I realize that everybody probably won't agree with me. . . . But in general I sincerely think that what I think I am trying to say is true.[25]

Insofar as our beliefs are in fact judgments that we are willing and able to defend, there is nothing we can or necessarily should do about removing them. But we can take thought about them as we read. Any administrator or board of trustees member could easily have said to himself, "Now let's see: which notion of the 'professor' makes better sense out of the details of this piece—the professor as wild-eyed radical or the professor who defends reason against irrationality?" Since at least a third of the details could not fit anybody's notion of an educated man, revolutionary or not, the second hypothesis, once tried on for size, is sure to prevail. The trick is in developing a habit of great skepticism about one's own hypothesis, and great flexibility in trying out alternatives. When these mental habits are missing, even a highly sensitive and learned mind can easily go astray, if the norms of a book violate the reader's own.

Needless to say, prejudice can operate on any axis of value; fixed notions of what makes a good literary form or technique can be as hampering as notions of what makes a good man (see I. A. Richards's "technical presuppositions" and "general critical preconceptions").

Since every reader carries a great load of prejudgments, since in fact he could not read anything without relying on them, one cannot exhort oneself simply to read with an "open mind." But the word "prejudice" suggests a value judgment, distinguishing what is idiosyncratic to the reader from prejudgments that are shared or sharable with

25. *Earlham Post*, 7 March 1970.

the relevant rhetorical community. Many of our prejudgments are entirely private—they amount to what Richards calls "mnemonic irrelevancies," being based on memory of private experience. By taking thought one can to some degree control the depredations of such privacies: "I know I am not a good judge of jokes about X, because I was frightened by one as a child." But the only true shield from them, again, is a healthy tentativeness about oneself and one's responses, until compared with those of other readers who seem not to be especially disqualified. Needless to say, those prejudices are most destructive that carry the strongest emotional load. As everyone knows, ironies that touch too close to sacred objects are almost certain to be misread.

## Lack of Practice

Everything that I said about the grooves of genre suggests that those who cannot recognize the grooves, however attentive, unprejudiced, or wise they are, will misread ironies. We need not try to settle here the current debate about whether at least some of our equipment for recognizing genres is innate. If we define such equipment at a more general level than I have implied, seeing it, say, as a capacity to recognize "such arrangements of subject-matter as produce crescendo, contrast, comparison, balance, repetition, disclosure, reversal, contraction, expansion, magnification, series," and so on, then I think that Kenneth Burke, from whom I borrow this list, is right in saying that we have certain "potentialities of appreciation which would seem to be inherent in the very germ-plasm of man, . . . innate forms of the mind."[26] But even if this is so, and even if we added the less secure belief that in a sense we have innate generic capacities for at least some basic forms like comedy and tragedy, we still are helpless in the face of elaborate and sophisticated ironies unless we have encountered a great many ironic varieties. To use complicated ironies on children is sadistic because even the brightest child lacks the experience—and it is not just "ignorance" in the sense described above—that would enable him to interpret irony. We must also admit the painful fact that some persons must be born with mental equipment below the threshold required for recognizing the ironic invitation. It must be, however, a fairly low threshold, because anyone who can develop a pattern of expectations,

26. "The Poetic Process," *Counter-Statement* (Los Altos, Calif., 1931; 2d ed., 1953), p. 46. Burke anticipates by some decades the kind of talk about innate universal linguistic potentialities that Chomsky stirred the world with in the fifties and sixties. And it was not original with him. But linguists generally ignored him and his sources until the climate was right.

and then recognize that it has been falsely suggested and then violated, can recognize irony. "I'm going to eat you," the father says to the two-year-old, and the child laughs in delight; a stranger says the same thing and the child looks troubled or bursts into tears.

We might think that in an age with so much irony as ours, everyone would have removed at least this one handicap. But if I am right about the dulling effect of unstable ironies, it is clear that a spate of uninterpretable ironies has the same effect as providing no experience in irony at all. In short, someone who sees ironies everywhere is almost as disqualified as someone who has had little or no experience. The quality of the experience is what counts.

### Emotional Inadequacy

In a catalog that will no doubt seem to some readers offensively elitest, this last defect will seem most offensive of all. But the fact is that some readers disqualify themselves by being either too ready to emote or too resistant to emotional appeals. The first kind may respond with sentiment to what is intended as a parody of sentiment; the second kind may protect themselves by laughing "ironically" at a great tragic scene. Sentimentality and coldness (as Longinus observed) are the faulty extremes of a human norm hard to define and harder to achieve. Whether the norm in fact exists, it is presupposed by much irony. So far as I can see, there is simply nothing one can do about this kind of inadequacy that is any simpler than amending one's whole life. Psychoanalysis, religious conversion, allowing ten years for general maturing—these may help the victim, but meanwhile the fault exists only as something for other people to take into account: in deciding which "experts" to pay attention to, when I try to obtain help in my own readings, I can legitimately rule out those who have shown themselves in other circumstances to be habitually sentimental or congenitally cold.[27]

### CONCLUSION: NEITHER RULES NOR RELATIVISM

These results may seem disappointing. I mean them to be—at least to all readers who would like to have useful general rules for judging literature. Everything I have said is too general to be of much use, because in the last analysis all rhetorical situations are unique. Unlike those sciences which deal in duplicatable (and therefore more or less

---

27. There are of course a host of other reading handicaps one could name. Hume lists, for example, lack of "good sense," which means for him inability to hit upon those judgments and responses that are commonly shared by men in a given culture—lack of *common* sense." But this can in practice always be reduced to one of the five.

completely rule-subjected) moments, the ironist and reader of irony deal in the unique in either of two senses:

1. If a given irony is intended to reinforce a rhetoric which sets out to achieve practical results in the future, it faces an audience with a question and subject combined in a moment which will never be the same again: *this* audience will be moved by such and such degrees and quantities of irony and no other. One can know in advance, of course, that most audiences will be delighted, for example, with the ancient ironic ploy: "My opponent has said (or done) X; he has also said (or done) Y, which visibly contradicts X. It is clear that only a fool or a knave could say (or do) both of these incompatible things." But the next step will vary from audience to audience and subject to subject: how much one leaves to inference, how much direct statement of faith in one's opponent's deep integrity or sharp intelligence will never be formulable as a general rule.

2. If, on the other hand, a given irony serves a rhetoric for a more nearly permanent, idealized audience, setting out to realize artistic effects in the "present (eternal) moment," the ironist's *particular* work will require kinds and quantities different from those of every other work; his audience is "the right reader" (in part made by the work itself) for *this* work. Though in one sense such a reader will not be unique because the work will have the power to reduplicate its proper readers, the ideal lineaments of implied author, implied reader, and shared work will be *this* rhetorical occasion, essentially unlike all others. And the proper kinds and amounts of irony—tragic, comic, satiric, dramatic, metaphysical, or whatever—will be determined by particular ends. Similarly, the degrees of concealment, of stability, or of scope will be unspecifiable in advance of recognizing the needs of this work, seen as a kind of rhetorical occasion.

The only seeming exception to this particularistic conclusion would be a work in which *being ironic* is itself the controlling purpose. One might think that if I set out to be ironic, I could at least discover some rules in advance about how it might best be done. But even here the possibilities are limited by the actual varieties of effects covered by the umbrella term "ironic," as we saw in our playful listing of the nineteen ironic genres.

As compared, then, with the heady generalizations that have been offered by many ironologists, my program for evaluation is comically arduous and chancy: work hard to remove your ignorance, pay attention, discount your "prejudices" (while relying on your sound prejudgments!), read a lot, so that you can recognize a generic demand when you see one—and you *may* then sometimes arrive at sound judgments of irony, judgments that will in themselves provide the best schooling in when and where to stop. But such disappointing caution should at least save us from the despair or recklessness of skepticism: some ironists really are better than others, and any one of us can learn how to join them in their splendid discriminations. As compared to the hopeless blur offered by some views of literary judgment, this perhaps ought to be enough.

That was a way of putting it—not very satisfactory:
A periphrastic study in a worn-out poetical fashion,
Leaving one still with the intolerable wrestle
With words and meanings.
                                    —T. S. Eliot, "East Coker, II"

If there is no meaning in a poem beyond what an author meant
it to mean, as soon as its inspiring influence has been exposed
all its meaning vanishes.
                                    —Michel Benamoŭ

Remember, Razumov, that women, children, and revolutionists
hate irony, which is the negation of all saving instincts, of all
faith, of all devotion, of all action.
                                    —Sophia Antonovna, in Conrad's *Under Western Eyes*

Irony is no joking matter.
                                    —Friedrich Schlegel

# PART III INSTABILITIES

I don't pretend that I quite understand
My own meaning when I would be *very* fine.
　　　　　　　　　　　　　　　—Byron, *Don Juan*

The one truth the new irony has to tell is that the man who uses
it has no place to stand except in momentary community with
those who seek to express a comparable alienation from other
groups. The one conviction it expresses is that there are really
no sides left: No virtue to oppose to corruption, no wisdom to
oppose to cant. The one standard it accepts is that on which the
simple man—the untutored non-ironist who fancies (in his dolt-
hood) that he knows what good and bad should mean—is regis-
tered as the zero of our world, a cipher worth nothing but uninterrupted contempt.
　　　　　　　　　　　　　　　—Benjamin DeMott

How shall a man live if he can no longer rely upon things turning out differently from what he thought?
　　　　—Jacob, in Thomas Mann's *Joseph and His Brothers*

# EIGHT | Reconstructing the Unreconstructable: Local Instabilities

hough the ironic works we have read so far have ranged widely in difficulty, most of them have been quite simple in two basic respects: the authors have offered us an unequivocal invitation to reconstruct, and the reconstructions have not themselves been later undermined. If there were victims (and there usually were) they were never the implied author (whatever victimized masks he assumed in passing) and they did not include the true implied reader; the reader and author were intended to stand, after their work was done, firmly and securely together. We cannot really claim to have read "A Modest Proposal" or *Tom Jones* or "Everything That Rises Must Converge" until we have discovered precisely where the implied author stands and performed the precise reconstruction asked of us. Even if we then choose to reject the new position as not compatible with our own, we still know where we have been asked to stand and we can define the grounds of our refusal.

But everyone knows that it is often difficult and sometimes impossible to find any such solid ground. In many works that are called ironic, very different demands are made, yielding very different and often incompatible rewards. By their nature, such rough beasts defy us. We can know in advance of any encounter that they will not yield to clear and final classification and that our interpretations will slip away from us even as they are made. But a closer look at how they relate to their stable cousins can illuminate the whole of our interpretative experience.

## THE CLASSIFICATION OF INTENDED IRONIES

The domains of irony will be mapped differently depending on one's critical purposes and principles. We could attempt, for example, to extend and codify my playful classification of literary kinds in chapter 7, leading toward a poetics of irony. It would be a very strange and imperialistic poetics, however, since stable irony can occur in almost every literary kind, and since unstable ironies tend to dissolve generic distinctions. Or we could attempt to classify the subject matters revealed or concealed by ironic methods: the different views of man, or of society, or of the universe; of how the mind works within its limits;

or of how social conditions undermine or support us; or of the moral ends violated or served by it.[1]

Rhetorical inquiry leads us to an ordering different from these, based on variations in how authors and readers relate. We first put to one side all ironies that are not in any sense rhetorical—that is, all that are not designed by one human being to be shared by at least one other—then we can see in those remaining three essential variables.

1. *Degree of openness or disguise.* How much secret work does the author require, if any? Ironies range from the most covert to flat assertion: "It is ironic that . . ."

2. *Degree of stability in the reconstruction.* How much reason does the reader have for thinking his immediate task completed once an asserted irony has been understood or a covert irony has been reconstructed?

3. *Scope of the "truth revealed,"* or ground covered by the reconstruction or assertion, ranging from local through grand-but-still-finite to "absolute infinite negativity." How far is the reader asked to travel on the road to complete negation, and how does he know when to stop?

When these three are placed against one another, the resulting grid yields a rough operational classification of ironies (see fig. 5).

It should be unnecessary at this late date in the twentieth century, the century of sociology, the century of matrices, to dwell on the dangers and limitations in talking of such types. Those I am distinguishing would be especially destructive if they were seen as what authors necessarily think of as they write. "I will write a piece of unstable-covert-infinite irony." "*Mine* will be unstable-overt-local." I am not classifying literary kinds but mutual operations, any one of which could be found in a variety of literary kinds.

1. The most complete survey of kinds of irony is, to repeat, that of D. C. Muecke in *The Compass of Irony*. In dealing with "rhetorical ironies," Muecke classifies them along two axes: (*a*) overt, covert, private, and (*b*) impersonal, self-disparaging, ingenu, and dramatized. The second one clearly combines—or so it seems to me—two questions: the relation of author to reader and the relations of author to his various speakers. Since Muecke is interested in descriptive completeness, according to degree of openness and the part played "by the ironist himself in relation to his irony," he obtains a much more detailed list of kinds than is useful for anyone concentrating on the relation of the ironist to his reader. The attempt by Norman Knox to classify *all* ironies, in his review of Muecke, is of even less help in our practical tasks. Though his classification is interesting in its own right, I think it contains a serious misreading of Muecke. ("On the Classification of Ironies," *Modern Philology* 70 [August 1972]: 53–62).

|  | COVERT | OVERT |
|---|---|---|
| STABLE | local | local |
| | infinite | infinite |
| UNSTABLE | local | local |
| | infinite | infinite |

Fig. 5

### Stable-Covert-Local

This is the clever quick sure-footed creature we pursued through the first seven chapters.

> It is a truth universally acknowledged that a single man in possession of a good fortune must be in want of a wife.

> He yaf nat of that text a pulled hen,
> That seith that hunters ben nat hooly men,
> Ne that a monk, when he is recchelees,
> Is likned til a fissh that is waterlees,—
> This is to seyn, a monk out of his cloystre.
> But thilke text heeld he nat worth an oystre;
> And I seyde his opinion was good.[2]

The meanings are hidden, but when they are discovered by the proper reader they are firm as a rock. Regardless of how much difference may be revealed in peripheral associations, the central irony is read identically by every qualified reader. It is simply unthinkable that later on we will discover that Jane Austen and Chaucer really believe what those words, on their surface, "say." Further, our reconstructions are not grand edifices—they are not primarily built of other, better universals but rather of delightful local truths about the marriage market and clergymen and the way people talk about them. But they are a good deal more weatherproof than most of what men think they have proved logically or scientifically. They have been stimulated by those lines for a long time now, and they have not changed a jot; nor will they change, as long as men can read.

As Muecke says, until well into the eighteenth century this was the main if not the only kind of irony men talked about, whether they used the *word* irony or not (p. 51).

2. Chaucer, *The Canterbury Tales,* General Prologue, lines 177–82.

## Stable-Overt

Here we shift to kinds of statement that are ironic only in a radically different sense. They require no special act of reconstitution or translation, because they *assert* an irony in things or events that the speaker has observed and wants to share. It is as if the ironist said (and sometimes he actually does say), "Isn't it ironic that . . ." or "Have you noticed how ironic it is that . . ."—as a preface to a statement which reads something like what the reader builds for himself when reconstructing covert ironies.

A great deal of what is called ironic literature is of this kind, and it is as different from stable-covert as day from night.

> Tell me where is Fancy bred,
> Or in the heart or in the head?
> How begot, how nourishèd?
>   Reply, reply.
> It is engender'd in the eyes,
> With gazing fed; and Fancy dies
> In the cradle where it lies.
>   Let us all ring Fancy's knell:
>   I'll begin it,—Ding, dong, bell!
> ALL:  Ding, dong, bell![3]

Like covert ironies, overt assertions about irony can range from the most minute local observations to claims about the infinite. Local assertions are made about every nook and cranny of our lives: "Ironic that while Mary was falling in love with John, John was falling in love with Louise"; "Oh, why does *that* have to happen, on top of all that has hit me lately?" But most such particular ironies can be easily turned into ironic generalizations, about the nature of man or woman, about the way things work, about love and sex. "The bigger they are, the harder they fall." "Have you ever noticed that doctors don't seem to live any longer than other men?" "Fancy dies / In the cradle where it lies." "Quis custodiet ipsos / Custodes?" "Oh, who takes care of the caretaker's daughter / When the caretaker's gone away?" "Physician, heal thyself."

For the determined ironist any anomaly or incongruity is ironic, and almost any phenomenon can be seen as incongruous in some light or other: what is not incongruous viewed locally will be found so when placed in a larger context. It may be the workings of fate—

3. *The Merchant of Venice*, III.ii.63–72.

> Lollai, lollai, little child!
> The foot is on the wheel.
> Thou knowest not if it will turn
> To woe or weal.[4]

or the destructive power of death and time—

> VINDICI:
> Does the Silke-worme expend her yellow labours
> For thee? . . .
> Does euery proud and self-afflecting Dame
> Camphire her face for this, and grieue her Maker
> In sinfull baths of milke? . . . see
> Ladies, with false formes
> You deceiue men, but cannot deceiue wormes.[5]

or the ironic reversals of the Kingdom of Glory—

> But he that is greatest among you shall be your servant. And whosoever shall exalt himself shall be abased; and he that shall humble himself shall be exalted. [Matt. 23: 11–12]

There must be thousands of works asserting, in neat classical form, the formless ironies of man's nature or condition. Everyone knows Hamlet's lamentations on the subject, but he was working in a vein that seems never to have exhausted itself:

> Oh of what contraries consists a man!
> Of what impossible mixtures! Vice and virtue,
> Corruption, and eternnesse, at one time,
> And in one subject, let together loose![6]

But ironists do not stop with man's nature. The obvious next step is toward the universe that made him, or failed to make him right and continues to treat him wrong.

### HAP

> If but some vengeful god would call to me
> From up the sky, and laugh: "Thou suffering thing,
> Know that thy sorrow is my ecstasy,
> That thy love's loss is my hate's profiting!"

---

4. Fourteenth-century Anglo-Irish Lullaby, as quoted by Earle Birney, "English Irony before Chaucer," *University of Toronto Quarterly* 6 (1936–37): 544.

5. Tourneur, *The Revenger's Tragedy*, III.v.

6. Chapman, *The Tragedy of Charles, Duke of Byron*, V.iii. Citation from Muecke. See also other quotations given by him, p. 124, and chap. 6, passim.

Then would I bear it, clench myself, and die,
Steeled by the sense of ire unmerited;
Half-eased in that a Powerfuller than I
Had willed and meted me the tears I shed.

But not so. How arrives it joy lies slain,
And why unblooms the best hope ever sown?
—Crass casualty obstructs the sun and rain,
And dicing Time for gladness casts a moan. . . .
These purblind Doomsters had as readily strown
Blisses about my pilgrimage as pain.

Thomas Hardy's assertion about the irony of existence is as
stable, as final, as unquestioned (rhetorically speaking) as if he were
preaching a non-ironic message on behalf of belief in Jehovah. Everyone would call the poem ironic, I suppose, but the cosmic ironies it
asserts are not like the ironies we have been dealing with. In terms of
my metaphor of reconstruction, the poem *asserts* only one location, or
if there are two, one is enclosed within the other (see fig. 6).

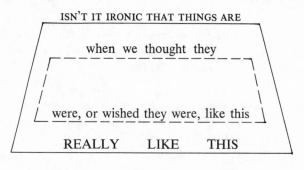

Fig. 6

Some of the finest effects of modern literature have been achieved
by authors who have learned how to shift their assertions of irony from
local to universal and back again, being more or less overt all the
while, seldom calling for reconstructions of covert irony but at the same
time demanding of the reader an intensity of attention comparable to
that required for reading covert irony. Often these asserted ironies are
spoken to us by a dramatized character who speaks for the implied
author on certain subjects but not on others (as in the example from
Wright Morris, pp. 169–71). Most narrators or reflecting conscious-
nesses in modern fiction have in fact been ambiguously covert, as it were
—asserting overt ironies part of the time and implying, in their distortions, covert reconstructions the rest of the time. Such characters

are useful for many reasons, not the least being that their authors can protect themselves behind them, as if to say, "Remember it is Folly, and a woman who speaks," or, with Swift's Grub Street hack in *A Tale of a Tub,* "where I am not understood, it shall be concluded, that something very useful and profound is couched underneath" ("The Author's Preface"). "I have sometimes heard," he says, "of an Iliad in a nutshell; but it has been my fortune to have much oftener seen a nutshell in an Iliad" (sec. VII). The asserted deflation could not be more direct—unless, of course, we are not clear about what it means, in which case we are likely to blame the hack rather than Swift.

One of the most successful and most daring uses of overt stable irony in modern literature is Saul Bellow's in *Mr. Sammler's Planet.* Here a fully modern man dares to create a character who is unambiguously (though of course haltingly) wise, wise and—what is perhaps even harder—good. I think that no such character could succeed —certainly not for modern readers—unless his own vision were relentlessly ironic; he must be clearly capable of seeing every ironic discounting, and he must be willing to discount everything except whatever is essential to his wisdom and goodness. He must not for a moment seem to preach any sort of affirmation that has not taken into account what can be said against that affirmation. Only a master craftsman could create for us a character whose asserted ironies would seem so clear and yet so shrewd as Sammler's:

> Sammler in his *Gymnasium* days once translated from Saint Augustine: "The Devil hath established his cities in the North." He thought of this often. In Cracow before World War I he had had another version of it—desperate darkness, the dreary liquid yellow mud to a depth of two inches over cobblestones in the Jewish streets. . . . Without the power of the North, its mines, its industries, the world would never have reached its astonishing modern form. And regardless of Augustine, Sammler had always loved his Northern cities, especially London, the blessings of its gloom, of coal smoke, gray rains, and the mental and human opportunities of a dark muffled environment. There one came to terms with obscurity, with low tones, one did not demand full clarity of mind or motives. But now Augustine's odd statement required a new interpretation. Listening to Angela carefully [as she talked of her sexual explorations], Sammler perceived different developments. The labor of Puritanism now was ending. The dark satanic mills changing into light satanic mills. The reprobates converted into children of joy, the sexual ways of the seraglio and of the Congo bush adopted by the emancipated masses of New York, Amsterdam, London. Old Sammler with

his screwy visions! He saw the increasing triumph of Enlightenment—Liberty, Fraternity, Equality, Adultery! Enlightenment,
universal education, universal suffrage, the rights of the majority
acknowledged by all governments, the rights of women, the rights
of children, the rights of criminals, the unity of the different races
affirmed, Social Security, public health, the dignity of the person,
the right to justice—the struggles of three revolutionary centuries
being won while the feudal bonds of Church and Family weakened and the privileges of aristocracy (without any duties) spread
wide, democratized, especially the libidinous privileges, the right
to be uninhibited, spontaneous, urinating, defecating, belching,
coupling in all positions, tripling, quadrupling, polymorphous,
noble in being natural, primitive, combining the leisure and luxu-
rious inventiveness of Versailles with the hibiscus-covered erotic
ease of Samoa. Dark romanticism now took hold [pp. 31–33].

No one who reads these words can have trouble with the few
ironies that, in isolation, might be called covert: e.g., The "triumph of
Enlightenment—Liberty, Fraternity, Equality, Adultery!" The subtlety
here is not in the invitation to difficult translations. The ironic anti-
climaxes that follow are available to everyone. The subtlety lies within
a vision that encompasses ironies but is itself not finally undercut with
irony. We are not invited to see beyond what Sammler sees but to see
with him.

Overt irony is thus always in one way more vulnerable than
covert: if I decide even for a moment that Sammler's vision is flawed in
essential ways that neither he nor Bellow suspects, the novel is diminished. It is not surprising that critics of Bellow have objected to his
characters' affirmations, since he seems to stand behind those affirmations with his full authorial power. Those who believe the curious
dogma that only negations can be properly and unashamedly affirmed
are troubled when Herzog and Sammler and Henderson, the Rain
King, find what the critics think of as unearned joy.

## UNSTABLE IRONY

At last we cross that formidable chasm that I have so long anticipated
—the fundamental distinction between stable ironies and ironies in
which the truth asserted or implied is that no stable reconstruction can
be made out of the ruins revealed through the irony. The author—
insofar as we can discover him, and he is often very remote indeed—
refuses to declare himself, however subtly, *for* any stable proposition,
even the opposite of whatever proposition his irony vigorously denies.
The only sure affirmation is that negation that begins all ironic play:
"*this* affirmation must be rejected," leaving the possibility, and in in-

finite ironies the clear implication, that since the universe (or at least the universe of discourse) is inherently absurd, all statements are subject to ironic undermining. No statement can really "mean what it says."[7]

The consequences of the differences between these kinds are immense. What we do with a work, or what it does with us, will depend on our decision, conscious or unconscious, about whether we are asked by it to push through its confusions to some final point of clarity or to see through it to a possibly infinite series of further confusions. No

7. Everyone who writes on irony with any seriousness seems to face this transition sooner or later. For Muecke, it is the transition from "specific irony" (corrective and normative) to "general irony"; "life itself or any general aspect of life seen as fundamentally and inescapably an ironic state of affairs. No longer is it a case of isolated victims; we are all victims; we are all victims of impossible situations, of universal Ironies of Dilemma, of Amiel's Law of Irony, and of Kierkegaard's World Irony" (p. 120). But for his purposes Muecke collapses three distinctions that are important to us: between the infinite and local unstable ironies; between covert and overt infinite ironies; and between intended ironies and ironies of event or of nature. In studying irony as rhetoric there is all the difference in the world between my stumbling upon an irony in the events of my own life and interpreting an assertion by another human being about similar ironies.

We should note that the new territory we now face is still sharply delimited by our interest in intended ironies only. In choosing this limitation, I do not mean to reject all criticism that does not; it is just that we have a great deal of it, and we have very little about the precise problems I am grappling with. Those other works might be divided into three kinds: (1) Critical works that stress ironies wrought by time (what some of our confreres in France might call the "diachronically determined"). It is ironic that Jane Austen's stabilities can be seen as a last expression of an order that crumbled even as she wrote; or that the works of Céline should have fallen into the hands of a reader like me, crippled by radically opposed moral views; or that "Snow White and the Seven Dwarfs" should be exploited by Donald Barthelme's *Snow White*. (2) Critical works that stress ironies wrought by the author's unconscious. It is ironic that Lewis Carroll did not understand how his feelings about little girls and about himself would deflect *Alice in Wonderland* from being the simple story it seems to set out to be. Such a deflection, if real, cannot be handled by my distinction between meaning and significance: many authors seem finally to create works that go deeper or further than their conscious art could ever plan for, and a complete Rhetoric of Irony would, I suppose, account for the deeper communings that such works invite us to. Insofar as such instabilities are "intended by the work" (regardless of the author) they would in theory enter our subject, but I'm afraid that what I see done by others when they attempt to describe their reconstructions of such works too often confirms my caution about making the attempt. In any case, this book is about the meeting of conscious minds through irony, not the meeting of the critic's conscious mind with the artist's unconscious. Since in fact most artists know more about their work than most of us ever discover, our subject is still vast enough to keep us humble.

other step in the never completed process of mastering the arts of interpretation is more important than discovering how and when to cross
and recross this borderline with agility and confidence. The job is not
made easier (though the excitement is increased) by the fact that the
very existence of the borderline is denied by some of the extreme ironists who choose to dwell entirely on "the other side" and then claim
that everyone is in the same position, whether he knows it or not. The
decision about which side of the line we are on is once again a decision
about the total intention of the author implied by the work. Just how
deep, we ask, runs this author's love affair with irony?

There is a very old story about an Eastern prophet who taught
that the world rests on the back of an elephant, which in turn stands
on the back of another elephant. When one of his disciples finally took
courage and asked him what *that* elephant stands on, he confided,
"There are elephants *all the way down*." Some authors, particularly in
this century, would give the same answer to our question: "My ironies
rest on other ironies all the way down." Many of them would, in fact,
repudiate (or so I must suppose) the whole enterprise of my first two
parts, even while depending, in much of their practice, on the securities
of stable irony.

Any written or spoken word of stable irony, I have assumed, is a
structure of meanings, an order which rules out some readings as entirely fallacious, shows other readings to be partially so, and confirms
others as more or less adequate. Though no reader can hope to be fully
successful with any but the simplest ironies, I have written as if every
reader will want to come as close as possible to seeing all there is in a
work as it really is, no less and no more, which of course presupposes
that a work "really is" something. Such an assumption, which cannot be
proved but which is confirmed as fruitful whenever a passage is in fact
read as an author intends, can be harmonized with many different
aesthetic theories, but the important point here is that it cannot be
harmonized with the belief that the work "means" whatever any reader
honestly sees in it. (It does not, of course, rule out the possibility of
many other assumptions leading to other kinds of inquiry. To assume
that a work is an order of "meanings" deflects us from interesting questions that would arise if we assumed, rather, that it is a made object,
and thus an order of what might be called not meanings but smaller
objects—characters, events, circumstances [e.g., "poetic" criticism in
the neo-Aristotelian mode]; or that it is an order of truths or realities
(political, religious, philosophical) that exist independently of authors
and readers; and so on. Thus inquiry in many non-rhetorical modes
could be *compatible* with what we have done; even a criticism that cut

*Circular*

242

itself free of terms like order and intentions might be compatible in the sense of "not contradictory," since the questions asked would be totally different and hence the answers found could not possibly meet head-on.)

Nobody argues, of course, that a work offers no limits whatever on the reader. It would not be a refutation of those who deny my assumption to accuse them of allowing *any* interpretation, however capricious. It is no good saying to them, "Well, then, for you an interpretation claiming that 'A Modest Proposal' is about the sexual practices in a nunnery of the sixteenth century will be as valid as one claiming that it is a satire on political and economic abuses in Ireland in the eighteenth century." They can reply quite simply: "Do you offer your interpretation seriously?" And since I do not, there is no argument. The real debate is only about whether one must choose between two seriously offered interpretations if they conflict. So far I have assumed that there are many occasions, even in the most advanced, most sophisticated literature, when one must choose—which is not to deny that there are many occasions when one need not.

Along with the belief that all serious readings have equivalent standing has often gone the assertion that the value of a work is partly proved by its capacity to produce a large number of alternative interpretations. And this naturally leads to the notion—self-evidently true in one very limited sense only—that the value of art lies not in the work of art itself but only in the activity of the spectator. It follows, or seems to, that one trigger is as good as another. Poems produced by chance or mathematical formulas or machines force the reader to create meanings—if there are to be any. Whatever may be said for or against such works, they offer no handle for interpretation in our sense at all, or for debate among rival interpretations. They are deliberately indeterminate, and there cannot be an *art* of reading them—whatever their value as cultural shock or therapy. (There might be an art of reading interpretations of them.) It is of course a natural step from them to works which do not exist after the moment of creation—to "happenings" that happen only once; to the composition of John Cage, called "4½," which consists of four-and-a-half minutes of silence; to the machine exhibited at the Museum of Modern Art that was turned on— one time only—and then systematically destroyed itself, finally going up in "ironic" flames, the ultimate in ironic instability.

Since such works of anti-art offer us no invitation to reconstruct anything deeper or truer than their own surfaces, they are clearly not ironic according to the definition used in the first seven chapters. If they are ironic at all—and their *creators* at least are said to be—it is only in the sense that the attack on conventional art that they embody seems to reflect back upon themselves, as if the maker said: "I am pretending to make a work of art; take that as my surface meaning. But you will find, on close inspection, that I have not made a work of art and in fact that my work repudiates art; take that as its deeper meaning—if you must have a meaning at all."

Both of these assumptions about art have usually been accompanied or supported by a further assumption about the essentially ironic nature of man's existence—and of the entire meaningless chaos he inhabits. In a different kind of book, I should want to trace some of the varieties of spiritual and intellectual annihilation that have been seen as threatening one kind of traditional statement and calling for new kinds of anti-statement—or for silence. Dozens of books and thousands of articles have discussed the literary effort to cope with various nihilisms —with "the death of God," with emptiness, negation, denial, nothingness, the void, the abyss, the heart of darkness in man and in the universe.[8] But for our purposes it is enough to see clearly that the deeper a man's doubt runs, the harder it will be for him to write ironically *with the intention* that someone should cut through the ironies to some underlying true statement. At the extreme point of doubt, all statement becomes suspect.

One can, or so many have believed, peel off the onion skins of discredited truths about life or the universe and finally discover no core of truth, nothing but nothingness itself. At that extreme point, there is of course "nothing" to prevent one from writing ironic works: what could be more ironic than the making of statements about a world in which the making of statements is meaningless?

Pursued to its logical extremes, such a view would lead, I suppose, to the abandonment of all books of interpretation (or perhaps of all books), the dismissal of all classes in literature (or indeed in any subject), the cessation of all criticism, and finally to complete silence— a completely silent response to match the increasing approximations to silence in the works themselves. But "ironically enough" no one seems seriously inhibited from attempting to state the sociological or psychological or political or philosophical meanings of such tracts against the

8. E.g., *The Disappearance of God: Five Nineteenth-Century Writers,* by J. Hillis Miller (Cambridge, Mass., 1963); *Nil: Episodes in the Literary Conquest of Void during the 19th Century,* by Robert Martin Adams (New York, 1966); *Poems of Doubt and Belief: An Anthology of Modern Religious Poetry,* ed. Tom F. Driver and Robert Pack (New York, 1964). I have tried to meet the rhetoric of infinite negativity head on in *Modern Dogma and the Rhetoric of Assent* (Notre Dame and Chicago, 1974).

possibility of meaning. What is more important to us here, novelists, dramatists, and poets inevitably draw back from complete silence and in fact write works that embody their intentions and therefore have "meanings" of a kind—works of resignation, of lament, of complaint, of dark laughter at the chaos, of defiance, of pathos. And in doing so they usually provide—sometimes it seems almost with a sense of shame —some handle or other for interpreting their works at whatever level of instability or negation they have elected.

Underlying all these confusions, one thing is clear: wherever there are intentions, however obscure or unconventional, there are invitations to interpret. It is true that "works of art" entirely produced by chance defeat the quest for meaning and leave us able to talk only of significance. But the truth is that all the artists who really interest the world, even the modern world, have produced works of *art,* not chance. It is amusing to see that even those who plan aleatory elements into their works often justify them with talk about the artist's intentions, especially in terms of what the artist wants the audience to do—or more often not to do. John Cage, for example, who insists that he is always "anarchic," issues manifestos at a great rate, and they generally include exhortations about how we should behave: to open our eyes and ears, to get rid of traditional expectations, to stop insisting that art accomplish something. "It behooves us therefore to see each thing directly as it is, be it the sound of a tin whistle or the elegant *Lepiota procera.*"[9]

In any case, our special question forces us to draw back from a full encounter with the significance of modern experiments with anti-intentions and deal with the meaning of works that fall short of ideal meaninglessness.

What we find is a sequence of rising ambition or scope in unstable ironies, from (1) *overt limited* or local underminings; through (2) *limited covert*; on through (3) overt *assertions* of the infinity of the ironic vision; and finally to (4) *covert* or thoroughly disorienting implications of "absolute *infinite* negativity."

These distinctions are not unreal or merely analytical, since, loose as they are, the reading task is different for each of the four. But the decision about which kind of reading is called for is seldom easy and sometimes impossible. And of course it is *sometimes* not very important, since the difference in literary effect can be slight—indeed no difference here makes as much difference to the reader as the difference between asserted and covert stable ironies.

9. *Silence* (Middletown, Conn., 1961), p. 276.

## Unstable-Overt-Local

Modern literature is full of assertions about specific situations that are
shown to be "ironic" but which neither invite a reconstruction of some
sort of affirmation out of the destroyed places (as in all stable irony)
nor yet quite claim that "there are ironies all the way down." Such
ironies while unstable may be very local indeed, as in the aphorism
about the economic order, "If things can possibly go wrong, they will."
(Does it apply only to daily matters? Perhaps it is merely a lay wording
of the law of entropy? Or is the author a Manichaean? He could very
well be.) Though such ironies have an element of stability—we *know*
that something is being undermined—we don't really know where to
stop in our underminings. We may be dealing with ironies that will turn
into infinities if pursued. No clear counter-propositions or secure platforms emerge as the various local platforms are bombed out of existence.

Here are some local asserted ironies from that encyclopedia of
modern irony, Robert Musil's *The Man without Qualities*:[10]

Chapter I: Which, remarkably enough, does not get anyone anywhere.

The fact is—in every profession that is followed not for the
sake of money but for love, there comes a moment when the advancing years seem to be leading into the void [p. 16].

In a community with energies constantly flowing through it,
every road leads to a good goal, if one does not spend too much
time hesitating and thinking it over. . . . So far as happiness is
concerned it matters very little what one wants; the main thing is
that one should get it. Besides, zoology makes it clear that a sum
of reduced individuals may very well form a totality of
genius [p. 30].

For this "something" here once again the word "soul" must
be used.

This is a word that has already appeared frequently, though
not precisely in the clearest of connections. For instance, as that
which the present time has lost or that which cannot be combined
with civilization. As that which is in antagonism to physical urges
and connubial habits. As that which is stirred, not only into re-
pugnance, by a murderer. As that which was to be set free by the
Collateral Campaign. As religious meditation. . . . As a love of
metaphor and simile with many people. And so on. Of all the
peculiarities that this word "soul" has, however, the oddest is that
young people cannot pronounce it without laughing. . . . It is distinctly a word for older people. . . . [p. 215]

10. Trans. Eithne Wilkins and Ernst Kaiser (New York, 1965).

In each case, here, there are local negations that are clearly stable; for example, it is ironic that "soul" should suffer the fate that is described, and no reader can doubt that Musil intends the passage to be seen as irony. What is not clear is where we go from there: quoted out of context, the ironies may or may not be part of larger ironic views, and even in context they can leave one baffled.

Or consider this poem by Howard Nemerov.[11]

## BOOM!

### SEES BOOM IN RELIGION, TOO

*Atlantic City, June 23, 1957 (AP).—President Eisenhower's pastor said tonight that Americans are living in a period of "unprecedented religious activity" caused partially by paid vacations, the eight-hour day and modern conveniences.*

*"These fruits of material progress," said the Rev. Edward L. R. Elson of the National Presbyterian Church, Washington, "have provided the leisure, the energy, and the means for a level of human and spiritual values never before reached."*

Here at the Vespasian-Carlton, it's just one
religious activity after another; the sky
is constantly being crossed by cruciform
airplanes, in which nobody disbelieves
for a second, and the tide, the tide
of spiritual progress and prosperity
miraculously keeps rising, to a level
never before attained. The churches are full,
the beaches are full, and the filling-stations
are full, God's great ocean is full
of paid vacationers praying an eight-hour day
to the human and spiritual values, the fruits,
the leisure, the energy, and the means, Lord,
the means for the level, the unprecedented level,
and the modern conveniences, which also are full.
Never before, O Lord, have the prayers and praises
from belfry and phonebooth, from ballpark and barbecue
the sacrifices, so endlessly ascended.

It was not thus when Job in Palestine
sat in the dust and cried, cried bitterly;
when Damien kissed the lepers on their wounds
it was not thus; it was not thus

11. From *New and Selected Poems* (Chicago, 1960). Copyright © 1960 by Howard Nemerov. Reprinted by permission of the author and the University of Chicago Press.

when Francis worked a fourteen-hour day
strictly for the birds; when Dante took
a week's vacation without pay and it rained
part of the time, O Lord, it was not thus.
But now the gears mesh and the tires burn
and the ice chatters in the shaker and the priest
in the pulpit, and Thy Name, O Lord,
is kept before the public, while the fruits
ripen and religion booms and the level rises
and every modern convenience runneth over,
that it may never be with us as it hath been
with Athens and Karnak and Nagasaki,
nor Thy sun for one instant refrain from shining
on the rainbow Buick by the breezeway
or the Chris Craft with the uplift life raft;
that we may continue to be the just folks we are,
plain people with ordinary superliners and
disposable diaperliners, people of the stop'n'shop
'n' pray as you go, of hotel, motel, boatel,
the humble pilgrims of no deposit no return
and please adjust thy clothing, who will give to Thee
if Thee will keep us going, our annual
Miss Universe, for Thy Name's Sake, Amen.

Full of particular, local, and seemingly stable ironies that can be confidently enjoyed, this poem in its larger lines gives us no secure ground to stand on. We know that the poet deplores the hypocrisy of the "Reverend" and of the crowds who inhabit the poem. We know that he thinks the contrast between older religious attitudes and present religious claims ironic indeed. But we cannot tell, with any confidence, how far or in what direction the poem takes us beyond these openly asserted local ironies ("it was not thus when Job in Palestine . . ."). When he seems to be showing what a genuine religious spirit might have been, his speaker cannot help drawing back from it: "strictly for the birds" and "vacation without pay" are good jokes, but they leave us unsure about who or what the victim is. Does the poet believe that there is a God who is blasphemed by the attitudes mocked in the poem, or is he saying that in their religious confusions these men echo a universe that, in its infinite confusions, justifies only this kind of mocking prayer? Though one has no question but that St. Francis and Dante provide, in their genuine religious devotion, an ironic undercutting of the Reverend's silly substitute for religion, there is no way, I think, to reconstruct a true religious view opposing the corrupt pieties the poem attacks. I can feel sure that any statement I make about the poem as a whole will prove unstable in the eyes of the poet; he would no doubt be amused at the very effort to pin it down by claiming that it is representative of poems that cannot be pinned down. But the interests are still fairly local—the poem provides all the clues we need about "where to stop." It tells us, in effect, "Beyond this and this point against modern culture (about which we can be clear) you will find questions irrelevant to this poetry. Don't force it into your irrelevant world!"[12]

## Unstable-Covert-Local

We can now see that instability is in itself an extremely unstable concept. Having begun with the notion that it marks the irony which offers the reader no firm place on which to stand, what can we do with covert works that clearly attempt to keep the reader off balance but that yet insist on having a meaning? Note the terms used by Peter Brook in his introduction to the English translation of Peter Weiss's *The Persecution and Assassination of Jean-Paul Marat as Performed by the Inmates of the Asylum of Charenton under the Direction of the Marquis de Sade*:

> His force . . . is above all in the jangle produced by the clash of styles. Everything is put in its place by its neighbour—the serious by the comic, the noble by the popular, the literary by the crude, the intellectual by the physical: the abstraction is vivified by the stage image, the violence illuminated by the cool flow of thought. The strands of meaning of the play pass to and fro through its structure and the result is a very complex form: like in Genet it is a hall of mirrors or a corridor of echoes—and one must keep looking front and back all the time to reach the author's sense.

I see no suggestion here that there is no meaning. In such limited instabilities, it is as if the ironist said, "So much of what you believe or assert is absurd that I can easily keep you off balance reminding you

---

12. The ukase pertains, of course, only to meanings. If I am curious about Howard Nemerov, whose poems I have come to love, and about the twentieth century, the only one I have, I will of course move out from the individual poems to speculate about their significance for the author and his times. When I find, as I do, that many of his poems have the same wry "anti-religious" tone as does "Boom!" I can begin to construct my unwritten biography, relating it to my unwritten history of a century that produces ready-made readers who, like me, can savor poems like this:

> He smiles to see His children, born to sin,
> Digging those foxholes there are no atheists in.

("The God of This World," *Gnomes and Occasions* [Chicago, 1973], p. 8. [Copyright © 1973 by Howard Nemerov. Reprinted by permission of the author and the University of Chicago Press.] See also p. 11.)

of your absurdities; but meanwhile, don't forget that I have a secret wisdom that justifies my ironic stance—I know what is really worth caring about." When Weiss's troupe of madmen come marching toward the spectators at the end of *Marat/Sade,* they are disconcerted not with a sense that nothing matters to Weiss, but that he is asking them to care for a great deal without offering the usual helps: knocked off one's perch, one struggles to regain *some* perch, knowing from the look on Weiss's face that *he* certainly knows that we ought to be up and doing, fighting all that injustice and unhappiness somehow.

Whether I am right in placing Weiss's play in this precise slot— any honest dialectician knows how little security of interpretation anyone has in dealing with a play of this kind even when by an avowed "Marxist"—it is clear that there is a great difference between a work like this with a strong political or moral message, however "unstable" the technique, and the works we turn to next, in which the ironic undercuttings are not only innumerable in a technical sense (therefore unstable), but infinite in the negation of meanings.

It was not without cause, that so many excellent philosophers became Sceptics and Academics, and denied any certainty of knowledge or comprehension, and held opinions that the knowledge of man extended only to appearances and probabilities. It is true that in Socrates it was supposed to be but a form of irony, *Scientiam dissimulando simulavit,* for he used to dissemble his knowledge, to the end to enhance his knowledge.

—Bacon

. . . the purpose of asking a question may be twofold. One may ask a question for the purpose of obtaining an answer containing the desired content, so that the more one questions, the deeper and more meaningful becomes the answer; or one may ask a question, not in the interest of obtaining an answer, but to suck out the apparent content with a question and leave only an emptiness remaining. The first method naturally presupposes a content, the second an emptiness; the first is the speculative, the second the ironic. Now it was the latter method which was especially practiced by Socrates.

—Kierkegaard

. . . irony is a healthiness in so far as it rescues the soul from the snares of relativity; it is a sickness in so far as it is unable to tolerate the absolute except in the form of nothingness, and yet this sickness is an endemic fever which but few individuals contract, and even fewer overcome.

—Kierkegaard

Such waltzing was not easy.

—Theodore Roethke

# NINE | Infinite Instabilities

## Unstable-Overt-Infinite

The borderline between a poem like "Boom!" and works that assert infinite ironies may be dim, but there is nevertheless a real difference between the still quite local underminings in the one and the unqualified cosmic assertion that the universe—not just this or that effort of man to grasp it—is absurd: no truth, no passion, no political commitment, no moral judgment, will stand up under ironic examination.

Since many modern men have seen themselves teetering perilously on that borderline, unable to be sure either that the universe is meaningless or that they can discern any meaning, it is not surprising that many poems and novels hover, as it were, between limited ironies and the ultimate ironic denial:

### Black Rook in Rainy Weather
#### *Sylvia Plath*

On the stiff twig up there
Hunches a wet black rook
Arranging and rearranging its feathers in the rain.
I do not expect miracle
Or an accident

To set the sight on fire
In my eye, nor seek
Any more in the desultory weather some design,
But let spotted leaves fall as they fall,
Without ceremony, or portent.

Although, I admit, I desire,
Occasionally, some backtalk
From the mute sky, I can't honestly complain:
A certain minor light may still
Leap incandescent

Out of kitchen table or chair
As if a celestial burning took
Possession of the most obtuse objects now and then—
Thus hallowing an interval
Otherwise inconsequent

By bestowing largesse, honour,
One might say love. At any rate, I now walk
Wary (for it could happen
Even in this dull, ruinous landscape); sceptical,
Yet politic; ignorant

Of whatever angel may choose to flare
Suddenly at my elbow. I only know that a rook
Ordering its black feathers can so shine
As to seize my senses, haul
My eyelids up, and grant

A brief respite from fear
Of total neutrality. With luck,
Trekking stubborn through this season
Of fatigue, I shall
Patch together a content

Of sorts. Miracles occur,
If you care to call those spasmodic
Tricks of radiance miracles. The wait's begun again,
The long wait for the angel,
For that rare, random descent.

This fine, wrenching poem faces the threat of a "mute sky" and the "fear of total neutrality" more openly than anything we have yet seen, weaving ironies around the mood of forlorn hope for "random" miracles of radiance. There could be a limit. One could "patch together a content / Of sorts." It *could* happen, even in this "dull, ruinous landscape," even for the wary, skeptical, ignorant yet politic poet. But even the "miracles" that occur may be mere "tricks of radiance"—the ultimate ironic trick of non-God, if these rare and "random" descents are entirely deceptive. Still they might not be.

Portrayals of how it feels to stand on the edge, looking into a possibly bottomless abyss, can be found in countless modern works. Robert Graves shows what might be called the thing itself, the moment of discovery of infinite instability:

### Warning to Children

#### *Robert Graves*

Children, if you dare to think
Of the greatness, rareness, muchness,
Fewness of this precious only
Endless world in which you say
You live, you think of things like this:
Blocks of slate enclosing dappled
Red and green, enclosing tawny
Yellow nets, enclosing white
And black acres of dominoes,
Where a neat brown paper parcel
Tempts you to untie the string.
In the parcel a small island,

On the island a large tree,
On the tree a husky fruit.
Strip the husk and pare the rind off:
In the kernel you will see
Blocks of slate enclosed by dappled
Red and green, enclosed by tawny
Yellow nets, enclosed by white
And black acres of dominoes,
Where the same brown paper parcel—
Children, leave the string alone!
For who dares undo the parcel
Finds himself at once inside it,
On the island, in the fruit,
Blocks of slate about his head,
Finds himself enclosed by dappled
Green and red, enclosed by yellow
Tawny nets, enclosed by black
And white acres of dominoes,
With the same brown paper parcel
Still untied upon his knee.
And, if he then should dare to think
Of the fewness, muchness, rareness,
Greatness of this endless only
Precious world in which he says
He lives—he then unties the string.

It is interesting to draw back for a moment and think of how the progression of effects in this poem compares with the dramatic irony discussed in chapter 4. Dramatic irony always depends strictly on the reader's or spectator's knowing something about a character's situation that the character does not know: Tartuffe makes love to Orgon's wife, not knowing that Orgon is hiding—visible to us in the audience—under the table; or Blifil, the villain of *Tom Jones,* tricks Allworthy into banishing Tom, the hero, and we know as we watch that he is making a mistake that will certainly be discovered later on; or Othello strangles Desdemona, believing she has betrayed him, while we, watching in horror, know for a certainty that she is innocent. Moments of this kind are possible, as we have seen, only when the author is sure that *we know that he knows that we know*—which is to say, the author and the audience stand together watching the characters from above as they make their mistakes. Everyone in our culture has experienced many times the peculiar form of suspense that such irony yields—the sense of comic anticipation or tragic anguish with which we are impelled forward toward the discovery. It is a staple of movies and comic books

255

and TV shows—as it is of Shakespeare, Molière, Dickens, and Dostoevsky.

As we have seen, it is an effect that depends on an absolute sharing of certain knowledge. No spectator at *Twelfth Night,* however poor he may be at "reading" Shakespeare on his own, has ever missed the point when he hears Viola, on the stage, dressed as a man and in love with the Duke, saying "My father had a daughter lov'd a man, / As it might be perhaps, *were I a woman,*/ I should your lordship." No Greek required instruction from Sophocles to understand the irony of Oedipus' opening speech—"I, Oedipus, whom all men call the Great." Every Greek possessed, before he went to the play, all of the knowledge on which that irony was based.

If there is dramatic irony in "Warning to Children," it is of a radically different kind. It certainly does not allow the reader to stand securely on the author's pedestal and watch the children fumble with those baffling boxes-within-boxes. The author has no secure pedestal, despite the tone of soothsaying. If we try to describe the position of author, reader, and characters in the terms that fit *Tartuffe* or *Othello* or "Soliloquy of a Spanish Cloister," we get into difficulties at once. The author does have an advantage at the beginning, but it is hardly one that matters much by the end: he knows what the reader learns only at the end, that all of us—author, readers, and "children"—are in the same "box." His truth (at least in this poem) is that the truth is inaccessible. We cannot even learn, from the poem alone, whether this dizzying moment is meant by Graves as an expression of a persistent ironic view of life. It may be simply one fleeting evocation of a vision spoken by a mask covering a real man who believes, say, in the Trinity, or in Zoroastrianism. Only a study of Graves's other works, and indeed of his life outside his poetry, could give us confidence in saying what meanings, if any, he embraces beneath or beyond these husks and rinds and parcel wrappings. But the important point is that this poem, unlike most works we have discussed, does not even ask us to seek for a meaning behind the surface meaning: its meaning *is* its surface meaning, untranslatable into other language. About the closest we can come is to add, as we have done in other asserted ironies, an opening phrase like "The irony of it all, children, is this: If you dare . . ."

And yet there is something curious going on here that deserves a closer look. "The irony of it all is that . . ." is itself a statement of a "truth," a truth which Graves presumably sees as underlying the poem. We children are, in a very real sense, on the stage of life, like Tartuffe on his stage, opening our packages in the search for nonexistent truth; and the *ironic* Truth, dimly perceived by the author and reader together, stands on its promontory, presumably amused as the children below walk into the eternal trap. I spare the reader any graphic rendering of this pregnant scene, asking him only to imagine for a moment the confusing patterns of dotted lines and inferential arrows that would be required to get the rhetorical relations here into the terms used in figure 2, page 37.[1]

## Unstable-Covert-Infinite

In dealing with overt ironies, I have of course been led to cite works in which the author seems to be speaking in his own voice and telling us, more or less directly, just how ironic things are or how vulnerable to irony the whole universe is. But as most readers know, many modern authors will refuse even this degree of open declaration, leaving us to infer the depths of their ironies from superficial and deliberately ambiguous signs.

Samuel Beckett's novel *The Unnamable* begins as follows:

> Where now? Who now? When now? Unquestioning I, say I. Unbelieving. Questions, hypotheses, call them that. Keep going, going on, call that going, call that on. Can it be that one day, off it goes on, that one day I simply stayed in, in where, instead of going out, in the old way, out to spend day and night as far away as possible, it wasn't far. Perhaps that is how it began. You think you are simply resting, the better to act when the time comes, or for no reason, and you soon find yourself powerless ever to do anything again. No matter how it happened. It, say it, not knowing what. Perhaps I simply assented at last to an old thing. But I did nothing. I seem to speak, it is not I, about me, it is not about me. These few general remarks to begin with. What am I to do, what shall I do, what should I do, in my situation, how proceed? By aporia pure and simple? Or by affirmations and negations in-

---

1. It is even more amusing to think of what expedients anyone given to propositional analysis would be forced to, if he tried to trace the intricacies of this act in full detail. A student of Ted Cohen's, Tamara Horowitz, trying to develop a precise account of irony based on H. P. Grice's analysis of "utterer's meaning, sentence meaning, and word meaning," produced the following oversimplified definition of the ironic act: "By x, U meant $\phi$ iff $(\underset{\iota}{\,} \sigma)$ [U uttered $\sigma(x)$, and $(\underset{\iota}{\,} A)$ (U uttered $\sigma(x)$ intending to produce in A the effect [(i) that A should think U to . . . (and in some cases depending on the identification of . . . (ii) that A should via the fulfillment of (i) himself . . .] by means of A's recognition of that intention. The lacunae to be completed by writing $\sigma(\phi/x)$]." Grice's own brief but necessarily intricate comments on irony were made in his unpublished William James lectures (1966?), circulated in mimeographed form under the title "Logic and Conversation." For references to his widely discussed work, see n. 1, chap. 4 above.

validated as uttered, or sooner or later? Generally speaking. There
must be other shifts. Otherwise it would be quite hopeless. But it is
quite hopeless. I should mention before going any further, any
further on, that I say aporia without knowing what it means. Can
one be ephectic otherwise than unawares? I don't know. With the
yesses and noes it is different, they will come back to me as I go
along and how, like a bird, to shit on them all without exception.
The fact would seem to be, if in my situation one may speak of
facts, not only that I shall have to speak of things of which I cannot speak, but also, which is even more interesting, but also that
I, which is if possible even more interesting, that I shall have to,
I forget, no matter. And at the same time I am obliged to speak.
I shall never be silent. Never.

It would seem obvious that to attempt an interpretation of such
a passage is to invite ridicule. Beyond grammatical analysis, looking
up *ephectic* and *aporia*, if necessary, or noting the stylistic devices
imitating drift and despair, what can be said? To find meaning where
meaninglessness is asserted, to seek an art of interpretation of a passage
so clearly against interpretation is to risk appearing like one of
Beckett's own characters. The passage seems to challenge every notion
on which this book is based, and indeed every concept of any kind.
Nor is there anything in what follows in the novel to reassure us. As in
most of his other works, Beckett himself seems to assert nothing except,
perhaps, that everything is hopeless, or *perhaps* that there is some slight
hope, or *perhaps* that the act of speaking "of things of which I cannot
speak" is ultimately absurd, or *perhaps* that it is not, or *perhaps* that
one should "shit on them all without exception"—not just on the yesses
and noes but on those who assert them.

Everyone seems to see this non-meaning at the core of his work.
There is really little controversy among the commentators: they all
take him at his word, as he says again and again that this is "how it is"
—*comment c'est*—to live in a meaningless void. At the end of *Watt* he
summarizes the view in a little poem which a footnote tells us he could
not fit into the novel because of "fatigue and disgust":

> who may tell the tale
> of the old man?
> weigh absence in a scale?
> mete want with a span?
> the sum assess
> of the world's woes?
> nothingness
> in words enclose?

Even to say that such a poem asserts the meaninglessness of life, since the "sum" is equated with "nothingness," is to fall into the trap of overassertion; after all it only asks a wistful question about a condition taken for granted. But whether they talk of assertions or merely of assumptions, critics have generally found in these works an unlimited ironic undercutting; they attempt to portray—or perhaps one should say attempt to portray the attempt to portray—the ultimate negation of everything. The only meaning is that there is no meaning, and any reconstruction of an irony is as vulnerable to destruction as any other. It may be that in practice, when faced with the task of reading, say, "A Modest Proposal," Beckett would accept tentatively such implied norms as that cruelty to children is wicked or that those who conspire to perpetuate poverty are vile. But in his works he simply evokes, often with great comic power and always with poignancy, how it feels when all is chaos, when there is no point in living, when there is, in fact, no point in writing either. One writes because of an absurd need to "keep going, going on, call that going, call that on."

But—and here is where the fun for any foolhardy hermeneuticist begins—note how phrases like "great comic power" and "poignancy" creep into such accounts. Nobody seems to read these "empty" works without an intense emotional and intellectual response, and it may be that without too much absurdity we can make for ourselves a small opening into interpretation by looking at that response. Such effects are not likely to be produced accidentally, by the hopeless bumbler that Beckett's narrators—sometimes called "Sam" or "Samuel"—claim to be. As H. Porter Abbott says, "Beckett is far from being as helpless as he appears."[2]

We needn't be optimistic about it: whatever we arrive at will be radically inadequate, subject to the puncturings of Beckett's kind of irony. At best we can hope to complicate his ironies: here, perhaps, is a small bit of light in a world in which you have told us there is none. It is not light on "how it is," in the grand metaphysical sense taken by many of your readers. But perhaps light about "how reading Beckett works" would be something. And perhaps if there is something, something *is*? In which case . . .?

We should be quite clear about what we are doing. If we do find any yesses here that need not be shat on, they will be ironic underminings of Beckett's own professed beliefs, in his works and in personal statements outside them.[3] His intended ironies are all quite clearly

2. *The Fiction of Samuel Beckett* (Berkeley, 1973), p. 13.
3. See for example his famous dialogue with Georges Duthuit (1949), picked

stated, on the surface. We have thus now drifted to a position exactly opposite to the one we built in chapter 1. There we sought meanings that were intended, stable, covert, local, and finite. Here we are peering behind overt efforts to portray infinite negation, hoping to find some covert significance that will—in spite of the author's seeming intentions—have some degree of stability. The inherent arrogance of this quest would trouble me more if I did not find Beckett himself asserting, as it were, decade after decade, an extremely stable commitment to absurdist views.

It would seem legitimate to take a brief look at the validity of the assertion itself. A claim is being made about the world. Critics often praise Beckett for the validity of the claim, quite aside from the question of his artistic skill. When Beckett was awarded the Nobel Prize in 1970, Ronald Hayman wrote in *The Sunday Times* (April 1970):

> If it is true that all being aspires to the condition of non-being, Beckett is the poet of this process. . . . As Pinter has written: "The farther he goes the more good it does me. I don't want philosophies, tracts, dogmas, creeds, way outs, truths, answers, *nothing from the bargain basement*. He is the most courageous, remorseless writer going. . . . I'll buy his goods, hook, line and sinker, because he leaves no stone unturned and no maggot lonely."
>
> He is important because he reports with absolute integrity what he sees, and because he gets so close to seeing Nothing.

Such outbursts are in a sense more revealing than more considered criticism. The enthusiasts are caught with their inconsistencies showing, and they offer us clues about how Beckett consistently achieves what he again and again claims to be impossible: a thorough meeting of minds with us strangers, his readers.

1. Surely if there *is* a "process" to be a poet of, then *something is*: a praiseworthy process to be a praiseworthy poet of. But is the praiseworthiness *real* praiseworthiness or simply another phony, unreal value that should be seen through by the man of true perception? Talk about

---

up by Hugh Kenner, *Samuel Beckett: A Critical Study* (New York, 1961), pp. 30–31, by Abbott, pp. 5–6, 104, and by Muecke, *Compass of Irony*, p. 214:

"B. The situation is that of him who is helpless, cannot act, in the end cannot paint, since he is obliged to paint. The act is of him who, helpless, unable to act, acts, in the event paints, since he is obliged to paint.

"D. Why is he obliged to paint?

"B. I don't know.

"D. Why is he helpless to paint?

"B. Because there is nothing to paint and nothing to paint with."

nothingness is always caught in this ironic trap, as Beckett himself often points out with effects both comic and poignant.

Each of Pinter's words of praise is subject to this same ironic undermining. (*a*) Is the "good" that Beckett does Pinter by "going far" a genuine good or an illusory one? If the former, then there is such a thing as a real good, and total nothingness is denied. If the latter, why bother to make the meaningless statement? Does Pinter want to make converts to a "good" experience that is not in fact good? (*b*) Is the courage *real* courage? Of course. Then courage is a real value? Etc. I see no way for Pinter and Hayman to escape this point, unless they want to confess that their praise for Beckett's courage is itself meaningless. If courage is praiseworthy, then something is praiseworthy. All readers in fact believe that courage *is* praiseworthy, and they cannot resist responding to its portrayal. (*c*) Is it a good thing to leave no stone unturned? If so, etc. etc. (*d*) Is it a good thing to leave no maggot lonely? What's wrong with loneliness, if there is no meaning? And why maggots? Here we see a hint of the kind of value-sharing that consistently goes on in reading Beckett: he *cares* even for the "maggots," and there are few of us who do not admire such caring—whether we believe that no sparrow falls without God's concern or that the universe is hateful because it is indifferent to people, sparrows, and maggots alike. In short, in the Pinter-Hayman-Beckett world, there are goods, after all! Beckett, the prophet of the Meaningless, is seen as a good writer because he knows what real values and real virtues are. There's irony for you.

2. Pinter doesn't want "philosophies," "truths"—except, of course, the dogmatic truth discovered in the Denial of Meaning; he does not want tracts—except tracts that "remorselessly" attack Meaning; he does not want "answers"—except the final and apparently undiscussable truth, the final answer, that comes from pushing the "process" of denial to the bitter end. Irony.

3. Can Hayman's concluding statement be true? *Does* Beckett "report with absolute integrity on what he sees"? No, not really. We can't know, of course, all that Beckett the man really sees. All we know is what he makes. But one thing we do know that he "sees" is how to organize his life day by day to get his writing done, how to maintain a productive and obviously exhilarating verbal life while cashing checks and resisting the debilitating effects of world fame. His books do *not* report with absolute integrity on the creative side of his own life. There is no hint in them of how any man, "as things are," could possibly find enough constructive energy to put together the beautiful plays and novels Beckett himself writes, or, for that matter, how anyone could

ever read them. The whole shared world of his art is overtly denied, only covertly revealed.

Here is irony indeed, if we try to take the "abysmal" world view as a serious statement of *how things really are*. The very effort at ultimate negation is thus ironically trapped in its own inconsistencies, a truth the recognition of which seems to be leading Beckett into a more and more laconic pose. Only silence can "affirm" ultimate negation. Or, as Camus put the same point some decades ago,

> The revolutionary spirit, born of total negation, instinctively felt that, as well as refusal, there was also consent to be found in art; that there was a risk of contemplation counterbalancing action, beauty, and injustice, and that in certain cases beauty itself was a form of injustice from which there was no appeal. Equally well, no form of art can survive on total denial alone. Just as all thought, and primarily that of non-signification, signifies something, so there is no art that has no signification. Man can allow himself to denounce the total injustice of the world and then demand a total justice that he alone will create. But he cannot affirm the total hideousness of the world. To create beauty, he must simultaneously reject reality and exalt certain of its aspects.[4]

I am not arguing that Beckett should try to do justice in his works to "the constructive side of his life." But I am arguing against swallowing whole, as many critics seem to, the implied claim that his vision is the whole truth. Good literature can be produced based on radically limited and even downright erroneous views. The harm is done only when readers take the literature for philosophy and think that Beckett's marvelously funny and moving portraits of despair add real evidence to the case for nihilism, forgetting that the evidence before them paradoxically undermines its own claims.

4. "If it is true that all being aspires to the condition of non-being, Beckett is the poet of this process. . . . He is important because he reports with absolute integrity . . ." But what happens if this unsupported belief is not true? What if some "being," like Samuel Beckett and his works, aspires to the condition not of non-being but of perfected being? Does Beckett cease to be important? Hundreds of shoddy writers in this century have presented visions that are, in intellectual terms, as empty as Beckett's. Why then is his superior? The fashion in Nothingness goes on—"call that going, call that on." Since the view is by now hackneyed, it is surprising that it should still be possible to earn praise for originality or honesty or courage by embracing it. To think

4. Albert Camus, *The Rebel: An Essay on Man in Revolt,* trans. Anthony Bower (New York, 1956), p. 258.

that Beckett's achievement lies in his coming closer to Nothingness than others have come is to insult his genuine artistry: it is exactly like telling T. S. Eliot that his poetry is great primarily because he has dared to affirm Christian values against the predominant nihilism.

If the intellectual position underlying such works is as vulnerable as all this, how then can we account for their powerful effect, on believers and unbelievers alike? I suggest—still aware of the spirit of irony hovering over my work—that we have here a curious and complex version of the process we saw working in the simplest ironies. In essence, our reading of these "indecipherable" ironies depends, once again, on a silent act of reconstruction of the author's superior edifice, and on our ascent to dwell with him in silent communion while the "meaningless" drama enacts itself down below, on the surface of things.

What values do we share with this enigmatic author whose lineaments are implied both by the works and by the tortured portraits that stare at us from the dust jackets of most of them? The answer is in part implied by what I have said so far. He is *courageous,* not just in being able to fight against the void but in being able to do so with laughter. He tells us, in effect, that his vision is more *honest* than other men's, that the only honest statement is that every yes and no will be invalidated, sooner or later, that he would in fact like to shit upon all yesses and noes, without exception, *and yet* what he has really decided to do is to write a marvelous book about it all, generously, generously: it is a book for "us," those implied rare spirits who are qualified to catch the supreme ironies with which he plays. He has foreknown the worst that can be said about life; he *knows* the horrors better than anyone else could possibly know them. And yet, tortured as he is, he feels an immense *compassion* for all the torn lost creatures caught in his imaginative messes.

Honesty, courage, generosity, prophetic wisdom, a bitter passion for a justice that is denied us, and compassion—the only traditional virtue he may lack is temperance! If he were to unmask himself (as I risk doing to myself here) and assert these values in some "straight" medium, he would sound like Norman Vincent Peale. No wonder Pinter and Hayman fall into sermonizing. "He does us good." He does indeed. And thus all the debates about what he "means" are peripheral to the genuine communication of this "good" that takes place regardless of whether our metaphysics is cold like his or warm.

The effect of this covert affirmation is strongest, of course, for those of us who—intellectuals like him—can catch the details of his extraordinarily intricate play with traditional philosophies. We are the *true* insiders, or so he makes us feel; not only do we share all those other fine traditional virtues with him, but we share learning, too. He gives us a constant running allusiveness to the whole history of culture in these seemingly lean works; our sharing of the allusions takes precisely the structure that it takes when we read any traditional ironist. It is thus vulnerable—as the other shared virtues are not—to the traditional charge of elitism. When Lucky in *Waiting for Godot* brays his parody of Aquinas (and others), and I preen myself on having recognized even so obvious an allusion as the quacked *"qua, qua,"* the pleasure is a very old and conventional pleasure indeed, entirely amenable to the analysis we have given other stable ironies.[5]

It is probably still true, as I have argued elsewhere,[6] that the true believer in the Void receives a bonus from this kind of infinite irony that is denied to us skeptics. To feel oneself totally identified with the implied author in his elevated place is usually more exciting than to stand slightly above or below him. But I have known readers of Beckett who have paid a price for their metaphysical agreement—the price of hypersolemnity and self-pity and thus of failed comic effects. Mistaking his characters for Beckett, they have identified not with the elitest author but with his vermiform characters, and have—or so it seems to me—wallowed in self-pity as the maggots are put through their paces: there because of the unGrace of the nonGod crawl I. Beckett seems more and more to risk taking himself seriously in this same self-destructive vein—he has moved closer and closer to the silence which his overt position, taken seriously, would demand. But in his major works, the overt position of infinite negativity is always qualified by the essential artistic drive of the creative act in all its richness. Instead of self-pity, the works convey a positively bouncy verve, a joyfully rich inventiveness that is an inseparable part of the ironic reconstructions we are invited to make.

5. Critics have inevitably spent a good deal of energy explicating Beckett's allusions. See, for example, Hugh Kenner's comment on the intensely concentrated allusions in the short play *Happy Days* (in *Flaubert, Joyce, and Beckett* [Boston, 1962], pp. 98–100); H. Porter Abbott's probing of *Watt*'s religious and classical references and parallels (*Fiction of Beckett,* pp. 68–70). The twentieth century is, I believe, the only period in Western history when a major activity for critics has been spotting allusions in *contemporary* literature. When critics do so they are, in a sense, "reading between the lines," discovering an author who "means" something other than he "says," and they are thus engaged in a process very similar to the reading of stable irony: the little dance of relocation that I described in chapter 2 is performed in every respect *except* the retraction of the surface meaning; as in reading metaphor, reconstruction of allusions adds to rather than subtracts from the surface meaning.

6. *The Rhetoric of Fiction,* chap. 5.

My friends and I gather to read Beckett's *Watt* aloud to each other. We read about the two piano tuners, father and son, who comment on the freshly tuned piano:

The mice have returned, he [Mr. Gall Junior] said.
The elder said nothing. Watt wondered if he had heard.
Nine dampers remain, said the younger, and an equal number of hammers.
Not corresponding, I hope, said the elder.
In one case, said the younger.
The elder had nothing to say to this.
The strings are in flitters, said the younger.
The elder had nothing to say to this either.
The piano is doomed, in my opinion, said the younger.
The piano-tuner also, said the elder.
The pianist also, said the younger.
This was perhaps the principal incident of Watt's early days in Mr. Knott's house.
In a sense it resembled all the incidents of note proposed to Watt during his stay in Mr. Knott's house, and of which a certain number will be recorded in this place, without addition, or subtraction, and in a sense not.

And there we all are, laughing, recognizing and accepting together that we too are in flitters, doomed, doomed—and enjoying the whole show as if it were promising our salvation!

I have stressed, of course, the moments that most clearly contradict the picture of Beckett as inaccessible prophet of emptiness. Though he is scarcely a boon companion, he gets through to us somehow, his success depending precisely on the many moments when it seems that only murk can prevail. We must be constantly reminded that what we are doing is impossible, if we are to enjoy our brotherly achievement to the full.

I would not pretend to find any principle for the proper proportion, in such works, between intellectual undermining and dramatic clarity. Too much murk and all is lost; too many moments of clarity and we will wonder what all the fuss is about. The standards of excess and defect here are looser than in any of our previous forms; as we would expect, even the critics who share my admiration for Beckett cannot agree about when, if ever, he goes too far into the depths. But every favorable critic implies that somehow Beckett has found in *him* a rare kindred spirit.

It seems likely that in all "infinitely unstable" works that succeed, the same paradoxical communings will be found. The dramatic path of author and audience is somehow shared—that is after all what success is, in the rhetorical view. It is often only the intellectual superstructure that is "totally baffling." T. S. Eliot once suggested that "meaning" is the piece of meat the burglar distracts the housedog with. The intellect gnaws at the meaning, but the real work of the poem goes on elsewhere unobserved. This overstates the case, because part of the "real work" is the gnawing; but it at least tells us that the real work can be achieved even if the puzzles are not solved.

I noticed, after a recent production of Albee's *Tiny Alice* in London, that many reviewers (and some of my friends) said that they "didn't know what to make of it," yet it was evident that all were discussing the same questions. Every person at every performance had been forced to a sequence of innumerable precisely controlled inferences as the play progressed. One path, for example, runs something like this: The model of the castle in the center of the stage is somehow mysterious; these characters are not motivated by realistic psychology; ah, yes, the model has a *miraculous* relationship to the castle in which the characters are living—because when the real castle caught on fire the model castle emitted smoke; but in fact they all seem to have a worshipful attitude toward whoever or whatever inhabits it—perhaps Tiny Alice is a God inside the model; but somebody there said something about infinite negation, so it's perhaps not really God but nothingness; or perhaps the devil; now what on earth does that final crucifixion mean?—it simply cannot mean that Tiny Alice is really God, because . . . And on the other hand it cannot mean that Tiny Alice is the devil, because . . . And yet it cannot mean . . .

No one I have talked with has been able to solve the riddle, if by that we mean giving an unequivocal statement of the metaphysics underlying the drama. This confusion might be taken as evidence for ultimate instability about these infinite matters. But at the same time, everyone has seen the riddle in roughly similar terms, and this could be taken again as evidence for a curious kind of dramatic stability. And though different spectators have confessed to different levels of interest in solving the religious and metaphysical riddle—some growing bored early, some gripped to the end—no one has seen the riddle as no riddle, the play as "clear," the message as unequivocal. More important, everyone traces a somewhat similar emotional trajectory; without exception spectators feel more sympathy for the young Julian than for any other character, share his anguish about the central mystification, and grasp that in his final crucifixion he is intended to stand somehow for us. I may decide that the ending is a fairly weak attempt—compared, say, with Beckett's best—at confronting the horror of metaphysical nothingness. But I cannot help sharing the general intention: in my very puzzlement I am enacting what Albee has required me to.

## "Stable"-Covert-Infinite

The ambiguities of dealing with the ironies of Beckett and *Tiny Alice* lead us to a radical distinction which is of the greatest importance in reading infinite ironies. There are really two sharply distinct ways in which the vision of an infinite series of ironies, every one undermined by further ironies, can be turned upon life and the universe. And there are two basically different kinds of reading experience, depending on which form of the infinite rejection an author proposes.

We can say that all truths can be undermined with the irony of contrary truths *either* because the universe is essentially absurd and there is no such thing as coherent truth *or* because man's powers of knowing are inherently and incurably limited and partial. We can imagine, on the one hand, a chaos, a disjointed heap of absurdities impervious to man's statements because finally meaningless to the non-core; and on the other hand a cosmos, an order of truth so far beyond man's powers that any attempt at formulation is vulnerable to ironic discounting.[7] We face two radically different kinds of ironic reading, depending on which of these two grand ironic truths stands above us, laughing or weeping at our hopeless efforts to achieve final clarity. The difference depends on whether "the Gods" that Meredith's Adrian Harley saw laughing "in the background" at the "supreme ironic procession" are real or imaginary.[8]

If the universe is ultimately an absurd multiverse, then all propositions about or portraits of any part of it are ultimately absurd, all stories and poems are in at least one sense absurd, and the "readings" one gives can be infinitely various with no fundamental violation of the text; there is no such thing as a "fundamental violation" of any value. Indeed, the more variety the better, because only in absurd variety can the absurdities of things be echoed—though again one could ask how one defends use of a word like "better" in such a universe. Any statement should in theory be as good as any other statement; in practice, as we have seen, critics generally assume that the more ironies the better.

7. I cannot pretend to do justice here to the philosophical and religious issues that have been raised in debating these two views. By far the most important work on the contrast, as it relates specifically to irony, is Kierkegaard's *The Concept of Irony*. Kierkegaard is only incidentally interested in the rhetoric of irony. His game is from his own point of view much bigger: how does one "read" the universe itself? But his approach to the universe is through a brilliant reading of the Socratic irony that in his view will finally dissolve all truth.

8. *The Ordeal of Richard Feverel* (London, 1914), p. 8.

But if the "infinite" underminings of irony are conducted in a genuine universe—if value commitments need not finally be absurd—then differences in our interpretations make a difference; though no formulations will ever be fully adequate, some will be more nearly adequate than others, and the quest for truth and for truer interpretations will in itself be meaningful.

Clearly even in the second view any statement that implies a claim to cover "the way life is" will approach greater adequacy to the degree that it somehow takes into account its possible underminings. A simple affirmation is likely to seem simple indeed, compared to an affirmation that reveals at every stroke the author's awareness of how many threats the world presents to it. In contrast to the claim that "all good literature is ironic," the restraints here are not imposed by chosen critical theories but by everyone's inescapable experience of life; our "common" sense tells us that *if* a literary form aspires to show "how it is," it must somehow incorporate both the bliss and the bale, regardless of which side triumphs. Literary forms that deliberately select or distort, like some lyrics, fairy tales, or satire, thus face the special problem of making the reader accept the "unfair" selections. A lyric can celebrate a moment of joy, with no reminder that pain lies just around the corner. A short play like Synge's *Riders to the Sea* can dwell on almost total misery, with no hint that these people have ever known anything but pain. But longer works must either embrace some sort of "fantastic" convention which cancels the claim to reflect reality (farces, utopias) or satisfy our common awareness that the world is always and everywhere a mixture of joy, misery, and a great load of the "fair to middlin'."

In the terms of our figures of reconstruction, the first kind of irony, aspiring to infinite instability, could be said to present an invitation to the reader to join the author as he leaps into a bottomless abyss: it is the only noble thing to do. We cannot know what horrors we will discover as we descend, but it *is* the only noble thing to do. We may even discover that the concept of nobility is meaningless, but at least we shall be honest. We may discover that honesty is meaningless, but at least . . . well, at least we will have done what we have had to do. And we will thus somehow be superior, even in our doomed descent, to those who persist in their illusions.

In the kind we turn to finally, infinite but somehow stable, the ironist of infinities suggests that there is, after all, a Supreme Ironist, truth itself, standing in his temple above us, observing all authors and readers in their comic or pathetic or tragic efforts to climb and join him. For such an ironist it is not so much the whole of existence that is absurd as it is mankind in the proud claim to know something about it. His works may in some respects resemble Beckett's: every proposition will be doubted as soon as uttered, then undercut by some other proposition that in turn will prove inadequate. The meanings are finally covert. But both the effort to understand and the particular approximations, inadequate as they are, will be worthwhile: the values are stable.

The picture of God or Truth as supreme ironist, incomprehensible and infinitely distant, may superficially resemble the picture of an impersonal universe that indifferently (and hence brutally) frustrates all human effort at statement. But the form of "reading assignment" given by the two views is radically different. For the second, infinite ironies present finally a treadmill, each step exactly like every other, the final revelation always the same: *nada*. Since the universe is empty, life is empty of meaning, and every reading experience can finally be shaken out into the same empty and melancholy non-truth. But for the first, the universe, though deceptive, is infinitely, invitingly various; each flash of ironic insight can lead us toward others, in a game never ending but always meaningful and exhilarating. The ironies of the abyss not only destroy us but finally bore us as they destroy. But how could one be bored by an Ironist like the one described by Hegel? "Reason is as cunning as it is powerful. Its cunning, to speak generally, lies in the mediative action which, while it permits the Objects to follow their own [sc. finite or apparent] nature, and to act upon one another until they waste away, and does not itself directly interfere in the process, is yet only working out its own aims. With this explanation, divine Providence may be said to stand to the world and its process in the relation of absolute cunning. God lets men do as they please with their particular passions and interests; but the result is the accomplishment of —not their plans but his, and these differ decidedly from the ends primarily sought by those whom he employs."[9]

Perhaps the best schoolmaster for reading supreme ironies— certainly the one who means most to me—is Plato. The ironic Socrates, re-created for us in Plato's dialogues, is an ironist in almost every sense that we have dealt with so far. For one thing, he often employs covert ironies: the reader is expected to make quite literal translations of the kind we did with the ironies of chapters 1–3.

> Several times in the course of the discussion Thrasymachus had made an attempt to get the argument into his own hands,

9. G. R. G. Mure, *A Study of Hegel's Logic* (Oxford, 1950), p. 257; quoted in Muecke, p. 134.

and had been put down by the rest of the company, who wanted to hear the end. But when Polemarchus and I had done speaking and there was a pause, he could no longer hold his peace; and, gathering himself up, he came at us like a wild beast, seeking to devour us. We were quite panic-stricken at the sight of him.

He roared out to the whole company: What folly, Socrates, has taken possession of you all? And why, sillybillies, do you knock under to one another? I say that if you want really to know what justice is, you should not only ask but answer, and you should not seek honour to yourself from the refutation of an opponent, but have your own answer; for there is many a one who can ask and cannot answer. And now I will not have you say that justice is duty or advantage or profit or gain or interest, for this sort of nonsense will not do for me; I must have clearness and accuracy.

I was panic-stricken at his words, and could not look at him without trembling. Indeed I believe that if I had not fixed my eye upon him, I should have been struck dumb; but when I saw his fury rising, I looked at him first, and was therefore able to reply to him.

Thrasymachus, I said, with a quiver, don't be hard upon us. Polemarchus and I may have been guilty of a little mistake in the argument, but I can assure you that the error was not intentional. If we were seeking for a piece of gold, you would not imagine that we were "knocking under to one another," and so losing our chance of finding it. And why, when we are seeking for justice, a thing more precious than many pieces of gold, do you say that we are weakly yielding to one another and not doing our utmost to get at the truth? Nay, my good friend, we are most willing and anxious to do so, but the fact is that we cannot. And if so, you people who know all things should pity us and not be angry with us.[10]

Here there are some literal truths to be reconstructed from the ironies: e.g., "we were quite panic-stricken at the sight of him" means something like "we found his bull-like charge absurd"; "you people who know all things" means something like "you blustering fools"; and so on.

But there is a deeper kind of irony throughout the Socratic dialogues, an irony hinted at only toward the end of the passage just quoted: when Socrates claims to be the only man who knows that he knows nothing, he is echoing a claim that he repeats more fully in other contexts:

10. *The Republic* 336 (trans. B. Jowett).

. . . I will endeavour to explain to you the reason why I am called wise and have such an evil fame. Please to attend then. And although some of you may think I am joking, I declare that I will tell you the entire truth. Men of Athens, this reputation of mine has come of a certain sort of wisdom which I possess. If you ask me what kind of wisdom, I reply, wisdom such as may perhaps be attained by man, for to that extent I am inclined to believe that I am wise; whereas the persons of whom I was speaking have a superhuman wisdom, which I may fail to describe, because I have it not myself; and he who says that I have, speaks falsely, and is taking away my character. And here, O men of Athens, I must beg you not to interrupt me, even if I seem to say something extravagant. For the word which I will speak is not mine. I will refer you to a witness who is worthy of credit; that Witness shall be the God of Delphi—he will tell you about my wisdom, if I have any, and of what sort it is. You must have known Chaerephon; he was early a friend of mine, and also a friend of yours, for he shared in the recent exile of the people, and returned with you. Well, Chaerephon, as you know, was very impetuous in all his doings, and he went to Delphi and boldly asked the oracle to tell him whether—as I was saying, I must beg you not to interrupt— he asked the oracle to tell him whether any one was wiser than I was, and the Pythian prophetess answered, that there was no man wiser. Chaerephon is dead himself; but his brother, who is in court, will confirm the truth of what I am saying.

Why do I mention this? Because I am going to explain to you why I have such an evil name. When I heard the answer I said to myself, What can the god mean? and what is the interpretation of his riddle? for I know that I have no wisdom, small or great. What then can he mean when he says that I am the wisest of men? And yet he is a god, and cannot lie; that would be against his nature. After a long consideration, I thought of a method of trying the question. I reflected that if I could only find a man wiser than myself, then I might go to the god with a refutation in my hand. I should say to him, "Here is a man who is wiser than I am; but you said that I was the wisest." Accordingly I went to one who had the reputation of wisdom, and observed him—his name I need not mention; he was a politician whom I selected for examination—and the result was as follows: When I began to talk with him, I could not help thinking that he was not really wise, although he was thought wise by many, and still wiser by himself; and thereupon I tried to explain to him that he thought himself wise, but was not really wise; and the consequence was that he hated me, and his enmity was shared by several who were present and heard me. So I left him, saying to myself, as I went away: Well, although I do not suppose that either of us knows anything

271

really beautiful and good, I am better off than he is,—for he knows nothing, and thinks that he knows; I neither know nor think that I know. In this latter particular, then, I seem to have slightly the advantage of him. Then I went to another who had still higher pretensions to wisdom, and my conclusion was exactly the same. Whereupon I made another enemy of him, and of many others besides him.

Then I went to one man after another, being not unconscious of the enmity which I provoked, and I lamented and feared this: But necessity was laid upon me,—the word of God, I thought, ought to be considered first. And I said to myself, Go I must to all who appear to know, and find out the meaning of the oracle. And I swear to you, Athenians, by the dog I swear!— for I must tell you the truth—the result of my mission was just this: I found that the men most in repute were all but the most foolish; and the others less esteemed were really wiser and better. I will tell you the tale of my wanderings and of the "Herculean" labours, as I may call them, which I endured only to find at last the oracle irrefutable. After the politicians, I went to the poets; tragic, dithyrambic, and all sorts. And there, I said to myself, you will be instantly detected; now you will find out that you are more ignorant than they are. Accordingly, I took them some of the most elaborate passages in their own writings, and asked what was the meaning of them—thinking that they would teach me something. Will you believe me? I am almost ashamed to confess the truth, but I must say that there is hardly a person present who would not have talked better about their poetry than they did themselves. Then I knew that not by wisdom do poets write poetry, but by a sort of genius and inspiration; they are like diviners or soothsayers who also say many fine things, but do not understand the meaning of them. The poets appeared to me to be much in the same case; and I further observed that upon the strength of their poetry they believed themselves to be the wisest of men in other things in which they were not wise. So I departed, conceiving myself to be superior to them for the same reason that I was superior to the politicians.[11]

The basic irony here runs deeper even than the passage itself, read in isolation, might seem to indicate. We might take it as meaning, for example, that Socrates knows what Beckett claims to know—that all statements (including this one) are meaningless. But the whole "Socratic" effort belies this charge, whether we try to reconstruct the historical Socrates behind Plato's dramatization (and Xenophon's quite different picture), or construct an ideal embodiment of the true

11. *Apology* 20–22 (trans. B. Jowett).

fulfillment of Socratic irony (as Kierkegaard does), or think about what Plato himself is saying with his portrait of the great ironist. Though Socrates may "know nothing," at the same time he has "slightly the advantage" of those who know *not* that they know nothing. Which can only mean that he "knows something."

One thing he always seems to know is that what is being said now will not seem adequate later, that this part of what we might say must be discounted or modified by all the other things one might say. In the *Phaedrus,* after Socrates has entered with such "dithyrambic frenzy" into his first speech on love, he stops suddenly and says:

> My good friend, when I was about to cross the stream, the spirit and the sign that usually comes to me came—it always holds me back from something I am about to do—and I thought I heard a voice from it which forbade my going away before clearing my conscience, as if I had committed some sin against deity. . . . A dreadful speech it was, a dreadful speech, the one you brought with you, and the one you made me speak.[12]

Then he gives the speech which culminates in the allegory of love, leading to a grand paean to love and philosophic discourse. But then even this seemingly unqualified oration is further qualified, with a discussion of the nature of true rhetoric and the limitations of speech-making and writing: the only true "writing," Socrates says, is what is written on the soul in philosophical discussion, with the give and take of dialogue preventing the distortions that every reader must have imposed on him as he tries to make out a written text.

But what, then, is *Plato* doing as he writes all this down? He clearly knew from the beginning what each stage of the dialogue would be. He it was who planned the sudden reversal, for example, when the divine voice interrupts Socrates at the stream. Plato has thus built into this long *written* piece the inescapable critique of writing conveyed by this particular and final ordering. In short, no reader can ever doubt that for Plato the quest for truth, even in written form, is meaningful. The Supreme Ironist laughs harder at some than at others.

But the same is really true of Socrates. The final prayer, for example, is not in the least ironic: we feel that in spite of what the Romantic Germans and Kierkegaard made of Socrates' "absolute infinite negativity" we have reached here a platform on which Socrates, Phaedrus, Plato, and the reader can stand as they meditate on the rich ironies of the dialogue: "O beloved Pan and all ye other gods of this place, grant

12. *Phaedrus* 242 (trans. H. N. Fowler).

to me that I be made beautiful in my soul within, and that all external possessions be in harmony with my inner man. May I consider the wise man rich; and may I have such wealth as only the self-restrained man can bear or endure" (279). Those who believe that no knowledge is really possible will presumably take even this prayer as paradoxical; on the other hand, those who believe that truth can be fixed in literal propositions, unambiguous for all men if they will only study them closely, will be likely to see this conclusion as much more final than it really is. If one really believed either that nobody could know anything, or that knowledge is found only in literal, scientific statement, then it would be a foolish bit of futility to conduct Socratic dialogues in real life, or to write them down as Plato did.

But Socrates (to leave Plato aside for a moment) believed in *something* sufficiently to give his life for it: the value of the city and its laws, the value of conversation with his fellow citizens, the value of (finally inaccessible) truth itself. And Plato, even more obviously, believes that it is possible to master the ironies of Socrates by fighting through them to a comprehensive ironic vision that will encompass all negations. No one can read many Platonic dialogues without becoming convinced of Plato's conviction that he and Socrates both know a good deal. For one thing, they know how to discover error through rigorously thoughtful conversation: they know a method. They know that every statement of truth can be questioned from *some* point of view, and then with hard thought made more nearly adequate.

And there is never a hint that wisdom is undesirable. The wise man will always be the one who knows that there are ironic limitations on every pretension to wisdom, no matter how profound he may become, no matter how careful his formulations. All inquiry is at best tentative, approximate, to be used as a stimulation of further dialogue rather than as final statements of truth. But it *can* be genuine inquiry.

We can see what this means by considering other intellectual schemes that assume an objective order toward which limited human statements move without ever finally arriving at the destination. The natural sciences, for example, could be called infinitely ironic, because every honest scientist knows that his formulations will almost certainly be revised by later scientists. Goethe, as Muecke reminds us, claimed that to be a good scientist one must have a sense of irony. But Muecke is surely right in his statement of the limits to the irony of science:

> For although the dialectic of science accepts the possibility of contradiction, its eye is fixed more firmly on that other possibility, the possibility of reunification. It continually looks beyond

the possible antithesis to the possible synthesis; its ideals are simplicity and unity. Irony [that is, "General Irony," which is unstable and finally infinite irony], on the other hand, needs and looks for contradictions and dualities.[13]

One can imagine, of course, a good scientist whose whole endeavor would be to undermine the inadequate formulations of other scientists: *der Geist der stets verneint* would be a good assistant to have in any laboratory. But most scientists seem to think of themselves as on a quest for harmonies, not negations. The pursuit of truth for them is not meaningless, because there is a real difference between erroneous opinion and the knowledge that has been tested in the fire of scientific dialogue.

Most men do not like to test their opinions, and Plato as philosopher-dramatist can deal with such people ironically as he watches them charge blindly, like Thrasymachus, into traps that he has long since foreseen; the dialogues are thus full of quite literal and local dramatic irony. But even the few men who "know that they do not know" are dealt with ironically by Truth itself, which in this kind of irony plays toward both reader and author the role that we saw Swift playing toward his characters in "A Modest Proposal." Though Socrates knows more than Thrasymachus, and Plato knows more even than his characters (including Socrates), Plato, Socrates, and the reader all know that the Discoverer of their errors looms above them observing in ironic wisdom as they all charge, *almost* as blind as Thrasymachus, into other unforeseen traps.[14]

Thus the true philosopher lives in self-corrective dialogue, in which the inadequacies of one attempt lead inevitably to another one, and then to yet another. And since he knows that all literal statements mislead, it is not surprising that many of the dialogues finally leave the literal realm altogether, soaring into mythological statements which try to give, in metaphorical form, a still closer approximation to truth. Still misleading, of course, they are less dangerous, because even the most frozen literalist cannot easily reduce them to a final message.

13. Muecke, p. 129. He quotes Eugenio d'Ors, from "Glosa a Ramiro de Maeztu," *Glosario,* 1911: "Science is irony: science is in a sense aesthetic like art. At every point of its progress, science accepts implicitly, notes in its own margin, the possibility of contradiction, the progress to come." See also Muecke's discussion of Musil on scientific knowledge and irony, pp. 152–58.
14. Plato often personifies "the argument" and gives it an ironic vision, as at the end of *Protagoras:* "For if the argument had a human voice, that voice would be heard laughing at us, pointing out precisely how it has led the human weaklings to reverse themselves" (p. 361).

I reluctantly resist quoting at length from the conclusion to *The Symposium,* or from the heavenly vision at the end of *The Republic.* They are, of course, ironic passages—indeterminately ironic and thus deliciously skeptical about the literal-minded sureties in this book.

## A FINAL NOTE ON EVALUATION

There would be no point in trying at last to show that ironists should go only so far and no farther. Philosophers and scientists and literary critics differ greatly about the value of clear literal statement, and about the availability of an unequivocal hold on any aspect of the truth. I think that none of the major philosophers has gone as far in repudiating them as Beckett asks us to go in *The Unnamable*; their sentences and paragraphs, unlike his, make logical (not just dramatic) sense, and their paragraphs, unlike many of his, "track" or "follow" in a describable, logical order. Even the most extreme nihilists have not repudiated, as he *seems* to do, the very possibility of communicable speech. His position, if it can be called that, seems to me (and apparently to him) self-defeating, illogical, and untenable.

But to say this is not to say that because we cannot reconstruct his ultimate ambiguities, or because they contradict the assumptions of my book, Beckett should not write them. In the first place, nobody knows, in fact, what works men "should write" until they have been written. If Beckett can write works showing "how it feels" to believe that this is "how it is," then no theory of criticism can show that he should not have done so. There can be no guidebook to tell us how much irony a work *should* contain; the artist himself will show us how much of it a work *can* contain and still succeed with us. There is probably no area of taste about which we feel more deeply than this: we all tend to mistrust both those who have less of a stomach for underminings and unspoken negations than ourselves and those who can happily accommodate more. But if we will let the work (in its implicit genre) be its own rule-maker, we can be open to makings in all modes, without surrendering to complete relativism. Though in one sense it remains true that each reader must decide for himself the level of irony he will tolerate, once again we must say that there are just not that many levels to go around: we join authors and other readers even in our most "private" choices.

Secondly, we should be able to accept, in novels, plays, and poems, the emotional power and interest of many views which we think untrue. I do not, for example, place very much weight on my mistrust of "absurdism" when I come to reading Beckett and Albee, even though it will be decisive when I am reading a philosophical argument that the universe is absurd. I can enter into the plight of characters and authors who feel lost in the abyss—and not only because I have been there on occasion myself. The totally ironic view is, we should know by now, one of the plausible views of the human condition; intelligent people have held it in the past and will hold it in the future, and it is thus not inherently ridiculous for an author to ask us to take it seriously. Though I think that literary critics are criminally negligent when they accept the view as self proving and ignore all that can be said against it, I see no reason to apply the same strictures to poor Watt or Murphy or Malone.

Finally, I am convinced that on the whole even more harm is done by those who prematurely shut out a given literary experience than by those who accept everything new because their standards are flabby. The worst enemy of good reading as of good criticism is the application of abstract rules that violate the life of particular works. Whether we decide that the greatest works must be supremely ironic or that they must finally affirm something behind whatever ironies are on the surface, we should be able to admit that important writing has been done from both points of view. We can poison our reading experience both by failing to reconstruct when stable ironies are intended and by insisting on literal translation when the whole point is to heighten instabilities. To turn "A Modest Proposal" into a statement that defends equally the position of the speaker *and* the view that would condemn him is to make hash of a great work, but to try to find one single summary of Plato's philosophy, or to insist that the "Godot" Beckett's characters wait for must or must not be God, is to commit a kind of pedantry that deserves the touch of a clever ironist.

# Bibliography

Since everything is ironic in one definition or another, any list of works about irony must be brutally selective. Even if we limit our interest to the intended ironies discussed in this book, we face tens of thousands of books and articles purporting to show that this or that work is or is not intentionally ironic, and the tide swells daily. Only a few of them, however, offer reflection on how one properly argues such matters, and the list that follows is limited mainly to these. It is true that listing only the methodologically explicit means ruling out much that is valuable, including many works cited in the text and many uncited works that I have found useful or sound. But I hope that the list, supplemented by my index and by D. C. Muecke's and Norman Knox's bibliographies, covers most of the sustained work on "how we do it." It also includes a few works on the nature of irony and on general principles of interpretation—those that I have found either helpful or representative. I warn only that my exclusions are not made simply on lines of critical agreement: the reader who asks, "But where is Tieck, and where is Donaldson, and where is Stanley Fish?" can only guess about my prejudices, my carelessness, or my ignorance.

The latter is displayed by the discovery, just as I send the book to press, of a Portuguese work on irony (Maria Helena de Novais Paiva, *Contribução para uma Estilística da Ironia* [Lisbon, 1961]). Five hundred and forty three pages, in a language I cannot read! The irony of this event was not intended by any human author, but my account of it, overt, local, and finite, is. A complete bibliography of intended ironies would thus include this moment as one item, under some such head as "Flirting with Casaubon's Fate: On Compiling a Key to All Ironology without Knowing All That Has Been Written about It."

Allemann, Beda. "Ironie als literarisches Prinzip." In *Ironie und Dichtung,* edited by Albert Schaefer, pp. 11–38. Munich: C. H. Beck, 1970.

Austin, J. L. *How to Do Things with Words.* Oxford: Clarendon Press, 1962.

Baumgart, Reinhard. *Das Ironische und die Ironie in den Werken Thomas Manns.* Munich: C. Hanser, 1964.

Beardsley, Monroe C. *Aesthetics: Problems in the Philosophy of Criticism.* New York: Harcourt, Brace, 1958.

Brackman, Jacob. "The Put-On." *The New Yorker,* 24 June 1967, pp. 34–73.

Brooks, Cleanth. "Irony as a Principle of Structure." In *Literary Opinion in America,* edited by Morton Dauwen Zabel, pp. 729–41. New York: Harper and Brothers, 1951.

————. "Irony and 'Ironic' Poetry." *College English* 9 (1948): 231–37.

————. *Modern Poetry and the Tradition*. Chapel Hill, N.C.: University of North Carolina Press, 1939.

————. *The Well Wrought Urn: Studies in the Structure of Poetry*. New York: Reynal and Hitchcock, 1947.

Brower, Reuben. *The Fields of Light: An Experiment in Critical Reading*. New York: Oxford University Press, 1962.

————. *Alexander Pope: The Poetry of Allusion*. Oxford: Clarendon Press, 1959.

Burke, Kenneth. *Attitudes toward History*. Editorial Publications, 1937. 2d. rev. ed. Los Altos, Calif.: Hermes Publications, 1959.

————. *Counter-Statement*. Los Altos, Calif.: Hermes Publications, 1931.

————. *A Grammar of Motives*. Englewood Cliffs, N.J.: Prentice-Hall, 1945.

————. *Language as Symbolic Action: Essays on Life, Literature, and Method*. Berkeley: University of California Press, 1966.

————. *The Philosophy of Literary Form: Studies in Symbolic Action*. 2d ed. Baton Rouge, La.: Louisiana State University Press, 1967.

————. *A Rhetoric of Motives*. New York: George Braziller, 1950.

Chevalier, Haakon M. *The Ironic Temper: Anatole France and His Time*. New York: Oxford University Press, 1932.

Clough, W. O. "Irony: A French Approach." *Sewanee Review* 47 (1939): 175–83.

Cohen, Ted. "Illocutions and Perlocutions." *Foundations of Language* 9 (1973): 492–503.

[Collins, Anthony.] *A Discourse concerning Ridicule and Irony in Writing, in a Letter to the Reverend Dr. Nathanael Marshall*. London, 1729.

Crane, R. S. "The Critical Monism of Cleanth Brooks." In *Critics and Criticism, Ancient and Modern*. Edited by R. S. Crane. Chicago: University of Chicago Press, 1952.

Culler, Jonathan. "Structural Semantics and Poetics." *Centrum* 1 (1973): 5–20.

Davis, Herbert. *The Satire of Jonathan Swift*. New York: Macmillan Co., 1947.

————. "Swift's Use of Irony." See Novak below.

DeMott, Benjamin. "The New Irony: Sicknicks and Others." *The American Scholar* 31 (1961–62): 108–19.

Dyson, A. E. *The Crazy Fabric: Essays in Irony*. New York: St. Martin's Press, 1965.

————. "Swift: The Metamorphosis of Irony." In *Essays and Studies: 1958*. Vol. 11, n.s. Essays and Studies Collected for the English Association. London: John Murray, 1958.

Ehrenpreis, Irwin. "Personae." In *Restoration and 18th Century Literature: Essays in Honor of A. D. McKillop*. Chicago: University of Chicago Press, 1963.

Empson, William. *Seven Types of Ambiguity*. London: Chatto and Windus, 1930.

————. "Tom Jones." *Kenyon Review* 20 (1958): 217–49.

Evans, Bertrand. *Shakespeare's Comedies*. Oxford: Clarendon Press, 1960.

Ewald, William B. *The Masks of Jonathan Swift*. Cambridge: Harvard University Press, 1954.

Fónagy, Ivan. "The Functions of Vocal Style." In *Literary Style: A Symposium*. Edited by Seymour Chapman. Oxford: Oxford University Press, 1971.

French, A. L. "Purposive Imitation: A Skirmish with Literary Theory." *Essays in Criticism* 22 (April 1972): 109–30.

Frye, Northrop. *Anatomy of Criticism: Four Essays*. Princeton, N.J.: Princeton University Press, 1957.

————. "The Nature of Satire." *University of Toronto Quarterly* 14 (1944): 75–89.

Good, Edwin M. *Irony in the Old Testament*. London: S.P.C.K., 1965.

Graff, Gerald. "A Report on Oxymoronism." *TriQuarterly* 18 (1970): 237–43.

Greimas, A. J. *Sémantique structurale*. Paris: Larousse, 1966.

Grice, H. P. "Utterer's Meaning and Intentions." *Philosophical Review* 78 (1969): 147–77.

Hatfield, Glenn W. *Henry Fielding and the Language of Irony*. Chicago: University of Chicago Press, 1968.

————. "The Serpent and the Dove: Fielding's Irony and the Prudence Theme in *Tom Jones*." *Modern Philology* 65 (1967): 17–32.

Heller, Eric. *The Ironic German: A Study of Thomas Mann*. London: Secker and Warburg, 1958.

Hernadi, Paul. *Beyond Genre: New Directions in Literary Classification*. Ithaca, N.Y.: Cornell University Press, 1972.

Hirsch, E. D., Jr. "Privileged Criteria in Literary Evaluation." *Problems of Literary Evaluation*. Yearbook of Comparative Criticism, vol. 2. Edited by Joseph Strelka. University Park, Pa.: Pennsylvania State University Press, 1969.

————. "Literary Evaluation as Knowledge." *Contemporary Literature* 9 (1968): 319–31.

————. *Validity in Interpretation*. New Haven, Conn.: Yale University Press, 1967.

Humphreys, A. R. "Fielding's Irony: Its Method and Effects." *Review of English Studies* 18 (1942): 183–96. Reprinted in *Fielding: A*

*Collection of Critical Essays.* Edited by Ronald Paulson. Englewood Cliffs, N.J.: Prentice-Hall, 1962.

Hutchens, Eleanor N. "The Identification of Irony." *ELH* 27 (1960):
352–63.

————. "Verbal Irony in Tom Jones." *PMLA* 77 (1962): 46–50.

Immerwahr, Raymond. "Friedrich Schlegel's Essay 'On Goethe's
*Meister.*'" *Monatshefte* 49 (1957): 1–22.

Jankélévitch, Vladimir. *L'Ironie ou la bonne conscience.* 2d ed. Paris:
Presses universitaires de France, 1950.

Kemper, Claudette. "Irony Anew with Occasional Reference to Byron
and Browning." *Studies in English Literature* 7 (1967): 705–19.

Kierkegaard, Søren. *The Concept of Irony, with Constant Reference to
Socrates.* Translated by Lee M. Capel. London: Collins, 1966.

Knox, Norman. "On the Classification of Ironies." *Modern Philology*
70 (1972): 53–62.

————. *The Word Irony and Its Context, 1500–1755.* Durham, N.C.:
Duke University Press, 1961.

Laffont-Bompiani. Article on irony [by Maurice Boucher?]. *Diction-
naire universel des lettres.* Paris: Société d'édition de dictionnaires
et encyclopédies, 1961.

Levine, Donald. *Wax and Gold.* Chicago: University of Chicago Press,
1965.

————. "Ambiguity and Modernity." Unpublished paper prepared for
the session on the Sociology of Knowledge, Fifth World Congress
of Sociology. Washington, D.C., 7 September 1962.

Levine, George R. *Henry Fielding and the Dry Mock: A Study of the
Techniques of Irony in His Early Works.* The Hague: Mouton &
Co., 1967.

Lisca, Peter. "*The Revenger's Tragedy*: A Study in Irony." *Philological
Quarterly* 38 (1959): 242–51.

Longinus. *On the Sublime.* Translated by Benedict Einarson. Introduction by Elder Olson. Chicago: Packard & Co., 1945.

McAlindon, T. "Language, Style, and Meaning in *Troilus and Cressida.*" *PMLA* 84 (1969): 29–43.

Marsh, Robert. "Historical Interpretation and the History of Criticism." In *Literary Criticism and Historical Understanding.* Selected papers from the English Institute. Edited by Phillip Damon.
New York: Columbia University Press, 1967. Other essays in the
volume are pertinent, especially "Two Boethian Speeches in
*Troilus and Criseyde* and Chaucerian Irony," by Peter Elbow.

Mudrick, Marvin. *Jane Austen: Irony as Defense and Discovery.*
Princeton: Princeton University Press, 1952.

Muecke, D. C. *The Compass of Irony.* London: Methuen & Co., 1969.

————. *Irony.* Critical Idiom Series, vol. 13. London: Methuen & Co.,
1970.

————. "The Communication of Verbal Irony." Unpublished paper read to the Twelfth International Congress of the Fédération Internationale des Langues et Littératures. Cambridge, 1972.

Novak, Maximillian E. "Defoe's *Shortest Way with the Dissenters: Hoax, Parody, Paradox, Fiction, Irony, Satire.*" *Modern Language Quarterly* 27 (1966): 402–17.

———. "Defoe's Use of Irony." In *The Uses of Irony*. Papers on Defoe and Swift read at the Clark Library Seminar, 2 April 1966, by Maximillian E. Novak and Herbert J. Davis. Los Angeles: Clark Library Seminar, 1966.

Olson, Elder. "Hamlet and the Hermeneutics of Drama." *Modern Philology* 61 (1964): 225–37. See also Longinus.

Palante, Georges. "L'ironie: étude psychologique." *Revue philosophique de la France et de l'étranger* 61 (1906): 147–63.

Paulson, Ronald. *Satire and the Novel in Eighteenth-Century England.* New Haven: Yale University Press, 1967.

Perrine, Laurence. "The Importance of Tone in the Interpretation of Literature." *College English* 24 (1963): 389–95.

Preisendanz, Wolfgang. "Ironie bei Heine." In *Ironie und Dichtung,* edited by Albert Schaefer, pp. 85–112. Munich: C. H. Beck, 1970.

Price, John Valdimir. *The Ironic Hume.* Austin, Tex.: University of Texas Press, 1965.

Quintilian. *Institutio oratoria.* Translated by H. E. Butler. (Loeb Classics). London: Heinemann, 1920–22.

Radcliffe-Brown, A. R. "On Joking Relationships." In *Structure and Function in Primitive Society.* New York: Free Press, 1965 (London, 1952).

Richards, I. A. *Interpretation in Teaching.* London: Routledge and Kegan Paul, 1938.

———. *Practical Criticism: A Study of Literary Judgment.* London: Kegan Paul, 1929.

———. *Principles of Literary Criticism.* London: Kegan Paul, Trench, Trubner, & Co., 1924.

Rosenheim, Edward W., Jr. *Swift and the Satirist's Art.* Chicago: University of Chicago Press, 1963.

Roth, Robert. "The Sophistication of W. H. Auden: A Sketch in Longinian Method." *Modern Philology* 48 (1950–51): 193–204.

Sacharoff, Mark, and McAlindon, T. "Critical Comment in Response to T. McAlindon's 'Language, Style, and Meaning in *Troilus and Cressida.*'" *PMLA* 87 (1972): 90–99.

Sacks, Sheldon. *Fiction and the Shape of Belief.* Berkeley: University of California Press, 1964.

Schaefer, Albert, ed. *Ironie und Dichtung.* (Six essays by Beda Allemann and others.) Munich: C. H. Beck, 1970.

Schaerer, René. "Le Mécanisme de l'ironie dans ses rapports avec la dialectique." *Revue de métaphysique et de morale* 48 (1941): 181–209.

Schlegel, Friedrich von. *Literary Notebooks, 1797–1801.* Edited by Hans Eichner. Toronto: University of Toronto Press, 1957.

Sedgewick, G. G. "Dramatic Irony: Studies in Its History, Its Definition, and Its Use Especially in Shakespeare and Sophocles." Ph.D. dissertation, Harvard University, 1913.

————. *Of Irony, Especially in Drama.* Toronto: University of Toronto Press, 1935.

Sharpe, Robert Boies. *Irony in the Drama: An Essay on Impersonation, Shock and Catharsis.* Chapel Hill, N.C.: University of North Carolina Press, 1959.

Sidgwick, Arthur. "On Some Forms of Irony in Literature." *Cornhill Magazine,* 3d ser. 22 (1907): 497–508.

Slepian, Barry. "The Ironic Intention of Swift's Verses on His Own Death." *Review of English Studies,* n.s. 14 (1963): 249–56.

Smith, Barbara Herrnstein. *Poetic Closure: A Study of How Poems End.* Chicago: University of Chicago Press, 1968.

States, Bert O. *Irony and Drama: A Poetics.* Ithaca, N.Y.: Cornell University Press, 1971.

Strauss, Leo. *Persecution and the Art of Writing.* Glencoe, Ill.: Free Press, 1962. Esp. chapter 2.

Strohschneider, Ingrid (Kohrs). *Die romantische Ironie in Theorie und Gestaltung.* Tübingen: M. Niemeyer, 1960.

Sutherland, James. *English Satire.* Cambridge: Cambridge University Press, 1958.

Tave, Stuart M. *Some Words of Jane Austen.* Chicago: University of Chicago Press, 1973.

Thirlwall, Connop. "On the Irony of Sophocles." *The Philological Museum.* Vol. 2. Cambridge: Deightons, 1833.

Thompson, Alan Reynolds. *The Dry Mock: A Study of Irony in Drama.* Berkeley: University of California Press, 1948.

Thomson, J. A. K. *Irony: An Historical Introduction.* London: George Allen and Unwin, 1926.

Ward, Hooker. "Irony and Absurdity in the Avant-Garde Theatre." *Kenyon Review* 22 (1960): 436–54.

Watt, Ian. "The Ironic Tradition in Augustan Prose from Swift to Johnson." *Restoration and Augustan Prose.* Papers delivered by James R. Sutherland and Ian Watt at Clark Library Seminar. Los Angeles: Clark Library Seminar, 1956 [?].

Winters, Yvor. *Privitivism and Decadence.* New York: Arrow Editions, 1937.

# Index

# Index

# Index

# Index

Shakespeare, 23–24, 40–41, 54, 63, 68 n, 88, 101, 125, 128, 132, 133, 134, 136, 214–15, 236, 237, 255, 256; *Julius Caesar,* 42; "My Mistress' Eyes," 123–26, 134
Shaw, Theodore L., 195 n
Shumaker, Wayne, 193 n
Significance, 94, 144, 241 n, 245. *See also* Meaning
Silence, 243–45, 262, 264
Simile, 7, 23, 98. *See also* Metaphor
Slepian, Barry, 121–23, 121–22 n
Smith, Barbara Herrnstein, 48 n
"Snow White and the Seven Dwarfs," 241 n
Socrates. *See* Plato
Soliloquies, 63
"Soliloquy of the Spanish Cloister" (Browning), 142–50, 256
Sophocles, *Oedipus Rex,* 208, 213, 256
Spinoza, 86
Steinmann, Martin, 15 n
Stendhal, 67 n
Sterne, Lawrence, 176; *Tristram Shandy,* 136, 151, 211
Stevens, Wallace, 177, 178
Stoppard, Tom, 18 n
Strelka, Joseph, 193 n
Structuralism, 35–36 n, 129 n
Structure of meanings. *See* Beliefs, structure of
Style, 67–73, 74, 183
Subjective-objective distinction, 16, 196, 222
Sublime, xiv, 178, 204
Swift, Jonathan, x, 12 n, 46, 47, 54, 88, 101–4, 105–23, 133, 194; *Gulliver's Travels,* 48, 82, 105, 201; "A Modest Proposal," 105–20, 134, 137, 142, 144, 175, 233, 243, 259, 275, 277; *A Tale of a Tub,* 25, 49, 105, 239; "Verses on His Own Death," 121–23
Symbolism, 177–78
*Symposium, The,* 276
Synge, John Millington, 268

*Tale of a Tub, A,* 25, 49, 105, 239
*Tartuffe,* 66–67, 255
Technical presuppositions, 225
Television, 256

*Tempest, The,* 54
Tennyson, Alfred Lord, 17
Theophrastus, 139
Thirlwall, Connop, 63 n
Thomas, Dylan, 176
Thomson, J. A. K., 63 n
Thurber, James, 57, 58, 212
*Tiny Alice* (Albee), 6, 212, 266–67
Tolstoy, Leo, 58, 202, 218
*Tom Jones,* 59, 60, 179–85, 233, 255
Topics, 33–37
Tourneur, Cyril, 27, 237 n
*Towards a Better Life* (Burke), 55–57
Tragedy, x, xiv, 204, 209 n, 213, 214, 226
*Tristram Shandy* (Sterne), 136, 151, 211
*Troilus and Cressida,* 68 n
Twain, Mark, xvii, 57, 61, 68, 70, 75, 76, 80, 141, 147, 176, 181 n, 210
*Twelfth Night,* 256

*Ulysses,* 47, 198
*Under the Volcano* (Lowry), 209
Understanding, as critical constant, 48, 204. *See also* Rhetoric; Rhetorical inquiry
Universe, irony as a reading of, 93, 175, 202, 241, 267, 267 n, part 3
*Unnamable, The* (Beckett), 257–58, 276

"Verses on His Own Death" (Swift), 121–23
Victims, 27–28, 39, 41, 48, 105, 123, 125, 233, 241 n
Voltaire, x, 10–12, 23, 39, 206
Vonnegut, Kurt, Jr., 174

*War and Peace,* 202
"Warning to Children" (Graves), 254–57
Warren, Robert Penn, 67 n
"Wasteland, The" (Eliot), 171, 212
*Watt* (Beckett), 75–76, 258, 265
Weimann, Robert, 36 n
Weiss, Peter, 249–50
Wharton, Edith, 13
White, E. B., 69, 71, 94–101, 102
Whyte, L. L., xv

291

*Index*

Whyte, William H., 76–80, 105
Willingham, Calder, 75 n
Wimsatt, W. K., 126 n
Wittgenstein, Ludwig, xii, xvi, 3 n, 127, 220, 220 n
Woolley, James, 121 n
Wordsworth, William, 17, 23, 219

Wright, Andrew H., 140 n, 179 n
Wright, Richard B., 93–94, 211

Xenophon, 272

Yeats, William Butler, 148, 178
*York Tilemakers' Play,* 28

WAYNE C. BOOTH is George M. Pullman Professor of English at the University of Chicago. His publications include *The Rhetoric of Fiction* and *Now Don't Try to Reason with Me.* He has edited *The Knowledge Most Worth Having.*

[1974]